ULISES ESTRADA LESCAILLE was born in Santiago de Cuba, on December 11, 1934, and was given the name Dámaso Lescaille. After the prolonged period of his clandestine activities and his use of the alias Ulises Estrada, he decided to legalize this name, using Lescaille, his father's surname, as a second last name.

At a very young age he joined the struggle against General Fulgencio Batista, who came to power in Cuba in a coup d'état on March 10, 1952. In 1955, he joined the July 26 Movement, founded after the attack led by Fidel Castro on the Moncada garrison, on July 26, 1953. This organization carried out clandestine work, both in Santiago de Cuba and in Havana.

Immediately after the revolution on January 1, 1959, he worked in different capacities in both the Inspection and the G-2 Intelligence Headquarters of the Rebel Army. He was provisional head of the G-2 Operations Division in the Escambray region, where counterrevolutionary bands, organized and financed by the Central Intelligence Agency (CIA), were active.

Ulises joined the newly formed Ministry of the Interior (MININT) in 1961, where he worked in the Technical Vice Ministry (VMT), the branch responsible for developing political intelligence strategies, under the command of Manuel Piñeiro (alias Barbarroja, XII, or Petronio). He fulfilled a number of Cuban missions in support of anti-imperialist struggles in Latin America under the direction of Piñeiro and Orlando Pantoja Tamayo (alias Olo).

In 1965, he worked in support of the guerrilla movement led by Ernesto Che Guevara in the Congo. Ulises organized and participated in Che's clandestine journey to Czechoslovakia, remaining with him during the first part of his stay while Che prepared his secret return to Cuba and departure for Bolivia. In 1966, he was appointed head of the Fifth General Command of the VMT in the MININT, specializing in Africa and Asia.

Four years later, he helped establish the General Command of National Liberation, which formed part of the MININT. Here he carried out a number of secret missions linked to the Cuban Revolution's solidarity with liberation struggles that were being waged in several countries of Latin America and the Caribbean. In 1975 he was appointed deputy chief of the newly established Americas Department of the Central Committee of the Cuban Communist Party (PCC).

After 1979, he was successively the Cuban ambassador to Jamaica, the People's Democratic Republic of Yemen, the People's Republic of Algeria, the Democratic Saharan Arab Republic, and the Islamic Republic of Mauritania. He headed Cuba's participation in the Movement of Non-Aligned Nations and the African and Middle Eastern departments in the Cuban Ministry of Foreign Affairs. He then took up a post heading the research department at the weekly newspaper *Granma International*; subsequently he joined the twice-weekly publication *El Habanero*. He has also worked with the newspaper *Juventud Rebelde*, with the magazine *Bohemia*, and with the stations Radio Havana and Radio Cadena Havana.

Since 2000 he has been the editor of *Tricontinental*, published by the Organization for Solidarity with the Peoples of Asia, Africa, and Latin America (OSPAAAL). He holds a degree in social sciences and is the co-author of *Tania the Unforgettable Guerrilla* and *Amilcar Cabral, un precursor de la independencia Africana* (Amilcar Cabral: A Forerunner of African Independence).

TANIA

UNDERCOVER WITH CHE GUEVARA IN BOLIVIA

ULISES ESTRADA

TANIA

UNDERCOVER WITH CHE GUEVARA IN BOLIVIA

Ocean Press
Melbourne ▪ New York
www.oceanbooks.com.au

Cover design ::maybe

Front cover photo: Haydée Tamara Bunke Bíder, or Tania, in Cuba.
Back cover photo: Ulises Estrada.

Edited by Luis Suárez

ISBN 10: 1-876175-43-5
ISBN 13: 978-1-876175-43-6
Library of Congress Catalog Card No: 2005925582

Published in Spanish as *Tania la Guerrillera* (ISBN 10: 1-920888-21-7)

Printed in Canada

PUBLISHED BY OCEAN PRESS
Australia: GPO Box 3279, Melbourne, Victoria 3001, Australia
          Fax: (61-3) 9329 5040 Tel: (61-3) 9326 4280
          E-mail: info@oceanbooks.com.au

USA: PO Box 1186, Old Chelsea Stn., New York, NY 10113-1186, USA
          Tel: (1-212) 260 3690

OCEAN PRESS TRADE DISTRIBUTORS
United States and Canada: **Consortium Book Sales and Distribution**
          Tel: 1-800-283-3572 www.cbsd.com

Australia and New Zealand: **Palgrave Macmillan**
          E-mail: customer.service@macmillan.com.au

UK and Europe: **Pluto Books**
          E-mail: pluto@plutobooks.com

Cuba and Latin America: **Ocean Press**
          E-mail: oceanhav@enet.cu

ocean

www.oceanbooks.com.au
info@oceanbooks.com.au

C O N T E N T S

APPENDICES

ACKNOWLEDGMENTS

It was not an easy task either to begin or to finish writing this book. That is why my first thanks go to Karen Lee Wald, a journalist and friend from the United States, who gave me her endless encouragement. In order that I would continue, she pointed me in the direction of Ocean Press. Without Karen's contagious enthusiasm, this book might never have been written.

José Gómez Abad (alias Diosdado), a *compañero* over many long years of work in the Technical Vice Ministry (VMT) and in the Directorate General of Intelligence of the Cuban Ministry of the Interior (MININT), took the book as seriously as if it were his own project. Not only did he pass on testimonies that had never before been made public, but he also helped to revive my memories, to locate some of the people who were involved in these events, and to relive those beautiful years of revolutionary struggle. His wife, Elsa Montero Maldonado, gave me endless editing assistance while we recalled the experiences we had been through together in the VMT and the Directorate General of Intelligence. To the Elsa of today, the Gina of yesterday, I owe my thanks.

I also owe my gratitude to Juan Carretero Ibáñez (alias Ariel) who, for the first time, gave his version of the role he played. Similarly, there is Iván Montero (alias Renán), a friend and *compañero* in the struggle for the liberation of Latin America, whose real identity remains enigmatic in the books that have been published on Che to date. Despite the fact that these books shed unfortunate doubt over his unquestionable revolutionary character, for the first time, and for this book only, Renán decided to relive publicly his memories of Tania. A very special thanks goes to him.

I am grateful to Onelia Chaveco, editor of the National Information Agency in Cienfuegos, and to Vitalia Acuña, who gave me much support in reconstructing Tania's period in this beautiful city in the center of Cuba.

Thanks to Ana Elisa García, who helped digitize this book, and to Aileen González García, who restored and gave me the photos of the belongings uncovered together with Tania's remains in Bolivia. Likewise, I am grateful to María del Carmen Ariet for her account of the details of that historic discovery.

My thanks go to everyone who helped with this book, and especially to the patient support of Ocean Press, in particular David Deutschmann and Javier Salado, and to the editor Luis Suárez. With the completion of this book, I pay profound tribute to an internationalist combatant I had the opportunity to know and love deeply.

PREFACE

ULISES ESTRADA

As will be seen over the following pages, I was deeply involved, on a personal and a professional level, with Haydée Tamara Bunke Bíder, known throughout the world as "Tania." Our relationship over the two final years of her stay in Cuba was so intense that before she left to undertake the mission that ultimately immortalized her, we agreed that once it was over we would share our lives and raise the children she dreamed of having.

Except for a very small number of *compañeros*, and Tania's parents and brother, our relationship was concealed from everyone until 1969, when I began to collaborate in the creation of the book *Tania the Unforgettable Guerrilla*.[1] At the request of Tania's wonderful mother, Nadia Bunke, and of my supervisors, I publicized the letter Tania had written telling her mother about our relationship. The letter was included in the book about Tania's exemplary revolutionary career that I was writing at the time, together with the well-known Cuban journalists Marta Rojas and Mirta Rodríguez Calderón.

Subsequently, in a posthumous tribute to Tania at the University of Havana, and in different interviews published in the Cuban newspapers *Granma* and *Juventud Rebelde*, Nadia identified me as the "*negrito*" [Afro-Cuban] whom her daughter had dreamed of marrying and with whom she would have many "*mulatito*" [little mulatto] kids when her clandestine mission to Bolivia had been completed.[2]

Because of my political, diplomatic, and clandestine work in Latin American and Caribbean countries (including Chile and Jamaica), and some photos in which I appeared next to Che Guevara in what was then known as Congo Leopoldville,[3] I became known as one of Manuel Piñeiro's men in certain international circles. The legendary Piñeiro, also known as Barbarroja [Red Beard], was closely linked to Cuba's unyielding politics of internationalism and solidarity.

Growing interest in the epic feats of Che and his *compañeros*—including the only woman to have taken part in the internationalist guerrilla force in Bolivia—has awoken in Latin American and European journalists, writers, and filmmakers, an interest in me. Consequently, around the 30th anniversary of their deaths, I selectively agreed to some requests for interviews, guided, like many of my Cuban *compañeros*, only by the desire to publicize as widely as possible the life and achievements of these heroes of the struggle for the definitive independence of all peoples.

Unfortunately, my aims did not coincide with those of most of my interviewers. In their respective publications, many of them distorted or falsified my account, for reasons either of profit or with the political objective of discrediting Che and Tania, as was the case with the French writer Pierre Kalfon,[4] and the Mexican intellectual and politician Jorge Castañeda. I spoke briefly to the latter only twice, on neither occasion giving him the information attributed to me in his "biography" of Che.[5]

Some of these works even portray Tania as the main character in a virtual spy novel, magically transforming her into the "lover" who had numerous romantic encounters with Che. Supposedly, they spent time together in Prague (a place where they were never together),[6] and in Bolivia. They were in fact together in Bolivia, but always surrounded by dozens of Argentine, Bolivian, Cuban, and Peruvian *compañeros*. This was between December 31, 1966, and January 2, 1967, as well as between March 20 and April 17 of the same year.[7]

These and other pen pushers tell Tania's story as if she were one of many agents to have infiltrated the ranks of the enemy on behalf of the supposedly omnipresent and omnipotent Cuban intelligence services. They do not investigate all the clandestine work she carried out in Bolivia—including her penetration of the highest spheres of government and right-wing circles— because it was not linked to classic espionage work. Yet it was this patient and prolonged preparation of conditions that finally allowed armed revolutionary struggle to begin in Bolivia.

Constantly having to read these crude lies gradually compelled me to write this book. In it, I provide insights into the final four years of Tania's life—in Cuba, Latin America, and Europe. For different reasons (the majority of which are linked to the security of specific individuals) this information could not be divulged in the various editions of *Tania the Unforgettable Guerrilla,* published first in Cuba and then in different countries after 1970.

This was the case, for example, with the complete report by the Guatemalan revolutionary Carlos Conrado de Jesús Alvarado Marín, who has since died, and who can only now be identified as the agent Mercy.[8] Some dates that appear in *Tania the Unforgettable Guerrilla* were deliberately altered to hide from the enemy the actual moment when our work had moved to an advanced operations level, which would have been apparent in Tania's training and in her infiltration in Bolivia. Now, however, the dates and places in this book correspond with the exact time of each of the events described.

To complete and complement my recollections of these events, and also to ensure the historical accuracy of my account, I am including in this book new testimonies by Cuban *compañeros* who were directly connected with Tania's training and her infiltration under the false identity of Laura Gutiérrez Bauer. She entered political, journalistic, and cultural circles of the Bolivian bourgeoisie who worked within the military dictatorship of General René

Barrientos (1964–69). I am also including, as appendices, a range of documents that have been either completely or partially unpublished until now.

Finally, it is superfluous to say that by providing more precise and in-depth information about the different facets of Tania's life, as well as about our personal and professional relationship, my sole aim is to pay a much-deserved tribute to her enduring example, to the magnificent friendship and infinite love she gave me from the time we met in Havana in March 1963.

Ulises Estrada, 2004

PROLOGUE

LUIS SUÁREZ

On August 31, 1967, after working clandestinely for over two years in La Paz and over five months in the ranks of the Bolivian National Liberation Army (ELN), Haydée Tamara Bunke Bíder—"Tania"—was killed in a Bolivian army ambush at Puerto Mauricio on the banks of the Río Grande. Ernesto Che Guevara had formally founded the ELN a few months earlier, on March 25, 1967.

Since then, with varying degrees of intensity, many people have hidden or denigrated the example of this extraordinary woman, born in Argentina on November 19, 1937. Some intellectuals linked to the ruling classes of the United States, Europe, and Latin America, and certain individuals on the Central Intelligence Agency (CIA) payroll, have tried to present Tania as a "femme fatale" whose "useless sacrifice" was the consequence of "her secret and sordid extramarital affair with Che."

Likewise, Tania has been accused of working as a spy for the Cuban intelligence services or of serving as a "triple agent," that is, for the East German State Secret Police (Stasi) and the Soviet State Security Committee (KGB). The claim is that she first infiltrated the Cuban Revolution and then under orders penetrated the "highest levels of the Bolivian government."

This book, in contrast, was born out of Ulises Estrada's deep love and admiration for Tania. Ulises, as well as being in charge of her training in espionage methods and techniques, was also Tania's partner during 1963 and 1964. In addition, Ulises also taught Tania urban and rural guerrilla warfare strategies, necessary for her to successfully accomplish the South American revolutionary mission assigned her by Che Guevara.

The author's involvement in the national liberation struggles of the peoples of Africa (including the Congo), and the compartment-alization typical of clandestine work, prevented Ulises from participating more directly in Tania's further training in different European countries (including Czechoslovakia). This was also the case in the subsequent secret contacts made with Tania in Bolivia, Brazil, and Mexico. Nevertheless, the author has unique access to different accounts by a number of Cuban comrades who had the privilege of knowing and working with Tania, and some of these are published here for the first time.

In the interests of historical accuracy the author once again reviewed classified documents on Tania, which are still filed in the archives of the Central Committee of the Communist Party of Cuba (PCC). Estrada also compared the information in these files — including an autobiographical essay written by Tania during her training — with accounts given by Tania's mother, Nadia Bunke, and other Cuban officials who, for various reasons, prefer to remain anonymous.

The inexorable laws of life and death unfortunately prevented Ulises Estrada from interviewing other Cuban, Peruvian, and Bolivian comrades who were directly linked to the guerrilla actions in which Tania participated as a member of Joaquín's column. This is also the case for those who accompanied Tania in her clandestine work, including the Bolivian Rodolfo Saldaña, who has since died, and the Cuban José María Martínez Tamayo (alias Papi). Tania worked with these comrades organizing the urban network that, in accordance with Che's instructions, operated in the Bolivian capital until mid-1967, when it was broken up by the repressive units (trained and guided by the CIA) of the military dictatorship of General René Barrientos.

In spite of Estrada's huge effort in searching for the accounts of other Bolivian comrades who worked with Tania in the urban network, no further information could be obtained for this book. Only Loyola Guzmán, one of the few survivors of the clandestine structure, was able to provide a recollection of Tania as a guerrilla fighter, whom she had met under the false identity of Laura Gutiérrez Bauer. Guzmán only discovered the surprising reality that this "Argentine bourgeois woman," well known in Bolivian social and official circles, was in fact Tania, when informed later by her clandestine contact.

Nevertheless, this book complements and enriches the information available on Tania's clandestine work and life in the guerrilla movement. It also offers, for the first time, information about some of the Cuban Revolution's solidarity work in different Latin American countries undertaken between 1962 and 1965, under the generic name of Operation Fantasma, in accordance with Che Guevara's instructions.

The book helps expose the claims of some biographers of Che Guevara that he had irreconcilable differences with the Cuban political leadership or that from March 1965 onward, these differences forced Che to abandon his family and his numerous posts in Cuba and "seek death," first in Africa and later in Latin America. In this regard, Ulises Estrada's unique testimony suggests incontrovertibly that Che's plans, drawn up from 1961 (and which incorporated Tania's work), included him personally joining the armed guerrilla struggle in the continent.

In addition to providing details of Tania's final four years, this book also contributes to the crucial reconstruction of one of the most heroic pages of the unfinished independence struggles of the Latin American and Caribbean peoples.

CHAPTER **1** |

HISTORICAL CONTEXT

To understand why Che Guevara chose to expand the Latin American liberation struggle and recruit the Argentine Haydée Tamara Bunke Bíder, I believe it is important to reflect on the situation prevailing in Latin America and the Caribbean during the first five years of the 1960s. Che's decision was in accordance with his personal determination to continue the struggle in other countries of the world and to pursue the internationalist policy set out by Fidel Castro and the Cuban Revolution.

As history has recorded, the Cuban Revolution, under the leadership of Fidel Castro, founder of the July 26 Movement and commander of the Rebel Army, was victorious in January 1959. That victory followed six years of bloody combat in the cities, plains, and mountains of Cuba against the dictatorship of General Fulgencio Batista, who had the ongoing political, economic, and military support of US administrations.[1] The young Argentine doctor Ernesto Che Guevara de la Serna was by Fidel's side continuously during that battle. Following the landing of the *Granma* (December 2, 1956) and the first military engagements, Che quickly became one of the most distinguished leaders of the Rebel Army.[2]

After the victory of the Cuban Revolution, new military dictatorships were established in Latin America, in addition to several bloody regimes already in power—such as those of François Duvalier in Haiti, Anastasio Somoza in Nicaragua, and Alfredo Stroessner in Paraguay. At the same time, so-called representative democratic governments were acting at the behest of the US government and the dominant economic and military circles in the United States.

One example of subordination to the White House was the silence of the majority of the continent's governments when Cuba was attacked by the United States, including during the Bay of Pigs operation. Likewise, the Organization of American States (OAS) decided, illegally, to expel Cuba in 1962 and to compel its member countries to break diplomatic, trade, and consular relations with Cuba in July 1964.[3] This decision was immediately adhered to by all Latin American governments and "independent" Caribbean countries, with the sole exception of Mexico.[4]

In spite of the declarations of the Alliance for Progress (officially established by the Kennedy administration during the OAS Social and Economic Council Meeting held at Punta del Este in Uruguay in August 1961) these governments were subjecting their peoples to extreme exploitation and repression, particularly after the successive coup d'états in Argentina (March 1962), Peru (July 1962), Ecuador (September 1962), the Dominican Republic (September 1963), Honduras (October 1963), Brazil (March 1964), and Bolivia (November 1964).[5]

The United States maintained colonial control over Puerto Rico and began a period of high-level aggression against African and Asian countries that had brought their colonial dependence on European imperialist powers to an end. During this period the White House was involved in the assassination of Patrice Lumumba, prime minister of the Congo, and in attacks against the peoples of Vietnam, Laos, and Cambodia. It intervened militarily in the Dominican Republic (April 1965) and subsequently installed, with OAS complicity, a government led by Joaquín Balaguer, one of former dictator Trujillo's front men.

The task of consolidating this and other regimes in Latin America was aided by disunity among the revolutionary organizations. Some of these were divided by Sino-Soviet disputes that had publicly surfaced during the International Conference of Communist and Workers Parties held in the Soviet Union in 1960.

In spite of being persecuted and in many countries banned, Latin American and Caribbean communist parties did not, generally, develop coherent policies that would lead to the seizure of political power because they believed that a Latin American revolution should be developed in two stages: democratic-bourgeois and then socialist. They adhered to the policy of weakening the enemy by making modest inroads into the distribution of power by working through trade unions and professional organizations, with the help of peasants and students. At the same time, organizations that existed legally campaigned to achieve representation within municipal governments and to win parliamentary seats, which only minimally contributed to the elimination of imperialist and oligarchic domination.

The example of Cuba's victory and resistance encouraged sectors of certain communist parties, particularly the youth, to question whether the tactics of their organizations were appropriate for the circumstances. These, like other organizations emerging from the dissolution of existing national reformist and social democratic parties, began to form what was then known as the New Left. It embraced a predominantly rural armed struggle as the main strategy for seizing political power and focused on the Cuban experience as its key point of reference.[6]

Leaders of the New Left traveled to Havana in search of political, economic, or military support for their revolutionary goals and the Cuban political leadership was open to their requests. This provoked sharp criticism from communist parties which, with the support of the Communist Party of the Soviet Union, argued that Cuban relations with these revolutionary organizations undermined their own political positions in Latin America. Nonetheless, while still maintaining friendly relations with the communist parties, Cuba, in accordance with its internationalist position, continued to support those Latin American and Caribbean revolutionary organizations that appealed for solidarity.

In this context, Che began to create the conditions that would facilitate the revolutionary struggle in other countries of the continent, particularly in his birthplace, Argentina. When he joined Fidel in Mexico in 1955, the two men agreed that Che would continue to fight for the liberation of other Latin American nations after the Cuban Revolution had taken place. After 1961, Che began to plan the logistics of this decision.

At that time the Colombian brothers Antonio, Juan Martín, and Patricio Larrotta González were in Cuba. They had arrived in Havana weeks after founding the Peasant Student Worker Movement (MOEC) in January 1959. Their decision to embrace revolutionary armed struggle brought them into contact with Che, who had a high opinion of Antonio's capabilities, forged through political debate and his work as president of the Colombian National Student Union.

Interested in receiving military training, Antonio and Juan Martín joined different units of the recently formed Cuban People's Defense Militia. From the ranks of this political and military organization, Antonio took part in the April 1961 Bay of Pigs battle against more than 1,200 mercenaries, trained and armed by the CIA and transported to the Cuban coast in US army ships. For his part, Juan Martín fought against counterrevolutionary bands that, also with the backing of the Kennedy administration, had waged an armed uprising in the Escambray Mountains in central Cuba.

Recognizing this solidarity and taking into account the Colombian government's increasing hostility toward the revolution,[7] the Cuban authorities supported the brothers in their determination to establish a guerrilla front in the Cauca River valley. According to Juan Martín, today a journalist with the Cuban magazine *Bohemia,* it was anticipated that he, together with Che, would join this guerrilla movement after it had become established. The plans failed, however, when Antonio and other MOEC leaders died in combat in May 1961.

Nevertheless, this setback did not in any way alter Che's decision. On the contrary, he maintained complete support for revolutionary guerrilla operations in rural and urban areas of Latin America. He continued to search for the path that would allow him to become directly involved in the armed struggle in the south of the continent until he could take the liberation struggle to his beloved Argentina.

With a view to establishing conditions that would allow him to achieve his goal—and as a result of a coup d'état against the reformist Argentine government of President Arturo Frondizi on March 29, 1962[8]—Che personally and decisively supported the political and military training of several Argentines who were in Cuba at that time. Among them were members of the Peronist Revolutionary Formation (named in honor of the deposed president and leader of the Justicialista Party, Juan Domingo Perón), under the leadership of distinguished individuals such as William Cooke and Alicia Eguren. Similarly, Che supported the organization of a select group of Argentine revolutionaries, led by his friend and companion, the prestigious Argentine journalist Jorge Ricardo Masetti, who had previously received military training in Cuba.

After January 1963, this group concluded its military training (which had begun in Cuba) in the recently liberated Democratic Republic of Algeria, with the aim of forming a guerrilla movement in the Salta region in northern Argentina.[9] At the same time, several officers from the Cuban Ministry of the Interior (MININT)[10] began to establish themselves in Bolivia by attaining legal documents. These were the circumstances in which Che ordered Manuel Piñeiro to select and train an Argentine citizen with the goal of establishing her clandestinely in La Paz.

Che's initial idea was that involvement would be at all times through coordination with the military wing of the Bolivian Communist Party (PCB), to avoid interfering with Bolivian internal affairs. The MININT officers would have to fulfill key tasks linked to the support of the revolutionary struggle in neighboring countries—Peru and, in the longer term, Paraguay. Above all, these tasks entailed preparing the conditions for the officers' eventual incorporation in the Argentine People's Guerrilla Army led by Masetti who, at that time, was known by the alias Commander Segundo.[11]

Masetti's disappearance, however, together with the capture or assassination in the months of March and April 1964 of some other *compañeros* in the struggle, once again postponed Che's aspirations. At the end of 1964, after speaking at the UN General Assembly, Che toured a number of Middle Eastern countries and north and central Africa. When he returned to Cuba, Fidel Castro approved Che's proposal to lead a group of Cubans to train and support guerrilla detachments for the Congo National Revolution Council.

In April 1965, Che secretly departed for Tanzania. From there he entered the southeastern territory of the Congo via Lake Tanganyika, a route also followed by over 100 Cuban internationalist combatants selected by the Ministry of Revolutionary Armed Forces. Toward the end of 1965, the Congolese political and military forces established in this area, following Mobuto's ascent to power, decided with the support of the Organization of African Unity to call military actions to a halt. The Cuban internationalists were therefore asked to withdraw. After a prolonged clandestine stay in the Cuban embassy in Tanzania, Che agreed to travel to Prague with the goal of recommencing the development of the revolutionary armed struggle in Latin America, especially in Bolivia, Peru, and Argentina.

Although Che never mentioned this while I accompanied him on this clandestine journey to the Congo or during the first part of his stay in Prague, I have always believed that his decision to focus on Latin America was influenced by the intensification of the people's resistance there—particularly the miners. The people fought against the dictatorship of the Bolivian General René Barrientos and against the coup d'état in Argentina led by the infamous General Juan Carlos Onganía, which on June 26, 1966, overthrew the "constitutional" government of Arturo Illía. The coup installed a dictatorship that lasted until May 1973 and, with US support, devastated this Latin American country.

It is false and offensive to argue as certain writers have, together with several traitors to the Cuban Revolution, that Che left Cuba for the Congo in April 1965 and then for Bolivia 17 months later on account of a conflict with Fidel and Raúl Castro.[12] On the contrary, during the course of the many conversations I held with Che after he left Africa, and while we were lodged clandestinely in a tiny apartment in Prague, he spoke to me of the positive nature of his relationship with Fidel. Che considered Fidel to be the person who had converted him into a true communist. Che's opinion of Raúl Castro was always framed with the highest respect and admiration for his abilities as a political and military leader.

According to what Che told me during those conversations, his decision was based on his identification with the need to support anti-imperialist struggles in different countries of the world, set out in his Farewell Letter to Fidel Castro and in his "Message to the Tricontinental," published in *Tricontinental*.[13] For the same reason, he was determined to step down from the high-ranking positions he occupied within the Cuban government and the United Party of the Socialist Revolution, later known as the Cuban Communist Party (PCC). Fidel authorized and supported all his activities with the national and social liberation struggles underway in Colombia, Guatemala, Nicaragua, Peru, and Venezuela.

Che's resolute decision linked my revolutionary career with certain facets of his internationalist activities. After the first months of 1963, it also linked me with the political career and personal life of the main character of this story, Haydée Tamara Bunke Bíder, citizen of the former German Democratic Republic (GDR), born in Argentina, who at that time was already known in different circles of Havana by her second name of Tamara.

OPERATION FANTASMA

In the early hours of one morning toward the end of June 1961 in a building on the corner of 5th Avenue and 14th Street in Miramar, headquarters at the time of the G-2 Operations Division of the newly formed MININT, Manuel Piñeiro suggested that I join the political intelligence branch of Department M. At that point I never imagined that for the rest of my life my entire professional and political career, and my personal life, would become inextricable from the Cuban Revolution's multifaceted work with the numerous democratic, anti-imperialist, national, and social struggles being waged by the peoples of Asia, Africa, Latin America, and the Caribbean.

Nor did I imagine that under the direct leadership of the renowned Manuel Piñeiro, for whom I had great admiration, friendship, and respect, I would fulfill a variety of political, military, operational, and conspiratorial missions in Latin America and Africa. These missions were headed by one of the most extraordinary and charismatic individuals involved in world revolutionary movements: Che Guevara, with the encouragement of commanders Fidel, Raúl, Almeida, Celia Sánchez, and other leaders.[1] The movement developed in tandem with the accelerated pace of hemispheric and international events, including intensified US hostility against my country.

It was even further from my mind that, during the years 1963 and 1964, these internationalist missions would link multiple facets of my personal, political, and professional life with Haydée Tamara

Bunke Bíder. Haydée, an intelligent, affectionate, knowledgable, selfless, and beautiful woman, became world famous after 1970. At that time, her numerous clandestine missions in Bolivia under Che's command, together with her involvement in the guerrilla column of the Bolivian ELN, became public knowledge with the publication of *Tania the Unforgettable Guerrilla.*

The first inkling I had in this respect was in October 1962, after being transferred from Department M to a second-in-command post at Department MM, which was the military intelligence branch. Piñeiro gave me a mission to assist my *compañero* and friend Olo Pantoja,[2] and other memorable Cuban *compañeros* (including Papi),[3] in organizing the Special Operations Division (MOE) of the Technical Vice Ministry (VMT) branch of the MININT.

In contrast to other sections and departments of this recently formed Cuban strategic intelligence branch, MOE would have sole responsibility for overseeing several clandestine operations linked to our country's solidarity work with the different revolutionary organizations and movements continually emerging in different Latin American countries. These movements had been inspired by the victory of the Cuban insurrection and formed in response to the pro-imperialist, antidemocratic, and unpopular policies of their respective governments.

The position of the Cuban Revolution regarding these new organizations and movements had been set out months previously in the Second Declaration of Havana.[4] The Cuban National Assembly adopted a firm commitment to the liberation of Latin America advocated from the end of the 19th century by José Martí, the preeminent fighter for Cuban independence and precursor of definitive independence for the peoples of Latin America and the Caribbean in the face of US imperialism.

The leadership of the Cuban Revolution foresaw that, given the critical economic, social, and political situation of the continent and the decision taken by various New Left organizations to embrace revolutionary armed struggle as the fundamental means of seizing political power, the Andes would become the setting for a new

Sierra Maestra. In other words, it would be the scene of a new insurrectionary movement against imperialism and the centuries-old domination of Latin America and the Caribbean.

Cuba's position differed from some of the strategies and tactics espoused by certain sectors of the leadership in the Soviet Union and the international communist and workers' movement (including some communist parties in Latin America), which embraced the effort for a peaceful coexistence between the exploiting and exploited. The Cuban Revolution declared that the duty of all revolutionaries (particularly Latin Americans) was to win complete political power for the people through revolutions.

In spite of my limited experience in international politics, for me this declaration was like a new call to just war against colonial and imperialist domination in Latin America and the Caribbean.[5] Together with Olo Pantoja, I dedicated myself enthusiastically to the organization of MOE, particularly to the variety of operational tasks which, during that period, linked me for the first time to a number of activists and revolutionary leaders who were working from, studying in, or regularly visiting our country.

My enthusiasm increased when I attended a meeting with Piñeiro in his house on 18th Street in Miramar.[6] In the 1960s, many discussions and debates were held there between different leaders of the Latin American revolutionary movement and Fidel Castro, Che, and Piñeiro. In the meeting, Piñeiro said to me that we should coordinate the range of operations being carried out by the Cuban Revolution in solidarity with revolutionary movements in Latin America. In his view, given the conditions in the continent and the intensification of enemy activities against our country and the Latin American revolutionary movement itself, these operations had to be carried out like "phantoms."

Put another way, this meant that they be organized with total secrecy, leaving no trace of our involvement to be discovered by our enemies, or even our friends—including those belonging to the socialist bloc and Latin American communist parties. It also meant that we had to avoid detection, at all costs, by enemy intelligence and counterintelligence units, particularly the CIA and the US intelligence community. The name Operation Fantasma emerged simply to identify the Cuban Revolution's various political and military operations in support of revolutionary organizations in Argentina, Colombia, Peru, Uruguay, and Venezuela.[7]

In line with Piñeiro's philosophy of decentralized work, I was given the opportunity to accompany him to meetings, together with certain Latin American revolutionary leaders. These meetings were generally held very late at night, with Fidel and particularly with Che, either in Piñeiro's home, in Che's office on the ninth floor of the Ministry of Industry building (situated in the historic Revolution Square), or in Che's private residence, which was at that time in Nuevo Vedado.[8]

My deep admiration and identification with the thinking of these Cuban leaders grew. I was proud of the fact that my direct relations with Che were strengthening, as well as those with some of his immediate *compañeros*, particularly José Manuel Manresa,[9] who was Che's office manager. In December 1962, immediately following the Missile Crisis, Piñeiro entrusted me with several tasks related to what were then known as Operations Matraca and Sombra.[10]

Both of these operations were based in Bolivia and required my participation, together with other MININT officers—including Abelardo Colomé (alias Fury), Papi, and Olo Pantoja—in addition to several members of the secret military wing of the PCB, such as Rodolfo Saldaña and the brothers Coco and Inti Peredo.[11] In the first operation, MOE contributed to preparing conditions for the clandestine entry of a small guerrilla detachment into Peru that planned later to begin armed attacks. The detachment developed into the Peruvian National Liberation Army (ELN), led by Héctor Béjar and comprising, among others, the young and distinguished revolutionary Peruvian poet, Javier Heraud.[12]

At the same time through Operation Sombra, preparations were underway for the arrival in Argentina of a group of revolutionary Argentine activists in the company of captain Hermes Peña and first lieutenant Alberto Castellanos. These Cuban officials, under the leadership of Jorge Ricardo Masetti and with the solidarity of the Algerian National Liberation Front, were under orders to establish a guerrilla front in the northern Salta Province. As we have seen, the foundation and consolidation of this guerrilla front constituted the embryonic plan drawn up by Che, with the aim of personally joining the armed revolutionary struggle in his *"patria chica"* [little homeland].

To conclude my initial role in these operations, Piñeiro sent me to take part in guerrilla exercises in Cuba. There were two groups of Peruvian revolutionaries being trained in Cuba at the time; I joined some members of the Movement of the Revolutionary Left, founded and led by Dr. Luis de la Puente Uceda, until his death in 1966.[13]

When this brief period of guerrilla training was over, Piñeiro entrusted me with the task of selecting from among the Latin Americans staying in Havana, "an Argentine *compañera*" who met the requirements within the framework of Operation Fantasma, a prolonged, dangerous, and important clandestine role in an unidentified Latin American country. Piñeiro mentioned that priority should be given to a *compañera* proposed by Che, whose name I heard then for the first time: Haydée Tamara Bunke Bíder.

Tamara, Piñeiro went on to say, worked as a German translator in the Ministry of Education and worked closely with the Cuban Institute for Friendship with the Peoples (ICAP). She also worked with the national leadership of the Federation of Cuban Women (FMC), through which she had close ties to its president Vilma Espín, and its then secretary of international relations, Lupe Véliz, and others.

In spite of these positive political references, Piñeiro also directed me to assess two other Argentine *compañeras* based in Havana: Isabel Larguía and the pianist Lidia Guerberoff. Piñeiro instructed a team of us to develop character profiles and to investigate the *compañeras*, before we decided which candidate could perform the delicate tasks planned, and who could finally be recommended to Che.

Given the fact that our intelligence apparatus was only recently formed, the task was complex. We would have to verify the political and personal characters and experiences of the three candidates, both in Cuba and in their respective countries. In the cases of Isabel and Lidia, we had to get in touch with our political and operational contacts in Argentina. In Tamara's case, in addition to verifying her family and political background in Argentina, we also had to obtain information from the GDR without disclosing to the East German Communist Party, intelligence, or counterintelligence services the operational nature of our interest in this *compañera*.

Piñeiro requested *compañero* Ramón Oroza Naberán (alias Demetrio) to discreetly undertake the relevant investigations and deliver the results to us as quickly as possible. Demetrio, head of the special counterintelligence unit and historically renowned in VMT circles, would later be acclaimed in the Directorate General of Intelligence and the General Command of National Liberation, which formed a part of the MININT.

CHAPTER 3

THE TANIA CASE

Thanks to the work of our intelligence services and our special counterintelligence unit, the process of investigating Isabel, Lidia, and Tamara was thorough and discreet. But when I received the report of these inquiries, a difficulty became apparent: all three candidates had excellent political and personal backgrounds. It was also clear that all three were committed to the liberation struggles of Latin America. Nonetheless, a single proposal had to be put to Piñeiro so that he, in turn, could forward it to Che.

After processing all the information gathered from different sources, I met with Piñeiro once again. Following a detailed assessment of the characteristics and abilities of each candidate, both of us selected Tamara. This choice was taken not only because she had been proposed by Che—which in itself was a compelling reference—but also because in our opinion the wide range of her experience in international relations work meant that she was closer to meeting the essential criteria for fulfilling the complex tasks we soon planned to undertake.

In addition, during the inquiries carried out in Havana, Buenos Aires, and East Berlin, both Tamara's and her parents' long-term and unequivocal political and personal commitment became clear. All three family members had been heavily involved in the struggle against fascism and were in support of socialist principles, both in Argentina and in the GDR. We also discovered evidence indicating that, after spending her childhood and adolescence in Argentina and immediately following her arrival in the GDR, Tamara—just 14 years old—joined the Free German Youth (FGY). She acquired a great deal of credibility within the youth organization and, at her own request, was promptly put forward as a candidate for membership of the German Unified Workers Socialist Party (GUWSP).

From the rank and file of these traditional communist organizations, Tamara actively participated in a variety of work with German political and cultural organizations. As a German-Spanish translator, she accompanied a number of Latin American leaders visiting the GDR, particularly those linked with the International Relations Department of the FGY. In addition to knowledge of the situation in Latin America, she acquired contacts through this work that strengthened her desire to return to the country of her birth and become involved in Argentina's democratic struggle.

Tamara had demonstrated solidarity with the Cuban people's struggle for liberation, keeping well informed about the revolutionary war in the Sierra Maestra. After the victory of the revolution on January 1, 1959, her commitment strengthened to the extent that she expressed interest in traveling to Cuba to take part, together with the Cuban people, in their difficult battle against US imperialism.

Tamara's enthusiasm grew when, in July 1959, she met Antonio Núñez Jiménez, captain in the Rebel Army, and Lieutenant Orlando Borrego, who were both in the the GDR capital. In addition, in December of the same year, she acted as an interpreter for Che Guevara during a meeting with East German and Latin American students. Che was visiting East Berlin for the first time as the head of a major delegation representing the National Bank of Cuba. From this time on, Tamara maintained close contact with Cuban delegations visiting the GDR throughout 1960.

Following successful overtures made by the Cuban prima ballerina Alicia Alonso (also founder of the Cuban National Ballet company), and after having obtained authorization from the GUWSP, Tamara finally arrived in Cuba in May 1961. She immediately became involved in a variety of translation work for ICAP, the Ministry of Education, the FMC, and the Ministry of Revolutionary Armed

Forces. She also interpreted for the first East German delegations that visited Havana.

Tamara worked with the organization known then as the Association of Young Rebels, which from April 4, 1962, was named the Union of Young Communists (UJC). She helped organize the International Student Union conference held in Havana in 1961. Tamara also devoted herself to a wide range of voluntary work, where at times she worked with Che.

Tamara joined the People's Defense Militia,[1] the uniform of which (olive green pants, denim blue shirt and white cap, together with a pistol on the belt), she proudly wore wherever she went in Havana. At the same time, she established and maintained relations with a number of Latin Americans who had traveled to Cuba seeking solidarity with their own struggles. Included among them was the Nicaraguan revolutionary Carlos Fonseca to whom she expressed her complete willingness to become immediately involved in the guerrilla struggle in Nicaragua.

Tamara was a highly educated woman. She spoke several languages and was well versed in literature and music. She had studied philosophy at Humboldt University in the GDR. She also played the piano, the guitar, and the accordion, performing Latin American folk music during gatherings hosted by different Latin Americans staying in Havana. Given that she was a conscientious student and constantly in search of new knowledge, she registered for a degree in journalism at the University of Havana. Finally, Tamara's personal conduct was irreproachable.

All these factors supported the validity of Che's proposal. Yet prior to presenting him with our conclusions, we needed to find out whether Tamara was willing to fulfill the mission. In the final days of March 1963, we arranged to meet her late one evening at Piñeiro's home. After greeting each other, she was invited into the mahogany furnished lounge, a room to the right of the main entrance, which had before been the library.

It was there that Tamara met for the first time the three officers who would be directly linked to her political destiny. The first was Piñeiro, a Rebel Army commander with a thick red beard, for whom we all held great respect. The second was a MININT officer, a robust white man we simply called Papi. Then there was me, Ulises, a tall, very slim Afro-Cuban man who was barely 25 years old. The three of us were casually dressed in our customary olive green uniforms. Tamara carried a pistol on her belt and wore her militia uniform with style.

Once the introductions were over and some comments made about the political and economic situation in Latin America, including the progress of the continent's revolutionary struggles, Piñeiro brought up the reason for the meeting. He told Tamara that we had asked to speak to her in order to propose that she carry out a secret mission, which, if she were to accept it, implied significant risks to her safety. The mission, he added, would be undertaken in a Latin American country with the utmost secrecy, to the extent that not even her closest friends could be informed of her whereabouts or the nature of her work. Her parents, in whom we already trusted completely, would also have to remain in the dark, as we could not burden them with the responsibility of keeping this secret.

Tamara interrupted, saying without hesitation that further explanations were not necessary. We could count on her to fulfill this mission for the Cuban Revolution, without concerning ourselves about the dangers she would have to face. Her excitement was apparent and Piñeiro tried to calm her by acknowledging her willingness to participate in the mission. Then he continued, explaining to Tamara that the sacrifice she would have to make would begin in Cuba, where none of her friends could be aware that she had been selected for this mission. Not even the officials who would assist in her military and operational training could know her real identity.

Tamara interrupted once again, to say that Piñeiro's request would not be easy, as her life in Cuba was very much connected with a number of Cuban and Latin American revolutionaries. In the latter case, she was involved with members of the United Nicaraguan Front—later known as the Sandinista National Liberation Front

(FSLN)—led by Carlos Fonseca, with whom she had planned to go and fight in Nicaragua. All of them would find it difficult to understand the (necessary) rift in their relationships with her. This could be seen as suspicious if it were not properly justified.

Piñeiro smiled, pleased that Tamara astutely grasped the nature of the situation she would have to confront. Trying to reassure her, he explained that the officials in charge of her operational training would map out the different cover stories she would have to use with each of her friends. These stories would complement each other but their accuracy could not be proven and they would be devised with her input, he said, reassuring her. In the meantime, however, it was crucial that she begin to distance herself from her closest friends, so as her training could go ahead unhindered, and so that when the training was concluded and she had to leave Cuba, her absence would be less noticeable.

At this point, with furrowed brow and tears in her eyes, but with her head held high, Tamara spoke of how much progress she had made since arriving in Cuba, in terms of her political and ideological development. She referred to the way in which her work here had contributed to her education, as had the warm friendships she had developed with Cubans and foreigners alike. Nevertheless, she said, she hoped that this mission would facilitate an even greater political development and, above all, would allow her to realize her dream of participating directly in the national struggles for the liberation of Latin America.

Piñeiro explained that the struggle Tamara dreamed of could be carried out in different ways, and in order for it to be successful various techniques and methods could be used in her clandestine work. From time to time, he stipulated, speaking from the perspective of a trainer, she would have to receive secret messages, messages vital to the success of a revolutionary operation or the safety of a *compañero*. In addition, the different ways to make contact with other agents that she would learn about would be essential in her future mission for outwitting surveillance of her activities by enemy intelligence.

Similarly, there would be coded or invisible messages she would learn to write. She would have to master techniques in preparing a dead drop,[2] or a secret place where she could leave messages, weapons, medicines, or money for other agents to pick up later. All these actions, Piñeiro concluded, separately or together, helped guarantee the efficiency and security of clandestine work that revolutionaries had to carry out. Tamara paid close attention to these explanations, but her face lit up when Piñeiro, unaware that he was predicting her future, said, "I cannot rule out, in any given situation, that should the occasion arise, you may have to join a guerrilla movement, for which you will receive the necessary military training."

At this stage of the conversation, the serious expression on her face told us that she had assimilated the complexity of the tasks she would have to confront. Piñeiro emphasized that she would receive the training required to successfully face the risks entailed. He went on to say that she would be assigned an alias—to be suggested at a later point—to identify her throughout her operational training, without revealing her real identity to anyone.

Evidently delighted, Tamara asked us to be allowed to choose the alias and immediately, as if she had thought about it long in advance, suggested Tania as her nom de guerre. Years later her mother, Nadia Bunke, told me this was the most subtle and solemn way her daughter could express her admiration for another woman who, also working clandestinely, had used this alias. Tamara was acknowledging the Soviet guerrilla Zoja Kosmodemjanskaja, detained, tortured, and assassinated in December 1941 by the fascists responsible for so much violence in her country. Even though at that time we were unaware of this story or of Tamara's political and emotional identification with this person, we all accepted the alias she had chosen.

A few days later I accompanied Piñeiro, Tamara, and Papi to Che's office in the Ministry of Industry. Che had previously asked Papi to get to know the *compañera* with whom he would participate in a mission in an urban organization in support of a guerrilla movement in a Latin American country. Tamara did not know whom we were going to see, and was delighted to see Che again. She was immensely pleased to learn that her mission would be linked, in one way or another, to Che—that compatriot whom she had written about in August 1960 to Antonio Núñez Jiménez, indicating that perhaps some day she would take him to Argentina "so that he could help bring about some changes in our country."[3]

For his part, Che had already worked alongside Tania with German and Argentine delegations and on voluntary workdays, and also in certain events related to the Argentine community in Cuba, such as the popular barbeque held in the grounds of ICAP on May 25, 1962, to celebrate the anniversary of Argentina's independence from Spanish colonialism. Che asked her about some of her compatriots. He also inquired about the progress of her work in the different Cuban organizations she was involved with, and other matters of general interest.

Engaging in this conversation, the experienced commander and political leader wanted to remove any initial tension from the meeting. When he felt certain that this was the case, he looked Tamara straight in the eye and told her to repeat to him what Piñeiro had told her and what her decision was, making it clear that the criteria for being accepted was that her choice had to be entirely voluntary. Should it be the case that she had changed her mind during the days since the last meeting, it would not lead to any problems for her, Che added. He knew that revolutionaries faced a whole range of challenges, including those entailing serious dangers, which she would have to confront if she decided to accept the mission he had offered her.

Without hesitation, though with a slight hint of irritation, Tamara answered that she had only one thing to say on this matter: she had already informed Piñeiro of her willingness to fulfill any mission that would contribute to the liberation of Latin America from imperialist exploitation. This struggle, in her opinion as a revolutionary, was much more important than any risk she would have to run.

Smiling, Che reassured Tamara and jovially reiterated that once the mission had been accepted she would have to be 100 percent committed. For that reason, he went on to say, he personally had to be convinced that this would be the case. Then and there he alluded to the significant emotional tension she would have to face as a consequence of being far away from people she loved, and as a result of operating in a capitalist world she had always despised for its selfish and exploitative nature in relation to our peoples. Moreover, she would have to run major risks that could lead to the loss of her life.

He began to discuss the political, economic, social, and military situation on the continent, the involvement—hidden for many—of US imperialism in the pillaging of the key sources of wealth in the region and the acquiescence of national governments that received, in exchange, only crumbs handed out to enrich local leaders. "You cannot be a revolutionary without being anti-imperialist," Che said with complete conviction. There was no alternative to the development of an open confrontation against the imperialist presence and against servile governments or military dictatorships in Latin America.

Her voice full of emotion, Tamara answered that she would be faithful to these principles whatever the price. From this point on, this would be the main goal in her life. She added that she had never expected to experience an occasion such as this, and even less to have Che talk directly with her and to trust her. She finished by saying, "I will never betray this trust while I am still alive and breathing."

In this way, the process of Tamara's selection ended, and from then on, in our technical language, we began to identify hers as the Tania Case. At that point, in accordance with Piñeiro's instructions, I took charge of the organization and management of a team of officers from the political intelligence division, the military training schools, and other MININT branches. These officers would be responsible for Tania's training in conspiracy methods and techniques necessary for the clandestine work she would have to carry out. Should the need arise, she would also be trained to take part in urban or rural armed struggle.

In close coordination with other specialists from my department, I would have to begin working on obtaining the documents that would be necessary for Tania's clandestine departure from our country. Above all, I would have to focus on the cover that would allow Tania to safely and secretly enter the Latin American country that would later be identified by Che at the appropriate moment.

OPERATIONAL TRAINING
IN CUBA

As agreed with Tania during our meeting with Che, I went to her Miramar apartment during the first few days of April 1963.[1] She looked startled when she saw that I had brought another *compañero* whom she had not met. I explained that he was Officer Salvador Prat (alias Juan Carlos) who would be with me throughout most of her training. Tania looked tense, expectant.

We drank a delicious cup of coffee she prepared Cuban style, before beginning to talk, as naturally as possible, about matters relating to the different activities she had been involved with here in Cuba. Then we cut straight to the point. As we had previously requested, Tania handed us an autobiographical essay, written in the third person (see appendix 1). We then informed her that her training would be prolonged and intensive, but that as Piñeiro had already mentioned, the first few days would be restricted to reviewing the cover stories we had prepared to explain the differences in her behavior to the people she knew.

We started to analyze, case by case, the Cuban organizations where she was working. Always bearing Tania's ideas in mind, we worked out what she would have to say to her bosses and friends to justify her gradual estrangement from them. Then we reviewed her closest personal relationships, beginning with a married couple from the United States, Lena and Louis Jones, who lived in Tania's building, on a floor above her apartment. Tania shared a close political affinity with them and they socialized every day. After studying the range of alternatives, we reached consensus about the explanation Tania would give to this couple.

We dealt with the special case of her parents, Nadia and Erich, in whom we had complete trust, politically speaking, as we had indicated to Tania during the conversation at Piñeiro's house. Nevertheless, we were not going to subject them to the anxieties that would undoubtedly arise were they to become aware of the truth about Tania's future clandestine activities. We agreed that in her letters to them, she would begin to mention a "special job" that she had taken with the Cuban armed forces. She would add that at some point these duties would "kidnap" her from her normal activities.

In this context, we insisted that the need to develop this cover did not imply a lack of trust in any of the Cuban or foreign revolutionaries Tania knew, but that the compartmentalization typical of clandestine work was an inviolable principle of our profession. For her part, Tania expressed her conviction that her parents, who had worked for years in the clandestine struggle against fascism, would understand the situation and would never ask about her "special job."

We went on to say that after some time had passed, we would look at the need to move her to another address unknown to her friends. In the meantime, in order to justify my continual visits to her apartment during the early hours of the morning, we agreed that she would say I was her boyfriend and that because of the sensitive nature of my work and due to other personal circumstances, I did not want to get to know her friends. Tania accepted this, certain that they would understand the situation without further explanations.

Having relaxed by this stage in the conversation Tania pointed out, with her typical frankness, that we needed to be entirely honest with her, including when we were discussing her mistakes or weak points. Indeed, she demanded that we be completely open when expressing all our views to her. Tania also asked if at any point she did not understand an instruction or lesson, she could be allowed to ask questions and make comments until she had fully internalized the issue. She knew how important discipline was in missions as complex and risky as those she would have to undertake, but this would only be possible when she had an in-depth understanding of what was required, obviously without violating at any point the necessary principle of compartmentalization.

Although we agreed with her, the reality is that in our profession we cannot, and could not, express our own opinions and I quickly became aware that Tania's understanding of discipline was unique. This was an omen that our work would be difficult and require patience. Nonetheless, both Juan Carlos and I left convinced that the goals of our first meeting with her had been accomplished satisfactorily.

From then on, our contact with Tania was on an almost daily basis. Most of the time our meetings were held at night and lasted to the early hours of the morning. Little by little, we got to know each other. During those times when we were both relaxed, we shared our respective tastes in music, literature, cinema, and sports. Sometimes Tania would take out her guitar and play the many Argentine folk songs she knew; on others she delighted us with her wonderful accordion interpretations of Soviet songs, including the famous "Moscow Nights."

In this way, chatting informally to each other, Tania's personal life became part of our daily routine. She was obviously happy to talk to us about herself, her parents' life (both of whom she adored), and the rest of her family. She was also pleased to talk about memories of her childhood and teenage years in Argentina, as well as the bustling lifestyle she led in the GDR as a consequence of her total commitment to revolutionary work.

For Juan Carlos and me these conversations were vital for getting to know Tania. As we explained to her, we would have to devise a cover of the new identity she would assume outside of Cuba. Our aim was to ensure that this cover was based as closely as possible on her real life.

The rest of her training was also very rigorous. We began by analyzing how the enemy worked. We pointed out that she was compelled to learn the methods employed by Latin American intelligence and counterintelligence. In many cases the methods were similar, since the majority of these repressive organizations had been trained by the CIA, the Federal Bureau of Investigation (FBI), and police officers and other agents from the United States.

Both Juan Carlos and I focused heavily on the surveillance and political control mechanisms employed by Bolivia's repressive apparatus, although we did not mention the country Tania would have to enter. In addition, we devoted whole days to studying the political, economic, and military situations prevailing in Latin American countries, as well as the links their corresponding governments had with the United States and its monopolies. We also taught Tania—based on the knowledge and experience we had already acquired—about the customs and lifestyles of each country's bourgeois classes.

After tackling these subjects we began to prepare Tania psychologically for the lessons she would receive in a range of operational tactics. These classes, we emphasized, would make her a true specialist in the methods employed by intelligence and counterintelligence enemy organizations, allowing her to detect, outwit, or neutralize operations undertaken against her. These enemy organizations were capable of using methods to detect her real motives, particularly during the early period of her arrival in a country, when she was beginning to frequent the circles of political and economic power as part of the routine crucial to her work.

In addition, as an essential aspect of her training, Tania began to learn how to carry out countersurveillance: the different methods she could use to detect a potential enemy's surveillance over her. She also learned how to observe identified targets.[2] When we were certain she had adequately assimilated the theoretical aspects of these lessons, we began to go out with her to conduct practical exercises in the area.

For example, we instructed her to discreetly follow a target —that is, a person chosen at random—and then to write us a report detailing all of that person's activities. Even though we initially had to correct some mistakes Tania made due to her lack of experience—especially when the target could have discovered they were being followed— Tania's attention to what had been said during our meetings and discussions, as well as her ability and intelligence, enabled her to overcome these deficiencies quickly. Indeed, for her, these practical operations were like a game.

When Tania described the movements of someone she had followed she did so with immense expressiveness, her beautiful face brightening with smiles. Gradually, she began to feel so sure of what she was doing that we had to work to avoid overconfidence, which could lead her to lower her guard. We emphasized that this behavior was not acceptable on clandestine missions. Distrust and constant vigilance were both invaluable virtues, as well as being principles that, as Che used to say in relation to the rural guerrilla, always had to be kept in mind.

In parallel, Juan Carlos and I also dedicated intensive sessions to showing Tania the different ways of passing along information to other agents, including through dead drops. The characteristics of the object to hide determined where it should be placed. For example, the underside of a park bench could be used as a place to stick a simple message, while a wall, a tree, or vacant land could be used to hide a larger object. Such objects would have to be duly camouflaged so that they would not be easily noticed and so no one could guess their content.

Much faster than we expected, Tania became an expert in these methods that were so crucial to the success of her future mission. We began to teach her how to theoretically use invisible writing codes, providing her with a general idea of lessons she would subsequently receive from *compañeros* who were specialists in operational techniques.

Similarly, Tania rapidly learned about telegraphy, radio transmission, and the reception of coded messages. We limited ourselves to explaining some of our own experiences and to making suggestions she could try out during the practical classes. Any doubts Tania had on the subject were resolved later in her practical classes.

Training aimed at teaching her to develop relations with unknown individuals was similarly successful. These classes were easy for Tania, given her education, charm, friendliness, and daring, as well as other personal qualities. As if it were yesterday, I remember a practical exercise she carried out in San Rafael Street, close to Galiano Avenue in Central Havana. At that time this neighborhood was a commercial district full of shops selling clothes, shoes, domestic appliances, and other products. Consequently, its streets were very busy during the afternoon.

One day, walking through the area with Tania, we asked her without warning to try to establish relations with a couple strolling along the street with their young daughter. Without hesitating, Tania approached them and asked for the address of a shop. The couple not only took her to the place, they also accompanied her while she made a few purchases and ended up inviting her home where they made her coffee. Accepting the invitation, she gave them fictitious information about Argentina and her stay in Cuba. The man was a civil servant employed by a cultural center and his wife was a teacher, which is why the conversation lasted a few hours, sufficient time for a friendship to be established. The friendship was maintained until we decided the right time had come to bring it to a close.

Juan Carlos and I taught Tania about another area of conspiracy work: the operational study of a military or economic target. She learned how to analyze the fundamental characteristics of a selected objective from a distance. We taught her how to gather and thoroughly evaluate all the available public information on a given military base: the range of security measures protecting it, the different means of accessing it, the weak areas that could be penetrated to gather information, and, in the case that this was the aim of the mission, the means to attack the target.

Tania showed no sign of insecurity, but we noticed that she reacted differently than she had during her training in other areas, where her ability to absorb the lessons had been very rapid. We had to convince her that her doubts and fears could be dispelled only through the practical classes she would subsequently receive from specialized instructors. Nevertheless, both Juan Carlos and I were certain that she had already acquired the tools necessary to undertake training at a higher level.

Based on our experiences in the struggle against Batista's dictatorship, we talked to Tania about our belief that without the support of an urban organization, it was very difficult for an armed revolutionary group to survive in rural areas, especially in its early stages. When the struggle had matured, the rural guerrilla force could achieve greater independence, but it would always require logistical support from contacts in an urban clandestine unit. The cells of such a unit, in addition to carrying out organizational work and providing information for the public, would facilitate links between the guerrilla force and the outside world.

We told Tania it was our understanding that this would be her main mission in the immediate future, although, as Piñeiro had made clear, we did not rule out the possibility that she may be required to participate in a rural guerrilla column. We informed her that in the following months she would receive military training in guerrilla fighting, allowing her to become skilled in the tactics essential to this type of warfare, including the use of different types of conventional weapons and explosives and the manufacture of more rudimentary weapons. We emphasized that in the Cuban situation the use of explosives as weapons of war—though never for terrorist attacks—had been important in confronting the enemy's troops and repressive forces.

When we concluded Tania's theoretical training, we contacted the first lieutenant of the Rebel Army, Neuris Trutié (alias Teobaldo). He had received orders from his superiors to oversee the technical instructors who were responsible for Tania's training. Teobaldo recalls that Piñeiro had summoned him in early April 1963 to inform him that he was to coordinate, in conjunction with me, the training of a *compañera* I would introduce to him, and that he was to ensure that her training was comprehensive. Piñeiro also gave him precise instructions regarding the areas that should be covered in Tania's training.

In order to achieve this, the plan I drew up with Teobaldo would seemingly train Tania as a regular agent of Cuban domestic intelligence and not as an internationalist undertaking a clandestine mission in support of a Latin American revolutionary movement. The lessons were divided into three stages: the first would take place in the city, the second in a remote territory (preferably a mountainous region), and the last was a practical exercise in three-way radio transmissions.

According to records handed to me by Teobaldo, *compañera* Laura[3] instructed Tania in invisible writing and secret codes. Classes in photography, microfilm, development, and secret compartments were taught by *compañero* Medina, while classes linked to passing information, making contacts, and devising cover stories, were given by *compañeros* Mauricio and Galardy. Practical instruction on surveillance and countersurveillance was Mauricio's responsibility.

Castilla and Carlos Puig Espinosa (alias Manuel) were her tutors in communications and in the arming, disarming, installing, and preparing of equipment for receiving and transmitting messages— particularly through a mini-transmitter that had been confiscated from CIA agents discovered in Cuba. In addition, Manuel and Payret taught her about radiotelegraphy; the latter was highly experienced in this field since, as a Cuban counterintelligence agent, he had participated in an operational mission against the counter-revolutionary bands active in the Escambray Mountains.

Tania's technical training lasted almost a year. Teobaldo recalls that throughout this period she stood out for her ability to act with complete discretion. Although he spoke to her several times about his personal experiences in the struggle against Batista, as well as the clandestine operations he had fulfilled abroad, he never discovered Tania's real identity, and she never revealed anything about her future mission. She stood out for her self-discipline (he never received any complaints about her conduct), her ability to quickly absorb everything she was taught, and the fact that she made very few mistakes. These mistakes were so few that, in spite of the years that have passed, Teobaldo still recalls them. On one occasion, during a practical exercise, Tania had to hand over information in the Pinar del Río train station, in the western part of Cuba. After carrying out the task satisfactorily, she then returned to the station to talk to the *compañero* to whom she had handed the information, thereby infringing security measures established for this kind of operation.

He once gave her a warning because during a practical exercise in radio communication, a MININT officer pretending to be an amateur radio ham interrupted the transmission to ask Tania questions directed at finding out who was transmitting, where they were transmitting from, and what equipment they were using. In this situation she did not cut off communication quickly enough. In a real situation, this would mean her location could rapidly be identified by the enemy. On another occasion, Teobaldo had to reprimand Tania because of the way she dressed, in a style not common in those days in Cuba and which, together with her attractive appearance, made her stand out wherever she went.

In spite of her headstrong personality, Tania took these criticisms well. Teobaldo now recalls her as a person "with a pleasant nature, easy to talk to, neither too extroverted nor too introverted," and who was "politically and culturally highly aware." Tania also knew how to adapt to the "surroundings in which she found herself and behave in accordance with the basic principles she had been taught." Teobaldo concludes that these qualities enabled Tania to "positively assimilate lessons taught her, without which, together with her intelligence and personal daring, she could not have successfully worked throughout the time she was in Bolivia operating under an assumed identity."

Manuel, who was working at the time as a radio and radio-telegraphy technician in the VMT and who was also one of Tania's instructors, has a similar opinion of Tania's qualities. She was introduced to him in 1963, in a house used for training purposes on the corner of 9th Avenue and 26th Street, in Miramar. He trained her in the use of radiotelegraphy and radio transmission and reception. Tania learned to operate several types of radios, including one confiscated from the CIA: a very small piece of equipment with a powerful broadcasting range. We affectionately nicknamed it Pancho. Once she had learned these techniques, Tania carried out a number of practical communication exercises with other correspondents located in different operations houses in Havana and other areas of the country.[4] Likewise, she learned how to construct a radio.

According to Puig, the only difficulty Tania had in the beginning of her training was in learning international radiotelegraphy, since in order to achieve greater communications security and to ensure that messages were not easily decipherable by the enemy, our technicians had introduced some modifications into the conventional code. Nonetheless, using Morse code and pretending to be a radio ham, Tania managed to perfect the technique, allowing her to establish contact with Venezuela and other countries in the continent. She went through a similar process learning how to put together a radio using materials that were easily available from electronic supply stores. In spite of her initial difficulties, Tania finally managed to construct a 75-watt appliance, allowing her to communicate with all the countries of Latin America.

Tania's training to join a guerrilla movement required theoretical and practical lessons in several military areas: arming and disarming light weapons, shooting, creating explosives, designing tactics, and surviving in mountainous regions where water and food had to be gathered from the surrounding environment. One of her instructors in explosives was Carlos Alberto González Méndez (alias Pascual).

Pascual remembers that he began to train Tania in June 1963. Classes were held in an operations house off the Medio Día highway, to the west of Havana. Juan Carlos introduced Tania to him in this house, proposing that her training include learning about CIA-manufactured explosives used in Cuba by counterrevolutionary elements. Likewise, her training had to cover conventional explosives and homemade varieties that could be useful in urban and rural guerrilla struggles.

According to Pascual, in their first conversation he explained to Tania the innumerable risks involved in handling explosives and the importance of adhering to strict security measures. Going by his own experience in the Cuban insurrectionary struggle, he also emphasized that these deadly weapons should only be used in direct attacks against the repressive forces of the enemy and should never cause injury to innocent people or civilians. Over the course of his daily contact with Tania he developed an opinion of her as "a jovial, open, and modest person who enjoyed conversation and asked a lot of questions, but who was highly disciplined given that this was one of the inviolable rules in the handling of explosives."

He also recalls, "I did not know what nationality she was or her real identity," but as she almost always came dressed in militia uniform with a pistol on her belt, he felt obliged to warn Tania that her attire could draw attention to her, given that very few foreigners based in Cuba dressed like that or carried a pistol. Even though he said this "jokingly, so that she would not take it as a criticism," from that day onward Tania "stopped wearing a militia uniform" and began to turn up without her gun.

When they were manufacturing explosives, mainly with powder ingredients, their clothes and hair ended up full of dust and Tania joked that she was going gray. When hand grenades were being made, Tania was initially concerned about using cans because they exploded into shrapnel, but little by little she became skilled in the best way to combine these materials. Very calmly, and with no hint of nervousness or fear, she learned how to throw grenades and take cover on the ground while awaiting the explosion.

Pascual says that while Tania "enjoyed conversation," Tania never disclosed any details that could reveal her real identity, in spite of the fact that during her training they were almost always alone— Juan Carlos, who took her to the house, rarely stayed to observe the practical exercises. On the contrary, she kept to all the rules of clandestine work and never asked Pascual about his personal life. Hence, it was not until news about Tania's death became public that Pascual realized whom he had been training years before. He still recalls her as "a young person, full of life, very dedicated to her beliefs, and very intelligent."

These accounts, and others not included here, strongly suggest that throughout her intensive training Tania developed a very clearly defined approach to clandestine work. She also consolidated the principles that govern the lives of men and women devoted to revolutionary activity: hatred of the enemy, ideological steadfastness, discipline, constant self-improvement, willingness to sacrifice, confidence in victory, and the absence of any ambition beyond that of having fulfilled one's duty.

Tania worked on her new identity. She fully understood the need to eliminate from her conversation any references to revolution and its practice and theory. She learned that she would have to choose words that would portray a cold distance from other people and characterize the vague, exploitative language of the bourgeoisie. She could no longer use the appellative *compañero*; she incorporated the words *señor, señorita,* and *señora* into her vocabulary. Her militia uniform became a memory, and, while still keeping her clothing simple, she began to dress like a petty-bourgeois woman. At the same time, she learned how the ruling classes behaved and was willing and able to imitate their conduct with sheer artistry.

This part of Tania's training had come to an end. It was time for the final phase of her operational training in Cuba: comprehensive practical exercises to determine whether Tania had absorbed her theoretical training and could succeed in the international mission entrusted to her by Che. Based on agreements with MININT counterintelligence units, these exercises would be performed in the city of Cienfuegos. Tania would have to travel to this city under a different identity and operate in circumstances resembling, as closely as possible, those she would have to face when she departed from Cuba.

CHAPTER **5 |**

PREPARING FOR LATIN
AMERICA

Tania's Practical Operational Plan for Cienfuegos was drawn up rigorously. Given the complexity of the assignments involved, Juan Carlos and I analyzed and discussed its contents with her on several occasions. We warned her of the difficulties that could arise as well as the measures she should take if she were detected by community surveillance or by the MININT Department of State Security (G-2) in Cienfuegos.

These difficulties could turn out to be significant, because in this practical exercise Tania would be playing the role of a foreign agent undertaking intelligence and sabotage missions in one of the largest cities in the Las Villas Province. This area had been one of the main sites of triumphant battles waged by the Cuban people against CIA-backed counterrevolutionary gangs, and consequently all MININT departments in the area, as well as the Committees for the Defense of the Revolution (CDRs), had acquired significant experience in confronting enemy activities.

The difficulties implied for Tania would be even more formidable, because we were going to inform the authorities of a "foreign enemy presence" in the city and Cuban counterintelligence forces would therefore be doing their utmost to detect her. Tania would have to fulfill all aspects of her Practical Operational Plan and do everything possible to escape detection by the revolutionary community surveillance forces and by whatever measures taken by Cuban state security.

I traveled to Cienfuegos in the first week of February 1964 to coordinate all the details of this exercise. Once there, I met with *compañero* Manuel Abstengo Carmenate (who died in 1978), then head of the department of state security in this region. I requested a surveillance team from him in order to try to follow Tania's activities in the city and surrounding areas. We agreed that the only information we would give to the officers involved would be that this mission was linked to the presence of a foreign woman who gave us "strong reason to suspect she was linked to enemy activities." In line with the principle of compartmentalization, none of Abstengo's subordinates were aware that the VMT had organized this exercise.

We also asked Abstengo to let us use his home for radio transmissions and receptions. Likewise, we asked if his wife, Vitalia Lorenzo, could accompany Tania from time to time, introducing her as a cousin if it were absolutely necessary. In order to lend this supposed family tie some credibility, Tania would travel under the name Tamara Lorenzo. She would also carry an identity card stating her occupation as a translator for the Ministry of Industry and she would be lodged at the Jagua hotel, one of the most popular tourist hotels in the city known as the "Pearl of the South."

From my point of view, everything was completely ready. Still, one week before traveling to Cienfuegos to conduct the mission, and without talking to Piñeiro first (who approved my decision when he was informed of it after the exercise was over), I asked *compañero* Diosdado to come with me to visit Tania. He accompanied me to the Miramar apartment, on the corner of 20th Street and 9th Avenue, where we had moved Tania shortly after her initial training. I had a close personal and professional relationship with Diosdado, who was then head of the VMT department responsible for underground work in the Latin American countries that were hostile to the Cuban Revolution. Without violating the principle of compartmentalization, my aim was for Diosdado to talk with Tania from the point of view of his professional experience in training secret agents. I wanted him to analyze with me the Practical Operational Plan she was to fulfill in Cienfuegos and to assess, as a colleague, her level of training, her aptitude, and ability to accomplish the goals.

Diosdado, Juan Carlos, and I visited Tania after 10 p.m. on February 12, 1964, a week prior to the departure date initially scheduled for Cienfuegos. When we arrived, I knocked on the door. A few minutes passed. Just when we thought no one was home, she opened the door apologizing for the delay: she had been finishing the reception of a radio message.

Years later, I finally managed to get around Diosdado's many excuses for not giving me his testimony for this book when I tried to talk with him. So thoroughly trained in compartmentalizing his life—and very modest—he had difficulty talking about experiences in his clandestine work. He finally opened up and told me that, at the time, it had caught his attention that Tania explained the situation without using words; she had relied, instead, on a range of gestures, demonstrating how much she had learned from the principles of secrecy we had taught her. One such vital principle was the need to take constant precautions against the possibility that the enemy had hidden listening devices in her home.

As soon as we entered the apartment, I introduced Diosdado to Tania simply as "a *compañero* from work." For the first few minutes she watched him closely; it was clear she was trying to figure out who the unexpected visitor was. He also watched her, although, objectively speaking, he had the upper hand because I had previously given him her file. Diosdado had prior notice about some of Tania's personality traits; he had also been told that it was not easy to change her mind if she believed she knew the truth, or if she doubted or failed to clearly understand instructions.

We quickly began to joke and laugh and soon created an ambience which facilitated the dialogue we wanted. The four of us sat in Tania's study where, to my relief, none of the tools she used for clandestine exercises were visible. This was partly because she had organized her place with a delicate, unique touch, suitable for both work and relaxation. Her guitar and some books were placed around the radio receiver, helping to camouflage the equipment.

The conversation continued in this atmosphere until the early hours of the morning. Tania had initially been on the defensive, almost certainly because of the presence of the stranger; she gradually came to believe that this was a normal work meeting. She began to relax and her state of mind helped her search for broader and more objective responses to our questions. The session became very intense, with just a few breaks for coffee and to refresh our minds. Tania performed well during the conversation. All that remained was to make a final few adjustments to the practical exercise. Among other things, this exercise would allow us to identify what steps were necessary to complete her training during the short period of time remaining before she left Cuba.

Two days after the date initially scheduled, on February 20, 1964, I traveled to Cienfuegos in the company of *compañero* Renán.[1] Renán was then training as a radiotelegrapher to the view of joining the Argentine People's Guerrilla Army, which had clandestinely entered Argentina a few months before, under Masetti's leadership and as part of Operation Sombra.[2] Renán was to participate in the exercise as one of the correspondents who would have radio contact with Tania. We also decided that Manuel, Tania's instructor, would accompany us to provide support in the case it were required.

At 2 a.m. on February 21, 1964, under the name of Tamara Lorenzo, Tania arrived in Cienfuegos. I had previously arranged with Abstengo to deposit a briefcase in Tania's room at the Jagua hotel. The briefcase had a false lining, containing the equipment and materials Tania would need throughout the practical exercise. Under cover and in unfamiliar terrain, she would have to prove her command of her training, as well as her ability to detect and avoid the operation being carried out against her by the experienced Department of State Security (G-2).

As is recorded in her Practical Operational Plan (see appendix 2), Tania would have to apply her knowledge of radio transmission and radiotelegraphy, the use of codes, secret writing, and the ability to develop both regular photos and photos of documents. Likewise, she would have to conduct dead drops, make personal contacts, use communication plans, and maintain security and clandestine measures. Similarly, she would have to put into practice methods of the urban guerrilla struggle, and obtain the information required to place, undetected, a package resembling an explosive device in an industrial complex that would serve as a pretend military base for the exercise.

Accomplishing all these tasks in the 11-day period scheduled for the exercise would reinforce Tania's confidence in the clandestine methods and techniques she had been taught. It would also strengthen her habits and experience using different security measures, such as writing reports on hard and smooth surfaces and communicating discreetly on the telephone, or in cars, houses, or other enclosed places. She would have to leave indications on her clothes and belongings that would reveal whether they had been secretly searched in her absence. To avoid being tape-recorded or photographed by the enemy, she would need to observe objects and people in restaurants, clubs, cinemas, and other public establishments chosen for contacts. Completing all these tasks would strengthen Tania's confidence in her ability to carry out overseas clandestine work.

There were some unexpected incidents at Abstengo's house and a few misunderstandings with Manuel over the set-up of the two radio antennae (see appendix 3). But Tania fulfilled the majority of the assigned tasks, despite having to concentrate on many things at the same time. In fact, the only tasks not accomplished in her Practical Operational Plan were practical exercises in the construction and use of explosive devices near the beautiful Cienfuegos Bay.

She could not accomplish this assignment because of an accident on the MININT-owned boat I was traveling in together with Renán; Manuel; Osvaldo Morejón Rodríguez, the head of the Office of the Struggle against Counterrevolutionaries in Cienfuegos; and Valentín, the captain of the ship. We were crossing Cienfuegos Bay in order to drop Renán at Cayo Ocampo (from where he would broadcast radio transmissions). At the same site, we were planning to bury in the sand the explosives that Tania would need to find for her practical exercise. A fire broke out on board when we were in the middle of the bay, and I made the decision to throw all the explosives we were carrying overboard, thereby canceling the operation.

Our observations during the course of the exercise, as well as Tania's written report (see appendix 3), were evidence of her command of all the areas in which she had been trained. Testimonies given years later by two counterintelligence officers who were part of the surveillance team deployed against Tania exemplify her work.

Major Sergio Izaguirre, an officer of the region's Information Division of the Department of State Security (who is now retired), remembers:

> One morning the chief at that time, Abstengo, called and informed us that a foreign woman from a capitalist country was operating in the city and that she had to be located and observed. Years later I discovered that it was Tania. A unit was assigned to follow her everywhere. Tania moved around a lot, even in poorer neighborhoods, and we realized she had to be very intelligent to outwit the surveillance units and slip away. I clearly recall the "bomb" episode. This was one objective of the exercise, to attack an industrial target, and she managed to put the package in the old Prado and Dorticós electricity generator, where the bowling alley is now.

Francisco Guerrero Véliz, who at that time was an officer in the section of the Department of State Security responsible for operations against the counterrevolutionary groups working out of Trinidad, tells of the following experience:

> I traveled to Cienfuegos on other business, but I was approached about participating in a surveillance operation—not in gathering information, but in the operation itself. I was told that this was part of a training session. I covered the "mail box" Tania had to use in the gardens or

parking lot of the Jagua hotel. My job, together with another *compañero* whose name I cannot recall, was to see whether she made any mistakes; if she did, the session had to be terminated.

It was night. She arrived, stopped, took all the proper surveillance and countersurveillance precautions, collected the "mail," and blended in with guests. I then reported that the *compañera* had completed the task satisfactorily.

Tania's "cousin," Vitalia Lorenzo, told me some memories that are still vivid despite the years that have passed:

In February 1964, I lived in Cienfuegos and my husband, Manuel Abstengo, worked for the state security. He approached me one day and said, "Tali" (that was what he called me), "a *compañera* is coming to stay in the house, acting as your cousin (we both had the last name Lorenzo). I need you to give her the spare room so that she can work. You shouldn't touch anything she brings or ask any questions. She won't be sleeping here but will come during the day to work." She arrived with my husband, he introduced us and I took her to the room where we had placed a desk. Later, my husband brought her a radio; we did not have any radios in my house at that time. Another day he came home with a portable electric stove and took it to the room. She came and left practically without talking to me. One day, when I was out on the balcony, she came over to talk to me and to my surprise asked, "Why don't you work? Haven't you ever worked?" I said I worked when I was single, but when I married and became pregnant I suffered health problems and was ordered to rest, which is why I had to stop working. In the end, I lost the baby.

One day she asked me to accompany her to get a manicure in a house near my home. My husband asked me once to go with her to the terrace, where she was doing an important job. While there, I saw that she and another *compañero* were setting up an aerial in the same place as the television antennae.

She always tidied the room and there was nothing visible to reveal the type of work she was doing. When she was leaving, we sometimes invited her to eat with us, but she never stayed. She was very reserved. I remember her as petite, wearing tight-fitting black trousers, and carrying a briefcase. I didn't know she was a foreigner; she spoke such good Spanish that I thought she was simply from Havana—people from

Havana speak differently from us. A long time afterwards my husband told me that the woman who had been in our home was Tania, the same person who is honored in Cuba.

As her trainer Manuel recalls, the final practical test in radio transmission and reception brought three correspondents together: a *compañero* undergoing training in Pinar del Río; Tania, who would be operating from Cienfuegos; and a trainer, deployed in the Oriente Province in the Sagua-Baracoa Mountains region, who would be the base between the two. Manuel met Tania on several occasions in Cienfuegos to find out whether she had any doubts about the mission she was carrying out. He also went to Abstengo and Vitalia's house, from where Tania was to make the radio transmissions, in order to help her install the radio antennae. Tania made it very clear to him that she knew what she needed to do and that she had studied the *compañeros* from state security who had her under surveillance, although she was not sure exactly who was watching her. In reality, as Manuel has said, the people she had suspected were not part of our surveillance team that was watching her so closely.

Once the practical exercise in Cienfuegos had concluded, Diosdado and I visited Tania again in her Havana apartment on March 3, 1964. She radiated happiness and enthusiasm and was full of stories and experiences, barely letting us talk. Despite being in Cuba, she said, having assumed a different identity had provided her with enormous insight. As was reflected in her written report on the practical exercise (see appendix 3), Tania was self-critical with her evaluation, listing her shortcomings and those areas where she considered she had made mistakes, particularly in imagining that countersurveillance operations were being carried out against her when, in reality, most of the time these were groundless suspicions based on coincidences.

Nonetheless, Diosdado and I believed that this position was preferable to one of overconfidence and naiveté. At the same time, her attitude proved that Tania operated on red alert, although, as she herself acknowledged, she still had to make an effort to focus on people's physical characteristics, an ability she would acquire only through practice and time. Years later, reflecting on this meeting with Tania, Diosdado gave me the following comments:

> Today I am convinced that given the historical period we were living through and the scarce experience we had acquired, Tania was provided with the most comprehensive training we could have given her. We used sophisticated technical equipment taken from CIA agents by our counterespionage services. The Practical Operational Plan was extensive and intensive, filled with activities that were above and beyond those normally required abroad. It was important to test her abilities to the utmost. She filled the role very well and demonstrated that she was ready for the final part of her training, which would take place in Prague.
>
> Personally, before or after, in all my 30 years of training work, I have not met a woman who, at only 27 years old, was so highly motivated, so committed, and so willing to sacrifice herself in carrying out such a difficult and dangerous mission… Her commitment was exceptional. In retrospect, the facts, and not my personal opinion, have confirmed this appraisal. It is as though she were predestined for such a mission and its subsequent outcome. She was faithful to her beliefs and to her commitment.

All those involved in her training were convinced that the Cienfuegos practical exercise represented Tania's graduation as an expert in clandestine work, as a clandestine combatant. I informed Piñeiro, almost a year after the start of her operational training, that Tania had conclusively demonstrated she had acquired the necessary theoretical-practical and political-operational skills required to undertake her mission successfully. In order to organize her departure from Cuba, it was only necessary to finish preparing her cover story and the documents with which she would clandestinely enter Latin America.

We had planned at the outset that once she was settled in Prague, Tania's main goal would be to travel through Western Europe to gather information she would need to construct a plausible cover. She would do this using false documentation assigning her the temporary identity of an Argentine national, Marta Iriarte. Acting as

Iriarte, she would have to obtain the information needed to travel to Latin America as a woman of Italian-German descent: Vittoria Pancini. The beginnings of this cover had already been prepared; Tania would have to build upon this during a trip to West Germany and Italy.

Given the foreseeable difficulties during this delicate phase of her training, Piñeiro decided that when Tania returned to Prague after this trip, one of our officers would travel there to examine with her the results of Tania's journey through Western Europe and to make any necessary adjustments in her cover story. Piñeiro did not mention who this agent would be, although both Tania and I believed at that time that I would be assigned this mission. We set about working out how contact would be made between Tania and the agent who would be meeting her in Prague.

Once these planning procedures had been concluded, Piñeiro decided to organize a final meeting with Che. As on the previous occasion, I attended the meeting in the company of Piñeiro, Tania, and Papi, who was always called Tarzan because of his impressive physique. Papi was also the person who would temporarily occupy the security apartment that Tania had been living in for the past few months, after she left for Europe.

The meeting took place at the end of March 1964 and lasted several hours. Tania was clearly moved when the meeting began. She became even more emotional as Che asserted that she would need everything that she had learned about clandestine work to guarantee his safety and that of the revolutionaries who would be associated with her in the future. Tania learned then that Bolivia would be her final destination. She had studied the situation of Bolivia in depth, together with other Latin American countries. Papi had helped her during these studies; although she was not aware of this, he had traveled to different countries throughout Latin America, participating in Operation Sombra.[3]

Che informed Tania that during the first stage, her main goal was to acquire legal residency in La Paz and, using the cover of an expert in folklore and ethnography, to travel to different places, particularly rural areas of the country. She would also conduct a detailed study of the social, political, and economic characteristics of the country. Without raising suspicions, she also was to try to establish close links with people connected to the bourgeoisie, political power, the government, and the Bolivian armed forces.

At the appropriate time, one of our *compañeros* would contact Tania in La Paz and inform her of her precise role when, as Che explained with ambiguity, "definitive actions" commenced. Tania would have to be patient and wait for this contact; in the meantime, even if a situation she was confronting was difficult, she was not to communicate with, ask for help, or reveal her true identity to any individual, organization, or party of known revolutionaries in Bolivia. Her mistrust was to be total, generalized, and constant.

Tania, with her typical sincerity and depth, listened carefully to these instructions, talked them over with Che, asked for clarification on some aspects, and then told him that she was entirely prepared to leave Cuba. She was ready to fulfill the commitments she had made to him and realize her dream of becoming an internationalist combatant. Her words were deeply appreciated by all those participating in this historic and, until now, secret meeting.

CHAPTER **6** |

TANIA AND ULISES

As the time approached for Tania's clandestine departure for Prague, I found myself facing an acute, and unacknowledged, dilemma. On one hand, as an Operations Division officer, I felt immense personal satisfaction for having fulfilled my political and professional commitments to Piñeiro and Che—including co-ordinating the qualified instructors who had helped train Tania, as well as providing technical and professional support. All of this had transformed Tania into an expert in clandestine work: someone with a vast potential to fulfill a range of assignments linked to the different liberation struggles in Latin America.

On the other hand, I had subconsciously begun to weigh the concern her departure would cause me, not to mention the serious risks she would unavoidably run fulfilling her commitments to Che. Above all, I was worried that I could not follow the same path; on the contrary, I would have to remain in Havana sitting at a desk, in a supportive role. By that time, we were emotionally involved beyond the usual rapport between a superior and subordinate involved in an internationalist mission. In fact, our relationship, after deepening into a sincere friendship, had progressed step by step into a profound and powerful bond without us being aware of it.

During the many times we found ourselves alone throughout the months of her training, Tania, who was highly demanding of herself and who expressed an enormous trust in me, began to expect the same of me. She often used to say, with just cause, that she had told me the most intimate details of her personal and political life but that, in spite of our deep friendship, she only knew I was called Ulises. So, breaking the rules of the VMT, I began to take my two young daughters to visit Tania. I saw that this made her very happy: she adored children, and I knew she wanted to have her own. These "family get-togethers" were an opportunity to rest from the demands of her training and they took place not once, but several times.

Initially, I avoided disclosing details that would reveal my real identity to Tania. But little by little, I talked about aspects of my past, as well as my modest involvement in the urban clandestine struggle against the Batista dictatorship, first in Santiago de Cuba and then in Havana. I aimed to convey some experiences that, in my view, might be useful for her future mission. I also have to confess, however, that I began to talk to her about different aspects of my private life. These included the difficulties I was having in my marriage to the mother of my daughters, a wonderful person, whom I had decided to divorce. I made it clear to Tania that the reasons for this decision were entirely personal—in other words, I was not having an affair with another woman.

We began to visit the Baracoa beach, west of Havana, close to one of the roads that leads to the Pinar del Río Province. Tania really liked this place, and we went there often, very discreetly. We took so many security measures that not even Juan Carlos, my closest colleague, was aware of what was happening between us.

Our trips to Baracoa were entirely between Tania and me, or rather between Tamara and Dámaso.[1] One of the fascinating things about that beautiful Argentine-German woman was her ability to separate the parts of her life. As a professional she was compelled to be Tania, but at other times, she could reveal the depth of her personality and we could share feelings and personal experiences in places far removed from the sites of her training. During these moments I was with Haydée Tamara.

Our memorable political conversations in which Tania revealed her revolutionary commitment were interspersed with periods of relaxation in which she sang and played Argentine or Latin American folk songs on her guitar. Other times she thrilled me by playing "Moscow Nights" on her accordion. Since the first time she performed it for me, this has become one of my favorite pieces.

Another place we often visited was a small cinema designed by *compañero* Alfredo Guevara, then president of the Cuban Institute of Art and Cinema (ICAIC), where we frequently watched films about the extensive secret work undertaken by Soviet intelligence services against top German Nazi officials during World War II.

These films brought out the emotional dynamics of the characters, in addition to the methods and means employed by the KGB or Soviet military intelligence to penetrate enemy units, and the difficulties faced by agents in accomplishing their dangerous missions. Moved by these powerful stories, we discussed these films and compared them with our reality and the course our lives were taking.

I have never forgotten one of the films we saw in the "little ICAIC cinema." A Soviet agent had infiltrated the Gestapo and could not get in touch with his superiors. Looking into a mirror, using his real name, he asked himself what he should do. At that moment, at the height of the drama, Tania said to me very seriously, "I will always expect more than that Soviet agent because I trust all of you completely. Besides, I will always know what to do." My answer was brief and equally serious, "I wouldn't expect anything less of you."

In one of these intimate moments, on a night in 1963 (the exact date escapes my failing memory), the inevitable happened. Sitting on the sand at the beach in Baracoa, looking into each other's eyes, we spoke about our feelings, and yielded to them with all the passion of young people our age. We both knew that our relationship was forbidden in clandestine work, but we also knew that we could no longer restrain ourselves. We were convinced of the purity of our feelings and that these would not affect our professional relationship.

From that point on, although we tried to avoid it, there was constant eye contact, and the way in which we spoke to each other and the relationship between us changed. In spite of our efforts we sensed that those we worked with could pick up our feelings. We were so convinced of this that we decided to inform Juan Carlos who, although he had said nothing, had begun to suspect that my relationship with Tania went beyond professional boundaries. As a tribute to our deep friendship, he was the first discreet and, in fact, silent accomplice to what occurred between Tania and me. Our revelation to him relieved the tension that had grown during the meetings among the three of us when we had to worry about hiding our love.

From that time on she talked to me about the future, about her return to Cuba when her mission had been accomplished, and about getting married and having children—a lot of children. Even though I knew about the immense risks involved in her mission I began to share her dreams, relying on my conviction that in the revolutionary struggle we cannot think about death and defeat. But we both felt terrible.

Tania and I were always asking ourselves what else we should do. We could not blame ourselves; our feelings were profound and sincere. In my position as an instructor in charge of her training, I felt that I was a systematic part of her breaking the rules of discipline I myself had taught her. Tania, as a subordinate, regretted that she was not controlling and subordinating personal feelings to the requirements of clandestine work. Still, both of us were certain that in our case, personal relations would not lead us to betray the commitments we had made to the Cuban and Latin American revolution.

In any case, in order to resolve this painful predicament, we both decided that I should talk frankly with Piñeiro and explain what had occurred. One day, at his house, in the same wood-paneled room in which we had first met Tania and where on different occasions we had gathered with other revolutionary activists, I finally talked to him. I told him that what Tania and I felt was not just a passing fling, but something deeply rooted in our emotions.

His first reaction was critical, but with his typical broadmindedness, he eventually understood the situation. The only advice he offered, while stroking his thick red beard with his right hand, as was his habit, was to make sure no one else found out about the relationship. We could not run the risk, he pointed out, of establishing a negative precedent with the other VMT officials. On that occasion my only mistake was to conceal from my boss and friend Manuel Piñeiro that Juan Carlos was also aware of my romantic attachment to Tania, but I did not want to compromise the loyalty shown to us by our colleague.

Months later, after Tania had finished her practical exercise in Cienfuegos, I informed Piñeiro of my decision to take Diosdado to meet her in March 1964, to evaluate her practical exercises. But I didn't tell Piñeiro that at the meeting, Diosdado had noticed that beyond the immense respect and regard Tania and I obviously held for each other, there was "a delicate difference, a chemistry uniting [us] above and beyond professional ties."

Diosdado's strong belief is that, leaving aside exceptions that confirm the rule, "there should be no intimate relationships between officials and the subordinates they are training that might affect the mission assigned." As soon as we left Tania's apartment, Diosdado spoke to me of his concerns. I said immediately that for some time now Tania and I had been a couple, a decision we had discussed maturely and made based on a shared commitment that our emotional attachment would not affect her mission.

Persuaded, as Diosdado has since said, that "emotional ties between two people cannot be governed by a machine-like rigidity," and that our "infinite need for love," our "mutual respect and admiration," and our common ideals had brought about our decision, he, like Juan Carlos and Piñeiro, adopted a broad-minded and discreet attitude toward our relationship. Above all, he said when relating this testimony, he was aware that "Tania's maturity would never allow our emotional ties to interfere in the accomplishment of her mission." But he was worried that the situation could be harrowing for both of us, given that we knew, "sooner rather than later, she would depart to fulfill her heroic mission and could not look back. She would take with her only the memory of her beloved *compañero* in the struggle."

Without letting me know, Tania decided to share our secret with her parents. On April 11, 1964, alone in Prague, Tania wrote a letter to her mother about our relationship and our dreams. Indicating her total faith in the success of the mission and signing with her nickname Ita, she wrote to Nadia Bunke, "Well, another thing, if my *negrito* [Afro-Cuban] isn't stolen from me before I return, I am going to get married. Whether or not there will be *mulatitos* [little mulatto kids] right away I don't know, but it is very likely. What is he like? He is tall and slim, quite black, and a typical Cuban, very affectionate. Are you in favor? Ah, I have forgotten the most important part: he is very revolutionary, and he wants to marry a woman who is also very revolutionary."

I did not become aware of the existence of this letter until two years after Tania was killed in combat. At that time, under Piñeiro's orders, I became involved in writing a book with the journalists Marta Rojas and Mirta Rodríguez Calderón, published for the first time in 1970 under the title *Tania the Unforgettable Guerrilla*. At that time, I was still loyal to our relationship. Even though life separated us definitively, I divorced my first wife and waited for Tania a long time.

Years after Tania was killed, I remarried. Nevertheless, I have to confess that she still remains alive within me. Not just as Tania, but also as Haydée Tamara Bunke Bíder, the exceptional woman, *compañera*, and friend I once loved with all my heart. With deep personal pleasure, I can say that both sides of her have greatly enriched the course of my life—and still do. I recall both sides of her with a deep, personal pleasure. Both sides have sustained me—and continue to—during the sometimes turbulent but generally rewarding course of my long political and personal life.

CHAPTER **7** |

FAILED COVER

When all signs seemed to indicate that I would travel to Prague to coordinate the last stages of Tania's training and to assist in the final, crucial touches to her cover, Piñeiro notified me that *compañero* Diosdado had been assigned that task. (I had already informed Piñeiro that Diosdado had met Tania personally some weeks earlier.) Piñeiro explained this decision, pointing out that Diosdado had more extensive experience than I did in underground work.

There was no doubt that from a professional point of view, this argument was completely justified, but I knew there was a hidden agenda: Piñeiro wanted to separate me from Tania so that our personal relationship would not in any way negatively influence Tania's work in Western Europe. I also interpreted his decision as a kind of punishment for breaking the rules.

Although I was heartbroken, I accepted his decision without comment, even though it probably meant I would not see Tania again until she had accomplished her dangerous mission. Both of us had dreamed of being together until the very last moment she left Prague for La Paz. We were going to devote ourselves entirely to the successful conclusion of her training and to intensely experience every minute of the deep love we had for each other while privileged enough to be together. But reality intervened and woke us from this dream. Although Tania was as upset as I, and had no idea who would be my replacement in the work ahead, she also understood the reasoning behind the decision of those in command.

Full of these conflicting feelings, but determined to fulfill the mission as scheduled, Tania left Havana for Prague on April 9, 1964, using a Cuban passport identifying her as Haydée Bídel González. The following day she was met at the airport in Prague by *compañeros* from the Czech security services, who regularly welcomed numerous Latin American revolutionaries clandestinely entering from or departing to Havana. They lodged her in an operations house on the outskirts of Prague—the same place where I stayed with Che almost two years later when Tania was in Bolivia. After resting a little and making the necessary changes we had agreed on in Havana four days previously, Tania, with a passport in the name of the Argentine Marta Iriarte given to her by the Czech security services, traveled to West Germany and Italy.

The main goal of this trip was to gather the personal experiences necessary to strengthen the cover that she would use throughout her clandestine stay in Bolivia. At the outset we thought that in Bolivia Tania could use the identity of the Italian-German woman, Vittoria Pancini, whose passport had been handed to us by allies.

According to the cover story we had created in Cuba, Vittoria was born in 1939 in a small Tyrolean village in the north of Italy, close to the Austrian border. In 1944, as World War II was drawing to an end, Vittoria's parents, who were of fascist tendencies, sent her to Uruguay to live with a German family. Vittoria lived there until she was 18, when she went to continue her university studies in West Berlin. According to the cover story, she lived in West Berlin for a while before deciding to return to Latin America, specifically to Bolivia, and continue her ethnographic studies by researching the folklore of the Andean region.

After her tour of West Berlin, Tania traveled through West Germany, proceeding via Austria until she reached the Italian village where Vittoria Pancini had been born. Once there, Tania made contact with several people, taking photos of those she would present in the future as her family and friends (see appendix 4).

Tania had never visited these countries before and, with only a minimal grasp of Italian, came into contact for the first time with the lifestyle, customs, and traditions of "developed" capitalist countries. She was able to see for herself the class divisions, poverty in the middle of opulence, and the self-centeredness that characterizes these societies. She experienced first hand the range of social phenomena that she had learned about from her parents and in the GDR and Cuba through her studies of Marxism and the international situation.

Tania saw the enormous differences between the capitalist system of West Germany, and the immense social progress achieved by socialism in the GDR. To her regret, Tania was only able to see East Berlin from over the Berlin Wall, constructed a few years previously. Her nostalgia was acute; she had vivid memories of living in the GDR with *compañeros* and friends when she first arrived there in 1952 as an adolescent (see appendix 5).

In fact, Tania was staying near the western part of the Berlin Wall and could actually see the building in which her parents lived. She had not seen them since leaving for Cuba in 1961 and did not know when she would meet them again. She could have crossed the wall. No one would have found out. Her parents, who were lifelong communists, would have kept the secret. Nevertheless, she did not cross. How much did she suffer? How much did she reflect on and weigh her revolutionary duties? Whatever her pain and her deepest feelings, Tania—instilled with a sense of discipline, duty, and respect for the security measures governing clandestine work—chose to follow the rules.

As can be seen in the messages sent by Tania from Prague (see appendices 4 and 5), many difficulties arose during her first trip through Western Europe which Tania successfully tackled using the skills acquired in Cuba, as well as her broad imagination and professional boldness. From my point of view, this history is the most important for the insight it provides into Tania's personality and her deep humanity. These virtues were fully appreciated by Diosdado during the almost six-month period when he unexpectedly had to live with her in the operations house on the outskirts of Prague.

According to Diosdado's testimony, when he arrived in the city in early May 1964, Tania had returned from her travels in West Germany and Italy. Several Czech security service officers met him at the airport and took him to our embassy where he had to arrange, together with an encoder, the dispatch of his messages and the reception of those from Havana. He was then taken to the operations house where Tania was staying. It was on a small farm in an area called Ladvi, about 20 kilometers north of Prague. The house was around 30 meters from the road and the surrounding vegetation prevented it from being seen. It was reached only by a narrow dirt road.

Diosdado remembers that he arrived in mid-afternoon accompanied by a Czech *compañera*, called Maria by all the officers at the VMT center in Prague, although her real name was Janka. She was almost 50 years old and had been a communist all of her life. She had been involved in the resistance against the Nazi occupation of her country during World War II. She spoke perfect Spanish and lived in a beautiful area some distance from Prague called Mielnik, famous for its grapes and for being the confluence of the two most important rivers in Bohemia: the Volga and the Danube. Diosdado recalls that relations with Maria were always friendly. The attention and affection that Maria showed Tania was of great benefit; particularly her advice on clandestine work was given in a truly internationalist spirit.

Tania was aware that a *compañero* would arrive from Cuba to finalize the details of her departure for Bolivia, but she did not know who would be given this job. She was very surprised when she saw Diosdado. She ran to him and embraced him, saying, *"Coño, Flaco!"* [Damn, Skinny!] Who would have thought we were going to meet again?" Giving him no time to sit down and almost forgetting Maria's presence, she overwhelmed him with questions about her acquaintances in Cuba.

Diosdado remembers that Tania first inquired about me. As he had no letter from me, he answered with a fib. He told Tania that for the past month I had been posted on an international mission when in reality I had handed responsibility for Tania over to *compañero*

Ariel, then head of the Latin American Department of the VMT. In the meantime, Piñeiro had given me the job of coordinating and participating in the training of a group of former soldiers of the Brazilian armed forces who, after leading a failed rebellion in Rio de Janeiro, had arrived in Havana and requested training in guerrilla warfare techniques.

Tania, respecting the rules of compartmentalization, did not ask about the nature of the mission I was supposedly carrying out. Instead, she asked about Gordo, as Juan Carlos was affectionately known, and of whom she was especially fond. She also wanted to know about Tarzan (Papi), with whom, Tania told him, she had heatedly debated Cuban machismo during her many political and operational activities in Havana.

When Diosdado was still answering these questions, Maria said good-bye and left the house. Tania and he were alone. She accompanied him upstairs and showed him his room. She helped Diosdado unpack the few pieces of clothing he had brought in a small suitcase from Havana, since, as Piñeiro had calculated, his stay in Prague would only last a week.

After unpacking, they continued discussing Cuba and their closest friends. These included the married couple, the Joneses, and the Argentine Isabel Larguía. She also wanted to know about the sugar harvest; the work of the FMC; the health of its president, Vilma Espín; the distribution of goods; imperialist attacks on Cuba; the latest films being shown; and even about the "feelings" songs that were popular at that time.[1] "In spite of the short time she had been away from Cuba," Diosdado concludes, "Tania was desperate to know about the finest details of life on the island."

As Piñeiro had instructed, Diosdado's objective was to determine as quickly as possible, together with Tania, the feasibility of her cover story and the suitability of the documentation she was to use to travel to Bolivia. In addition, he was to detect any signs of enemy activity and any mistakes she could have made during her trip around Western Europe. Immediately after dinner they began their first work session, focusing on the latter two points.

Diosdado relates that during the trip between Havana and Prague, Tania did not notice anything out of the ordinary. When she left Prague for West Germany there was a *compañera* at the airport who had been a German translator in Havana, with whom Tania had been friendly. On account of Tania's excellent disguise, the woman did not recognize her. Traveling alone around Western Europe, a number of men had approached her. Some wanted to go out with her, some harassed her, and others only wanted to talk. She brushed them off cleverly without arousing suspicions.

In accordance with the cover story devised for her trip to Bolivia, Tania spent most of the time in Italy. Tania met a significant number of people, including a young Italian called Pacífico, who, unwittingly, provided the information she required about the characteristics of the place and its customs. She was also able to take photographs of the area and of her supposed friends and family that she could show as proof that she had been born and lived there. She became friendly for a few days with a young police officer called Tomaso, who did not conceal his romantic intentions toward her. He bragged about his work as a police officer, allowing Tania to obtain valuable information about police checkpoints in the border region between Italy, Austria, and Switzerland.

Although incidents took place and situations arose which certain people could have interpreted as possible threats to West German or Austrian security—for example, the case of an unidentified man Tania encountered on a train, who pretended to speak Spanish poorly, was critical of Catholic priests, and said he had been to Cuba—Diosdado and Tania concluded that there had been no enemy activity against her throughout this period. Diosdado was also convinced that Tania had not made any mistakes that could have revealed she was involved in clandestine activity.

Once this part of the meeting had finished, they began a serious assessment of the validity of her cover story. It was very late at night and they both were exhausted, so they decided to continue early in the morning. After less than four hours of sleep, Diosdado got up and went to the kitchen, where Tania had already prepared breakfast. They ate quickly and immediately started working.

Following several hours of discussion, they concluded that despite the information collected and the contacts Tania had made during her travel through Tyrol, it was clear that Tania's scant knowledge of Italian was a weakness. The experiences she had acquired to prepare her cover story were also poor. All this could mean that repressive enemy forces might discover her real identity.

To give credibility to the false identity of Vittoria Pancini, at least another year would be needed in the preparation phase, including Tania's study of Italian, which she had only just begun. We did not have time for this, and imposing a weak cover story on her could sabotage the success of the mission, especially considering that Tania would have to adopt this identity on a permanent basis and make it visibly convincing day after day. Tania's cover had to withstand questioning of all kinds, ranging from a possible admirer, to friends she would have to make when settled and working in Bolivia, to enemy agents.

It was necessary to find a more suitable cover, even though Tania had proven to herself that she had the skills to feign another identity. Consequently, that same night Tania drew up a report containing the details of her entire trip, including her impressions and concerns (see appendix 4). At the same time, Diosdado wrote his own report, which contained the following:

1. No proof existed of enemy activity;
2. Tania was highly motivated and very enthusiastic about her mission;
3. Tania's analytical and observational skills had been refined and she had also matured as a secret agent;
4. Tania had acquired important experience during her travels through Western Europe under the identity of the Argentine Marta Iriarte;
5. It was necessary to drop the Italian cover story, both on account of the language difficulty and because of its inability to withstand investigation;

6. The need to find another set of documents and draw up a new cover story was imperative.

Tania and Diosdado suggested that the nationality for a future cover be Argentine, with the aim of utilizing Tania's knowledge of that country. Details of a cover story could then be based on places, events and names that, at certain times, had been part of her real life.

On the following day, Diosdado traveled to the embassy in Prague and sent all this information in code to headquarters. That night he returned to the operations house to await instructions. A few days later, in response to a telephone call from the embassy, he returned there. He was handed a message approving the analysis and proposals sent to Havana. The communication also instructed him to make contact with the Czech security services to find out whether they would be willing to help obtain the Argentine documentation suggested and to authorize Tania's residency in Prague until she left for Latin America.

Through Maria, Diosdado requested an urgent meeting with one of the heads of the Czech security services. He was immediately granted the request and met with Colonel Yemla, who was second in command at the time. After hearing the explanation of the situation, and without asking details of Tania's mission, he immediately granted both requests in a significant gesture of solidarity. He asked Diosdado to meet on the following day with an expert in the field of forged documentation. Jointly, they would decide where to focus their efforts in order to obtain the documents required.

Less than 24 hours later, Diosdado met with the chief of the documentation department of the Czech security services. Maria served as interpreter during the meeting. After a wide-ranging analysis, without discussing the destination country or the mission Tania was to fulfill in the near future, both agreed that the best solution would be a blank Argentine passport. At that point, however, the Czech security services had no such document. It would have to be fabricated with all the technical skill demanded by an assignment of this nature. This of course would take some time.

Representatives of the Czech security services committed themselves in the interim to supporting Diosdado's work, providing information on the European border checkpoints and airports Tania would have to pass through before reaching Latin America. They also agreed to prepare a new physical disguise Tania would have to use with the Argentine documentation created for her.

That same day Diosdado returned to the Cuban embassy and, following established procedure, communicated these agreements to headquarters. A few days later, he received a message indicating acceptance of the commitments made by the Czechs. The message also instructed him to begin working with Tania on creating a new cover story. In this way, almost one month after his arrival in Prague, Diosdado had to start from scratch in this especially delicate assignment for which he had little experience or available resources. In these circumstances, he was entirely dependent on the solidarity of the Czech *compañeros*.

Consequently, a trip that was scheduled for one week lasted almost six months. During this time Diosdado had to revise the training plan in accordance with the new circumstances. Specifically, together with Tania he had to find ways in which she could actively and productively utilize the indefinite period of time until her departure for Bolivia. They did not know when Tania would leave for Bolivia, and they had a lot to accomplish before then.

CHAPTER 8

THE BIRTH OF LAURA GUTIÉRREZ BAUER

Diosdado—taking note of my recommendation to speak frankly with Tania about any problems that might arise, and in line with his own conclusions about her personal character—immediately informed Tania of the instructions from Havana and the delay in her departure for Bolivia. This entailed preparing a new Argentine passport, as both of them had suggested. He did all of this without breaking the compartmentalization agreement he had with the Czech security services.

Tania immediately understood the situation. Ensuring they would take full advantage of whatever time they were to remain in Prague, Tania and Diosdado drew up an intensive plan of daily activities. This included reading about, studying, and updating themselves on the current political situations in Argentina and the GDR. Even though they could not reach a decision on the Argentine false identity Tania would adopt, they used the time to agree on the bare outlines of Tania's new cover story. As both had indicated to headquarters, this cover story was to be based on real places and events known to Tania. People who really existed could be used or references devised that were associated with fictitious persons who would form parts of the plot of her new "biography."

In parallel, they drew up a program of daily physical exercise that involved hiking and finding, filling, and emptying dead drops in the forests and rural areas surrounding their operations house. Tania and Diosdado also organized radiotelegraphy receptions that Tania would have to undertake based on the plan sent from Cuba. Likewise, they carried out practice exercises in secret writing, photography, ciphering, and deciphering messages sent between Tania and headquarters.

They read the Cuban press, studied political texts, and had certain free-time activities, such as listening to Radio Havana at night or trips into Prague in the evening, to ensure that Tania did not lose her ability to get around in busy cities. These visits included exercises in personal contacts and clandestine activities in places previously selected by Diosdado.

Given the unexpected circumstances they found themselves in, it was crucially important to prevent inactivity becoming a cause for demoralization and weakening the abilities Tania had acquired during her intensive and extensive training in Cuba. In Diosdado's opinion, this was avoided due to Tania's high level of self-discipline and her thorough understanding of the situation that had arisen. She was able to make full use of what turned out to be a long waiting period.

Each day was planned, with Tania and Diosdado adding whatever elements either considered useful. According to him it seemed, "we were at a boarding school with a schedule of activities to complete." The only aspect they did not have programmed was the time each would go to their rooms at night to sleep. In order to fulfill the timetable they agreed to get up at 7:30 a.m., except on Sunday mornings when they rested.

At the same time, in order to help maintain the operations house, the Czech *compañeros* contracted an elderly woman who communicated with them using signs since she did not speak Spanish. She cooked lunch and cleaned the house. Before she arrived, Tania made breakfast while Diosdado took care of the shopping because Tania was not supposed to go out during the day in urban areas. At night both of them cooked dinner, but as Tania hated washing dishes, Diosdado agreed to do it. In exchange, she offered to do their clothes. Diosdado admits that it was a learning experience for him to live in the same house with a female *compañera* with whom he was not romantically involved.

From time to time they fought. According to Diosdado, who was 23 years old then and recently married to a Cuban woman, Tania tried to impose her "German discipline" on him. Tania herself constantly referred, either in jest or seriously, to what she described as his machismo. In Diosdado's view, it was generally Tania who provoked the arguments, for insignificant reasons, and they sometimes got angry and refused to talk to each other for a while. Nonetheless, their conflicts were only minor.

Looking back, Diosdado believes that arguing and then making up were a means of breaking the monotony of the daily routine and of seeking relief from the unexpected situation in which they found themselves. One activity was never suspended, regardless of the tension between them at any point in time: listening to the evening broadcasts of Radio Havana. That was a "religiously inviolable" ritual because it was their main link with our country and, since neither of them read Czech, it helped them remain up-to-date with the situation in Cuba, Latin America, and the world.

Throughout this time Tania and Diosdado had only one argument that was in any way serious. During July, after receiving instructions from Cuba, Diosdado had to travel urgently to Paris to carry out a delicate intelligence operation with another *compañero*. He told Tania nothing but that he would be absent for 15 days, traveling abroad for work.

Tania understood the situation; she even helped him pack his small amount of luggage. On arriving in France, Diosdado had to buy a pair of trousers and two decent shirts for daily use, as well as some comfortable sandals. Diosdado needed to make those purchases in light of the nature of his work in Paris, where the worn-out jacket and modest pair of trousers he had used to travel from Havana to Prague would have drawn attention.

When he returned from Paris, Tania, who had been expecting him for some days, welcomed him warmly. But he noticed she seemed slightly upset. When she helped him unpack his clothes, which she knew well since she was the one who washed them, she quickly spotted the new items. She held them up and asked where they had come from.

Diosdado explained that he had to buy them for the work he had been assigned. Tania, who was their treasurer, erupted in a fury, accusing him of incurring "unnecessary expenses," saying that until now she had tightly controlled their respective budgets. She reproached him for spending money on clothes that could have been used to feed them for several days.

Diosdado was taken aback, knowing that Tania's argument and particularly her anger were misplaced, and he tried to persuade her that she was wrong. He said that he had been austere, and also that when she returned from her trip abroad he had at no point questioned her about what she brought back, thinking it would have been a waste of time. He said it was sad that this was affecting their friendship and, above all, that it was affecting their professionalism. From that point on he would be forced to adopt another approach regarding any details or explanations of his work that he would give her. Tania broke down in tears, but not with anger. He waited for her to finish and when she did, Tania said, "I thought you bought those things on a whim."

This unexpected incident lasted no more than half an hour. Tania invited Diosdado to eat dessert with her and things returned to normal. Yet the whole event allowed Diosdado to observe other facets of Tania's character and virtues: her honesty and her keen sense of austerity. She was not extreme but she was highly economical. He also noticed how sensitive she was. On occasions she lost control, especially with people she was very close to and with whom she did not have to put up a front. And when, as on this occasion, she was shown to be wrong, Tania was sufficiently humble to acknowledge it with sincerity, to ask to be forgiven. Above all, she was not resentful.

Under normal circumstances, Tania had a great sense of humor. Diosdado told me that she designed two posters that she placed outside her bedroom door. From morning to evening, while they worked, one said, "Silence, geniuses at work." On those nights when, before Diosdado went to his room, both sat listening to Cuban music—particularly those boleros and the "feelings" songs Tania loved—she hung up the other poster that said, "Club Saudades." Saudades is a Portuguese word with different meanings (nostalgia or romanticism), but it basically refers to a feeling that resides in the deepest, most private part of human beings.

When Tania was in this mood, she liked to sing songs by Cuban musicians. Her favorites were by César Portillo de la Luz, José Antonio Méndez, Ignacio Villa (also known as Bola de Nieve), and Elena Burke. At these times Tania and Diosdado saw themselves as the "last romantics in the world."

Regardless of the time each went to their respective rooms at night, both were always up in the morning to exercise in the yard, one of Tania's favorite activities. On occasions they would hike in the surrounding countryside. Sometimes they left early in the morning, taking a picnic lunch with them in their backpacks, and returned at dusk. They called these hikes "doing guerrilla," and took advantage of the activity to practice photography (always making sure they never appeared together in photos). Diosdado recalls that Tania had great physical stamina, and would criticize him when he got tired. Tania also insisted that he quit smoking, especially because during the initial hikes he became dizzy at times. Some days they walked 30 kilometers.

When they were bored with the Czech dishes prepared by the housekeeper, they would head out at night and walk 200 meters to a tiny hotel called the Balnovka, where they dined in a small restaurant. They claimed to be a married couple from the Dominican Republic who worked in a factory in the nearest city. They never came across any other Latin Americans there—it was a remote place, a stopover restaurant. The restaurant workers got to know them and their tastes in food.

Diosdado was initially uncomfortable pretending he had a close relationship with Tania. She took the initiative, holding his hand or placing his arms around her waist. She joked with him saying, "You Cubans think you are so macho but right now you are so timid. It's all a stereotype." With the passing of time, they got to know each other better, and those pretenses became natural to them.

Throughout the time they lived under the same roof, they went to Prague together six times. They left in the late afternoon on a bus that took 40 minutes to reach the Pankrác stop, near the prison that had held the renowned Czech journalist and antifascist fighter Julius Fucík.[1] From there they took a tram and reached the city center around 7 p.m., when it was dark.

They walked separately, concerned they might meet people who knew Diosdado and his work and be able to connect Tania to him. If they dined they would sit at separate tables, a rule that was only broken the day Tania finally left for Bolivia. On that occasion they went to a very remote restaurant in order to avoid any unfortunate encounters.

In addition to their operational exercises, these evening excursions were a way of getting Tania out of the house. Diosdado traveled every week to Prague to send or receive information, but Tania remained in semi-confinement, which was why he called her the "little nun." In the beginning, because of work or when he missed the last bus home, Diosdado spent the night in Prague. When this happened, she sarcastically scolded him for leaving her all alone. She told him things to convince him not to do it again, such as that he had missed a great show on the radio with so-and-so singing, or that he had missed a dinner she knew he really liked.

He came to understand her need for company and tried to return home every evening. He also tried to use the time they were together to talk about matters not related to their endless discussions on clandestine work. During these conversations, Diosdado became aware that Tania had a very high level of political education.

Sometimes they had deep discussions about socialist countries, particularly the critical currents prevailing at that time in Cuba about the negative attitude of the socialist countries toward the movements of national liberation. During these discussions, Tania uncompromisingly supported the GDR and the Soviet Union, although she strongly criticized the mistakes of the Stalinist period, particularly Stalin's abuse of power and the persecutions that took place against his own *compañeros* in the struggle.

Tania argued that socialism in Cuba was different, that it had none of the defects she saw in other Eastern European countries, such as a loss of socialist consciousness and an obsession with consumerism. For her, the Cuban Revolution, although it had certain problems, was the example of a socialist country. She also considered that if we Cubans managed to reach the standard of living achieved at that time by the GDR, and emulate its work discipline, we would be invincible.

When Tania wrote letters to her parents and friends, she gave them to Diosdado to read so that he could submit them to what she called "censorship." Demonstrating her self-discipline, she accepted in good faith whatever comment he made on what should be erased or changed.

She did the same with the personal letters written for me. When Diosdado—on the basis of our mutual trust and my links with Operation Fantasma—refused to read them, Tania argued that there should be no exceptions since she could, without realizing it, say something she shouldn't. So Diosdado was forced to read letters written to me.

Diosdado said to me years later that reading these letters confirmed his belief that our relationship would never stand in the way of Tania's decision to fulfill the mission assigned to her. This was more so the case because from the very first day of his time in Prague he was compelled to confront a delicate situation that was affecting both Tania and me.

Prior to his departure from Cuba, I had asked Diosdado to keep an eye on Tania, because when we had said good-bye to each other, her period was overdue. Diosdado says he very discreetly expressed this concern to Tania and with María's help they went to see a gynecologist. Diosdado asked her, "What will you do if it turns out that you are pregnant?" She said nothing for a moment and then replied, "Listen, perhaps you don't understand how important it is for me to have a baby at my age and with the man I love, but this cannot be an obstacle to accomplishing the mission I have committed myself to. Some day, if I can, I will have a baby, if not, we will adopt one."

Diosdado did not expect this answer. He confesses that Tania's level of commitment impressed him. Diosdado had never before told me what Tania had said, because, as he explained almost four decades later, "I was afraid to hurt you, knowing how sensitive you are." Nevertheless, knowing Tania as I did, I was convinced that whatever happened, she would never have subordinated the mission assigned to her by Che to whatever changes that took place in our relationship. Fortunately, she was not pregnant. The delay was caused by nervous tension and, a few days later her menstrual cycle returned to normal. When the clinical diagnosis was confirmed, Tania said to Diosdado, "Tell the *negrito* to relax, for the moment there won't be any little mulattos, but he should get ready for the future."

Tania's commitment was confirmed some time later, when I learned the details of Tania's stay in Prague as well as the seriousness with which she undertook the preparation for her new identity and cover story. Following a great deal of work, on July 25, 1964, Diosdado sent headquarters the new cover story that had been drawn up for Tania's clandestine stay in Bolivia.

In accordance with the proposals that both had designed over the previous two months, Tania began to assume the identity of Laura Gutiérrez Bauer, an Argentine citizen who had lived for a substantial period of time in West Germany (see appendix 6). With this cover she would overcome the majority of the problems she had come up against previously, both in terms of her memories of where she had lived during her childhood in Argentina, and in terms of her knowledge of German language and customs.

Nonetheless, as Tania had traveled only once to West Germany, a much deeper acquaintance with this part of the world was necessary for the credibility of her cover story. With this aim in mind, she left on August 5 for West Germany once again. She traveled with the same passport she had used on the previous trip, issued in the name of the Argentine Marta Iriarte. On this occasion the main goal of the trip was to study the situation in West Germany and to acquire details about living there that could be incorporated into Laura Gutiérrez's cover story.

The journey was very fruitful and took place with no hitches. On Tania's return, she and Diosdado analyzed the details of the trip, arriving at the conclusion that Tania had internalized her cover and had coherently and consciously assimilated all the aspects of her new "biography." She affirmed this in a message to me sent before she left for West Germany (see appendix 5).[2] Tania indicated in this message that within a short period of time she would believe "the story" so much so that if people told her otherwise she would think they were crazy. On her second trip to West Germany, Tania strengthened her cover and acquired new facts in preparation for her clandestine entry into Bolivia, a date which was fortunately approaching, because when she returned to Prague her new Argentine passport was ready for the final steps.

The final step would have been to take her fingerprints for the passport, but following the advice from the experienced Czech specialists who had prepared her passport, Diosdado decided not to do this and instead used those of another person. According to them, if for any reason she was detained, she could not be accused of possessing a false passport if her fingerprints did not match those of the passport. This was a preventative measure and necessary in view of the situation; however, it forced Tania to undertake a risky operation to obtain later a similar document with her fingerprints on it that would allow her to apply for permanent residency in Bolivia.

In this way, at the end of September 1964, the final details were completed in the process of preparing for Tania's departure for Latin America. As Diosdado had agreed with Colonel Yemla, the Czech security services provided him with the wide-ranging information on border checkpoints and airport controls that he had requested.

Using this information, Diosdado drew up Tania's itinerary.

At the same time, Maria, always helpful, took Tania to a hairdresser outside the city where she had her hairstyle changed and her hair dyed a different color; she was then photographed for her new Argentine passport. The transformation was remarkable; darkening her hair color transformed Tania into a *trigueña,* as we call brunettes in Cuba. When she put on her glasses her deep blue eyes were hidden and she was unrecognizable to those who knew the beautiful blond hair that framed her soft, oval face and lovely fair skin.

Once Tania's appearance had been completely changed and her passport was ready, it was time for her final departure from Prague. Diosdado recalls that this was on October 3, 1964, exactly one day after his wife and *compañera* Elsa Montero's birthday. Diosdado, with his well-trained memory, also recalls that on that day, "Tania was quieter than usual… she was frowning. When I asked how she felt she said, 'I've been preparing myself psychologically for months, but so many things are going through my mind now. I remember so many people I would like to say good-bye to and yet we are alone, you and I. You've had to put up with me. You know me by now.'" He agreed in silence. He really did know and understand her.

Diosdado recalls that day: its gray sky and the golden color of the leaves announced the beginning of autumn. Respecting compartmentalization, no Czech *compañeros* visited the house. Maria had said good-bye the previous day and had cried when she hugged Tania and gave her a kiss. She must have wanted to say so many things but only managed to ask Tania to take care of herself and to wish her good luck.

Before leaving, Tania checked over her room once again in detail to ensure no compromising evidence had been left behind. Around 10 a.m. she and Diosdado left the house they had lived in together over the recent months. Some 200 meters down the road, they boarded a bus for Prague. They sat in separate seats for the 40-minute journey and when they arrived in the city they took a taxi, as it was very dangerous to always travel on foot. They waited for the hour when Tania would have to leave; her train for Austria was scheduled to depart at 9 p.m.

To pass the time, they went to a restaurant out of the city in the early evening. Apart from the discreet Balnovka hotel, it was the only time they shared a table in a restaurant. Diosdado recalls that they didn't speak much; Tania didn't feel like talking and he respected her desire for silence. They toasted the success of the mission and once again her blue eyes filled with tears. They left for a stroll but as the evening progressed they began to feel the cold. Tania was wearing a thin, black raincoat, and Diosdado suggested that she put on her coat instead, which she did. She handed Diosdado the raincoat and said, "Keep it. It's my birthday present to your wife." Diosdado accepted, and Elsa still has the raincoat.

Afterwards, Diosdado and Tania arrived at a spot just a few blocks from the train station; he accompanied her to that point only. Tania cried and said she wanted to be with him until the final moment. Diosdado had to force himself to remind her that according to rules of clandestine work, it was not advisable to stay together. She did not understand. He finally managed to calm her by promising to go with her to the platform, but separately, and wait for her to depart from there.

They embraced. She squeezed his hands and gave him a kiss, with these final words, "Forgive my behavior. I know that I've been hard to live with at times. You've been like a brother to me. Give my love to everyone and tell the commander that I will fulfill the mission he has given me, no matter how long it takes. And tell my *negrito* to wait for me." She hugged him again and walked away. Standing in the station at a distance, Diosdado watched Tania board the train. Before disappearing she turned her head toward him and their eyes met, some 50 meters separating them.

It was the last time that he saw her, but not the last time he heard of her. He continued working from a distance to support Tania in her mission. Nevertheless, in spite of his subsequent involvement in Operation Fantasma, it took some years for him to learn that the commander she was referring to when she said good-bye was not Piñeiro, as he had presumed, but Che.

"From that point on," Diosdado concludes, "the VMT took significant steps that allowed many *compañeros* in similar situations to follow the path taken by Tania. She was a forerunner. She was the first *compañera* who, with a false identity, settled abroad for an indefinite time. She led the way. Others followed."

CHAPTER 9

TANIA'S FIRST YEAR IN BOLIVIA

It was not until November 5, 1964, that Tania arrived in Peru en route to La Paz using the false identity of the Argentine woman Laura Gutiérrez Bauer. By pure historical coincidence, this was one or two days after the coup d'état led by the reactionary General René Barrientos, who had overthrown president Víctor Paz Estenssoro, the former leader of the Bolivian Revolution in 1952.[1] She arrived in La Paz on November 18 of that year, starting that very day on the procedures required to apply for permanent legal residency in the country to fulfill the complex mission that Che had assigned her.

According to the detailed report that she prepared on her arrival and her first year of residence in Bolivia (see appendix 9), Tania had previously traveled to Cuzco, the former capital of the powerful Inca Empire. There, she met a few people, including the lawyer Fernando Casafranca, director of a study group on the rich folklore of the region. After staying there for a few days, Tania traveled by train to Puno and then by small truck to Yunguyo, the last stop on the Peruvian border. Mounted on a mule, she entered Bolivia late in the afternoon of November 17.

Since there was no police presence at the Bolivian border post at this time, Tania went to the customs building to declare her belongings. Afterwards, she traveled to Copacabana. Once there, after having spent the night in a small hotel in the company of a

Spanish woman she had met in Cuzco and who had accompanied her on the trip, the next morning she went to the Bolivian police. After her arrival was registered in the country, she continued her journey to La Paz.

Tania devoted her first weeks in the city to tourism. She visited some places related to the vast pre-Columbian culture of the country, including the museum and famous ruins of the Tiahuanaco civilization just outside of La Paz.[2] Tania also established contact with people directly linked to studying the culture and ruins. Through the painter Moisés Chile Barrientos, cousin of the then head of the Bolivian military junta, she met Dr. Julia Elena Fortín, director of the Folklore Research Committee of the Ministry of Education.

Following her recommendation, Tania immediately established contact with Ricardo Arce, secretary of the Argentine embassy in La Paz. A few days later when he came across Tania at an event at the exclusive La Paz club, he introduced her to several people (some of whom belonged to the diplomatic corps) as "someone who worked in his embassy." Later, at the end of 1964, she saw him again at a folk festival held on the Bolivian shores of the majestic Lake Titicaca. Without realizing her intentions, Arce allowed Tania (by introducing her as his wife) to take part in a special lunch with General René Barrientos.

On that occasion Tania had the opportunity to hold a conversation and be photographed with the new Bolivian dictator (who lavished attention on her) and with several members of his government. She also met some members of the Protocol Office of the Ministry of Foreign Relations, with whom she kept in touch throughout her stay in Bolivia. They unwittingly helped her in several of her missions.

By now Tania had acquainted herself with a number of people in La Paz and had the legality of her passport acknowledged by the Argentine embassy. She had also made initial contact with several Bolivian intellectuals, key government members, and some people from the Latin American diplomatic corps accredited in the country (such as Ricardo Arce and the Mexican chargé d' affaires,

Juan Manuel Ramírez). At this point she left the busy La Paz hotel where she had been staying and moved into a guesthouse at 232 Juan José Pérez Street. The owner was a Bolivian woman, Alcira Dupley de Zamora, wife of the administrator of a large cement factory. This woman became close to Tania, treating her in a way that Tania described in her report as "maternal."

Tania became friendly with one of Alcira's daughters from her former marriage, Sonia Azurduy Dupley, who was employed as secretary to the minister of the Bolivian government's Bureau of Planning and Development. She also became friends with Sonia's husband, Marcelo Hurtado, who was a university student leader. Likewise, through contacts in the same guesthouse she had good relations with Ana Heinrich, who had previously held the post of Secretary of the Senate and because of this had excellent links with several Bolivian politicians. Around this time, Ana worked as secretary to Walter Guevara Arce, president of the right-wing Revolutionary Authentic Party, a faction which belonged to the political coalition that supported the military junta of generals René Barrientos and Alfredo Ovando Candia until 1966.[3]

This friendship with Ana also allowed Tania to establish contact with Mario Quiroga Santa Cruz, editor of the newspaper *El Sol*, which was being published in La Paz during those months. He was ideologically linked to Christian democracy and to the pro-fascist political group named the Bolivian Socialist Falange (FSB). He immediately offered Tania work as a proofreader for the newspaper. Though she rejected the offer, Quiroga still gave her the certificate of employment that Tania needed to begin procedures to obtain permanent residency in Bolivia.

At the same party, Tania established relations with Bolivian business people residing in Peru, including Oscar de la Fuente and René Segadan. Likewise, she became acquainted with the corrupt lawyer Alfonso Vascope Méndez, leader of the FSB Information Commission, who in Tania's opinion was connected to the security section of this right-wing political group. Nevertheless, he acted as a guarantor and informed her of tricks she could use to speed up the preparation of the documents needed to obtain residency in Bolivia. After receiving the certificate of employment from Mario Quiroga Santa Cruz, she needed a certificate of good conduct that the police had to issue. She acquired this in half an hour after paying a bribe of just over 5,000 Bolivian pesos.[4]

Thanks to these procedures, the Department of Immigration of the Government Ministry granted Tania her residency in Bolivia two or three days later. This represented a crucial step toward obtaining the identity card that certified her residency in the country. To avoid the comparison of her real fingerprints with the false fingerprints in her passport, Tania pretended to have lost the Argentine passport that the Czech security services had given her.

Because of the ingenious credibility of this fabrication (see appendix 9), as well as the creative way in which she had strengthened her cover and false identity as Laura Gutiérrez Bauer, Tania was able to sidestep the requirements. Posing as a folklore researcher, she received a letter from the Department of Folklore in the Ministry of Education requesting facilities for a trip to the interior of the country. The Department of Personal Identification and Foreign Affairs of the Government Ministry gave Tania the identity card, and to fully legalize her presence in Bolivia, Tania only had to register with the census. However, this step required the presentation of a passport she had supposedly lost and, inevitably, the comparison of her real fingerprints with those that were already in her passport.

On January 20, 1965, barely two months after having crossed the Peru-Bolivia border, Tania had obtained the documents necessary to remain in the country for an indefinite period. At the same time, she moved into a rented room in an apartment owned by a woman whose husband was the former Bolivian diplomat Alfredo Sanjinés. He had been progressive, but now was elderly, reactionary, and impoverished. The apartment was at 2521 Presbítero Medina Street, in the well-known Sopocachi neighborhood of La Paz.

Living in this apartment allowed Tania to meet other people in Sanjinés family who were well placed in La Paz society circles, Some of them were even close to members of the military junta.

In accordance with the plan drawn up in Havana, all Tania had to do was to find ways to justify her income and to acquire Bolivian citizenship.

First, Tania made contact with the renowned Bolivian painter Juan Ortega Leyton after developing relations with the Bolivian Folklore Research Committee and the National Tourism Headquarters, and after acquiring the support of Ana Heinrich. For his part, Ortega Leyton helped Tania get in touch with the journalist Gonzalo López Muñoz. At that time, prior to being appointed director of Information Services for the Bolivian presidency, López Muñoz was a correspondent of the well-known journal *Visión* and, together with other colleagues, was simultaneously publishing the Bolivian magazine *Esto es* and a weekly publication known as *Información Periodística* (*IPE*).

Using her proven ability to establish ties with individuals unknown to her, Tania received an offer of employment to work as a subscriptions agent for the journal *Visión* and the weekly publication *IPE*. Tania rejected the first offer for *Visión*, but worked briefly for *IPE* since this provided her with greater opportunities to fulfill her clandestine mission. She strengthened her bond with Ortega Leyton, who introduced her to López Muñoz and other members of his family, in addition to other journalists in the publications office.

Some of these people helped Tania find eight students for German lessons, which allowed her to justify her income and have the free time needed to strengthen her false identity by studying handmade ceramics. This work also permitted her to carry out voluntary anthropological research as part of the group of researchers registered with the Department of Folklore in the Ministry of Education. Her acknowledged research in this field served as a justification for her trips to different parts of Bolivia while her recordings of dozens of Bolivian musical performances allowed Tania to develop relations with some distinguished Bolivian intellectuals. She helped found the Bolivian Society of Ceramics and obtained other credentials to justify her trips out of the country.

To overcome the difficulties of registering with the Bolivian census and obtaining citizenship as soon as possible, on her own initiative and in line with one of the operational variants we had discussed in Havana, Tania focused on finding a Bolivian to marry. She needed a spouse who would trust her, who had no links with any left-wing political parties or organizations, and who would be willing to allow her the freedom of movement that would be crucial to her accomplishing the clandestine mission.

From a number of admirers dazzled by Tania's level of education, friendliness, and subtle beauty, after a careful (but incomplete) evaluation, she chose a young electrical engineering student named Mario Martínez Álvarez. She had met him along with his brother and some other students. After they started dating, Mario agreed to a secret wedding as he feared that if his brother and friends found out they would tell his father (a mining engineer who lived in Oruro),[5] who would not give his approval because he would suspect that the marriage might undermine his son's university studies, possibly making him drop out.

This was the information that Tania sent in a message to headquarters about the convenience of marrying Mario as a means of solving the problems created by the evidently weak aspect of her Argentine passport and also as a means obtaining Bolivian citizenship. Nevertheless, given the difficulties that were arising in our communications with each other, Tania was unable to obtain a reply to her inquiry. Therefore, based on her own analysis of the situation she was facing, she discreetly married the engineering student at the end of February 1966. The marriage facilitated her departure for Brazil, Uruguay, and Mexico a few days later.

In the first 15 months of her activities in Bolivia, by adopting and demonstrating conservative, anticommunist politics, Tania managed to establish a tight network of relations, in spite of the complex political situation that prevailed in the country and the difficulties in receiving instructions from headquarters. Her relations included a host of intellectuals, professionals, and politicians linked to right-wing parties, as well as some sectors of the bourgeoisie and high-level functionaries of the Bolivian military junta.

She was able to establish ties with the writer Tristán Marof (whose real name was Gustavo Navarro), the subscriptions agent of the journal *Visión*; Sergio Cobarrubias (who had falangist leanings); the journalist Luis Raúl Durán, press liaison in the state-owned company National Treasure Oil Reserves;[6] the Gonzalo López Muñoz brothers; and the journalists Alberto and Eduardo Olmedo López. The latter, even though he had been imprisoned on the charge of a "crime of passion," had been secretary to the overthrown president Víctor Paz Estenssoro.

Víctor Sanier, editor of *El Mundo* in Cochabamba, was included in Tania's social circle and was closely connected to the dictator René Barrientos, as was the business person Carlos Casi Goli, married to Colombia López Muñoz. He owned a business specializing in the sale of plastics, as well as a printing press that offered its services to the Bolivian government. In addition, there was the editor of the daily newspaper *Prensa Libre* in Cochabamba, Carlos Bekar; secretary of the university rector in Cochabamba and journalist with the newspaper *Extra*, Julio Mendoza López; the lawyer Erdulfo Val de Escobar who had certain professional ties with the OAS; and the well-known artist Rosario Sarabia. Tania knew distinguished Bolivian ceramicists too, such as Jorge Medina, Inés de Córdoba, and Yolanda Rivas, who were founders, together with Tania, of the Bolivian Association of Ceramicists.

These and other links allowed Tania to strengthen her false identity and cover story if the Bolivian repressive authorities would ever question it. Through these connections she was also able to carry out studies of the operational situation in the La Paz prison known as the *Panóptico* and the Criminal Investigations Headquarters (DIC) of the Government Ministry. In addition, she was able to acquire information on modifications of Bolivian repressive structures by the dictatorship of General René Barrientos. Likewise, she obtained information on the location of certain military units, including the Staff Military College in Calacoto, La Paz.

Tania obtained evidence of US involvement in this institution, acquired through her informal but active friendship with Álvaro

Cristian, one of the US professors who worked there. He had, according to what Tania so capably found out, in addition to a long "diplomatic" career, clear links with the FBI. Some of Tania's links, as was the case of the director of Information Services for the Bolivian presidency, Gonzalo López Muñoz, contributed unwittingly to Che's clandestine journeys through Bolivia when he arrived there in the beginning of November 1966.

Just three months after Tania's arrival in Bolivia, there were setbacks in her communications with headquarters. As I learned later (because during that time I was with Che in the Congo), Tania sent a new message in September 1965 requesting urgent personal contact with a Cuban officer from the VMT. This led to Piñeiro's decision to send the Guatemalan *compañero* Carlos Conrado de Jesús Alvarado Marín (alias Mercy) clandestinely to La Paz. At that time he was in Western Europe developing his cover story as a business person working for an international cosmetics firm. On the basis of this decision, he was instructed on a plan for his time in Bolivia that included these tasks:

1. Congratulate Tania on her work and notify her that she had been awarded membership in the Cuban Communist Party (PCC).
2. Give her news about her family and *compañeros* and inform her of developments of the Latin American and Cuban revolutionary process.
3. Investigate the possibility that Tania had been detected by the enemy through checking up on her several times before contacting her, to safeguard his own security.
4. Review with Tania the technical matters she had been taught in Havana and Prague which, as she informed us, she had begun to forget because of lack of use.
5. Undertake a study of the personal relations Tania had established in Bolivia and analyze with her the possibility of using some of these in revolutionary work.
6. Create the conditions for her departure for Mexico where

she would clandestinely meet with a Cuban VMT officer. In this contact the Argentine passport made in Czechoslovakia would be exchanged for another with the same identity and nationality, but with her actual fingerprints.

The new passport would allow Tania to complete the procedures related to her legal status, with as few risks as possible (except those entailed in her departure and arrival in Bolivia). This was in accordance with the analysis undertaken by *compañeros* in headquarters responsible for Tania, which led them to conclude that even if she decided to marry the student Mario Martínez Álvarez, she would need to present her Argentine passport as a first step toward acquiring Bolivian citizenship.

When the new Argentine passport was prepared and his cover as a business person was ready on November 22, 1965, Mercy received final instructions for his clandestine contact with Tania in La Paz. He was briefed on a message that Tania had sent a few days before, changing some of the meeting places they had agreed to beforehand. In addition, Mercy was given directions about the route he should follow on his trip to Bolivia (see appendix 7). He was also told about the procedures that he should conclude beforehand in Europe, as well as about the instructions Tania had to comply with to make the secret contact in Mexico scheduled for April 1966.

Mercy finally arrived in La Paz on January 1, 1966. Nevertheless, he did not make immediate contact with Tania as is evident from his subsequently compiled detailed report covering his time in La Paz and Cochabamba, as well as an unexpected stay in São Paulo, Brazil (see appendix 8). He did not make immediate contact with Tania because he was following instructions from headquarters to first learn about the operational situation there and, particularly, the places Tania visited.

At first, he could not locate Tania due to confusion at headquarters about the places she frequented. Mercy decided to follow Tania's movements from the moment when she left the Sanjinés family home where she was living at that time. After checking for several hours to ensure that there were no signs of enemy activity, at noon on January 6 he began to take the measures agreed upon to establish personal contact with Tania. After calling Tania to give her the signal that let her know that an emissary of headquarters had arrived in La Paz and wanted to meet her at the contact place agreed upon, Mercy continued to watch Tania surreptitiously. This gave him an opportunity to observe how content she was and how professionally she carried out her work in the city.

On the night of January 7, the two international combatants met for the first time, exchanging prearranged code words to be certain of each other's identity. In Mercy's words, "she smiled and extended her hand toward me; I greeted her and invited her to go somewhere to talk quietly." When, following Tania's suggestion, they arrived at the place she had chosen, he gave her messages sent by *compañeros*, as well as some instructions on the steps she should take to find a safe place to receive the mail he had for her and where both could work together over the following days (see appendix 8).

Tania could use her ceramicist friend Yolanda Rivas's house that was being built in the Calacoto neighborhood, but it would not be available for a few more days, so next time they met on the outskirts of the city. Tania used the time to collect and destroy the old secret codes that she had hidden in a place far from her house. Mercy had brought her new ones to use instead. They concluded by agreeing to meet again 48 hours later in the little house in Calacoto.

It was during this meeting that he was finally able to give Tania the message "stuffed" into his shoes. According to his report, "...she was overjoyed and while she read it I could see how happy she was, and from time to time she cried with emotion and said, 'I thought that they had forgotten me.' I told her, 'You mustn't think that way. The revolution will never forget you or anyone who serves it as you do.' She replied with emotion, 'It was a joke. I know that they haven't forgotten me...'" (See appendix 8.)

Immediately afterwards, Mercy gave Tania technical instructions on new surveillance and countersurveillance techniques. He also taught her some practical exercises linked to selecting verification points. Finally, they established the details of the following personal contact to be made 48 hours later in the same place. This contact was also made without any setbacks and Tania was given new theoretical classes, but they decided that the place was no longer safe or appropriate for all the work they had to do.

Given Tania's fear that making contact in open places could lead to an unwanted encounter with certain individuals (including an airport official who was always telling her to get her papers in order), they decided to continue with their contacts in the city of Cochabamba. However, because of tight police control on foreigners who visited the city, as well as the impossibility of acquiring a safe apartment in this and other cities close by, they returned to La Paz.

But they were not able to rent a safe apartment in La Paz (the only one that they found belonged to a woman who worked in the Bolivian Government Ministry). They decided to travel to Brazil even though this could mean certain difficulties with Tania's passport when she requested authorization to leave Bolivia by air.

In case of problems, they had planned an alternative route along the extensive land border between the two countries. Fortunately, this was not necessary as plans went ahead without any setbacks after she married Mario Martínez Álvarez (who helped her with the exit procedures). Using the pretext of a translation contract she had been offered in Brazil, Tania arrived in São Paolo at the end of February 1966. As they were not able to rent an apartment or a safe house within their budget restraints, on March 1 they moved to a rented apartment on the beach at Itarare de São Vicente, 78 kilometers to the southeast of São Paolo on the shores of the Atlantic Ocean.

Here, Mercy had to deal with some conflicts arising from what he called Tania's inappropriate tendency to be "too thrifty," and "her tendency to be argumentative" together with "strong emotional clashes" arising from their encounter and the previous "isolated situation in which she found herself." At the end of March, they achieved the safety and tranquility required for an intensive review and update of the techniques of clandestine work that Tania had acquired in Havana.

Once the training was over, in spite of Mercy's opposition, Tania took a brief trip between São Vicente and Montevideo, the Uruguayan capital. She wanted to strengthen her cover story by leading her Bolivian contacts to believe that she had been in Argentina since March 24. In Montevideo, Tania further developed her position as a member of the Bolivian Association of Ceramicists and was able to acquire information of some operational use.

All this led Mercy to state in his report, "I have reached the conclusion that in spite of the short period of time we had available for Tania's training, on account of her outstanding ability to assimilate information, she fully understood all that was taught. When she was not happy about something, I told her to raise the issue with her next contact and she was satisfied and content to do this."

He added, "In relation to her attitude toward our work, I believe that she is aware of the honor attached to being a link in the chain that will soon strangle imperialism and that she is proud of having been chosen to carry out special work for the Latin American revolution." In this contact, Mercy provided Tania with all the instructions she needed for her next clandestine contact in Mexico.

CHAPTER 10

AN ENCOUNTER WITH ARIEL

In line with the instructions Mercy had given her, Tania arrived in Mexico City from São Paolo, Brazil, at the beginning of April 1966. The goal of this trip was for Tania to have a clandestine meeting with a Cuban MOE officer. The officer would give her responses to the inquiries she had made and clear up any doubts remaining after her meetings with Mercy, who had related the problems with her Argentine passport. In spite of her recent marriage to Mario Martínez Álvarez, the passport issue continued to hinder progress toward obtaining Bolivian citizenship.

As Diosdado commented, according to Piñeiro's instructions, two Cuban *compañeros* traveled to the city: Ariel and Adolfo Valdés, whom we all knew as Adolfito up to the time of his death. During those years, Ariel replaced me in my work on the Tania Case after March 1964. He was head of the VMT Latin American Department, while Adolfito was one of the most distinguished officials in the Documentation Division of the department and was in charge of all undercover agents operating abroad under orders from the MININT Vice Ministry.

According to Ariel, before leaving for Mexico City he had received direct and precise orders from Che, who was residing clandestinely in Prague after the beginning of March 1966. He was to create all the necessary political and operational conditions that would allow

Tania to safely become involved with the support work for an international guerrilla movement which, in the following months, would be set up in Bolivia.

In this respect, Piñeiro advised Ariel that during his contacts with Tania he could count on the support of officers from the VMT branch that was located in Mexico, and they, in addition to Adolfito, would guarantee a definitive solution to the problems she was facing with the Argentine passport given to her in Czechoslovakia. Moreover, Ariel was to gather all the information Tania had obtained through her work in Bolivia, to assess the security of Tania's situation and to establish the conditions for a further clandestine contact that a representative sent by Che would have with her in La Paz.

Likewise, and without revealing exactly who this person would be or what the nature of her future work was, Tania was to have faith in the revolutionary importance of the mission she had been assigned. According to Ariel (who was not yet aware of the outcome of the meetings held between Mercy and Tania from the start of January to the end of March 1966), this was necessary because "it was possible that, after two years of successful and courageous clandestine work,[1] Tania might have questioned the significance of the mission she was fulfilling. Until then, she could not have perceived how directly she was participating in the movement of national liberation, which was her greatest revolutionary aspiration and what really inspired her to take on the job."

In accordance with Piñeiro's instructions, Ariel was to express to Tania how much Cuba valued all the work she had done and her talent for the secret services. He told Tania that she had been chosen because of her revolutionary career in Argentina and the GDR (see appendix 1), as well as the work she had accomplished in Cuba between 1961 and 1964. The high level of self-discipline she had demonstrated during her extended stay in Prague and the activities that she had undertaken in Bolivia for 15 months were deeply appreciated. Ariel was under orders to show Tania that she had been accepted, under her real name, as a member of the PCC.

To highlight the "extreme political importance" of this fact, on April 6, 1966, the card was personally signed by Fidel Castro.

All this work had to be carried out in a way that ensured that Tania's stay in Mexico was brief, because, according to Diosdado, "in spite of the fact that she had created a solid cover story that facilitated any trip abroad, she should only be away from Bolivia for as long as was strictly necessary." Consequently, "a swift operation was decided upon that would not jeopardize Tania." Therefore, they planned "no more than two personal contacts between Ariel and Tania, on different days and in different places, which were chosen and studied in detail in advance."

To guarantee the success of the meetings, Mercy had given Tania a variety of ways to make sure that contact was made in Mexico. The VMT officials in Mexico City had performed a series of operations to ensure that neither Tania nor Ariel were under enemy surveillance. According to Ariel, all these strict security measures were required because, in spite of the Mexican government's traditional position of solidarity with many popular causes, "the CIA and other US espionage and counterespionage agencies operated in Mexico City."

Everyone was pleased when, despite delays that took place for reasons beyond our control, Ariel arrived at the contact site and the operation took place as planned. Things went so well that on April 16, 1966, Tania was able to meet Ariel in person, accompanied by an official from the VMT center in Mexico City (see appendix 9). They examined the circumstances surrounding her arrival and stay in Bolivia and her different relations in the country, as well as the possibility that she could have been under suspicion by the police or under the surveillance of the Bolivian security apparatus. They also reviewed the problems surrounding the false fingerprints in the Argentine passport given to her by the Czech security services, as well as, in this context, the causes behind her decision to discreetly marry the Bolivian student.

In Tania's opinion, one of the main difficulties that she was facing was acquiring Bolivian citizenship. During her meeting with Ariel they also examined in detail what her options were on her return to Bolivia. She was to report back on Mario's willingness to respect the agreements made with her before the wedding through clandestine communication with headquarters.

Tania was determined to obtain the support of headquarters so that Mario could continue his studies in one of the countries bordering Bolivia or in one of the Eastern European socialist countries, which is what he wanted to do. She had encouraged him to consider this option and inspired him to make remarkable improvements in his grades at the university.

Tania's concern was all the more acute because she was aware that her new husband (whose potential links with the PCB she was asked to check) could become an obstacle to fulfilling the difficult clandestine work that lay ahead of her. Indeed, her worry was so great that she insisted that she would ask for a divorce once the problem of her Bolivian citizenship was resolved.

Ariel had initially learned about Tania through reading her file and listening to descriptions of her from "*compañeros* who had previously worked on her operational training." Such was Tania's positive attitude toward the struggle that, according to Ariel, when he met her personally he found her to be "a mature combatant, forged in the daily revolutionary struggle against the enemy." At the same time, she had "all the sweetness that a woman can offer when she loves and commits herself fully to a just cause."

During our conversations, Ariel added, "she always stressed her admiration for Fidel and Che as symbols of her highest Latin American aspirations." She also spoke of her "three greatest loves: her parents, Nadia and Erich Bunke; her Cuban *compañero* Ulises Estrada; and the revolutionary cause." Ariel went on to say, "I set up a new contact time in La Paz with a different Cuban representative who would give her instructions and explain that, from this point onward, she would have to prepare herself to take on new, important, and crucial tasks linked to the revolutionary continental struggle. For reasons to do with compartmentalization, I could not give her a detailed report on the steps being taken toward the organization of a guerrilla force, not to mention that she would be working directly with Che.

Diosdado recalls, "under the weight of the enormous responsibility of the mission, Adolfito took charge of Tania's new Argentine passport that loyal friends had passed to us with the entry and exit stamps from different countries, personal details, visas, etc. It contained all the information that appeared in the passport from the Czech security services that was going to be discarded." Because of compartmentalization, Adolfito was unaware up to the last moment that he was going to have personal contact with Tania. Diosdado added, "In normal circumstances at that time, this job would have required three or four specialists. Nevertheless, Adolfito's skills and abilities ensured that when the order was received to hand over the passport everything was ready in record time."

All that remained was to include Tania's fingerprints in the passport and to copy airport exit and entry stamps and visas previously received by her. The effort, Ariel believes, was very much appreciated by Tania, while "new recommendations on her future actions as Laura Gutiérrez Bauer encouraged her and gave her the confidence she needed to actively participate in those historic events for which she had been so intensively and patiently trained."

In the beginning of March 1966, Papi, following orders from Fidel Castro and Piñeiro, arrived in Prague to discuss Bolivia with Che. This was a few days after Che and I had arrived from Dar-es-Salaam, and just before the meeting between Ariel and Tania in Mexico. The idea was to consolidate plans Che had been working on since his clandestine stay in the Cuban embassy in the capital of Tanzania.[2]

During a lunch that I attended with Che, Papi, and José Luis Ojalvo (the head of the VMT center in Czechoslovakia), Che authorized Papi's trip to La Paz with the aim of reestablishing contacts with *compañeros* from the PCB. They had been working since 1962 on a series of support initiatives for what Piñeiro defined that same year as Operation Fantasma.

On that occasion, Che (who did not know that Tania was in

Brazil at that time) stressed to Papi that under no circumstances should he make contact with her. Even if they were to bump into each other in the streets of La Paz, they could not greet each other. They had to preserve Tania's false identity and cover story for future missions he would personally assign her. Following these instructions, Papi traveled to Bolivia where he contacted the Bolivian Party and, after quick stops in a number of countries, he made a stopover in Havana and returned to Prague once again. This time he was accompanied by another MININT officer whose identity still cannot be revealed.

Che decided that Papi and the unidentified officer were to return to Bolivia and that the latter would remain in La Paz to help prepare for the future clandestine arrival of Cuban combatants who were being selected in Cuba on the basis of a list that Che himself had drawn up. They could not, however, stay in La Paz, and after a few days the two officers returned to Prague.

Always careful to compartmentalize, Che excluded José Luis and me from the following meeting with both *compañeros*. Nevertheless, through Papi, I learned of the other officer's return to Havana. Furthermore, Papi told me, in a very general way and without breaking the rules of compartmentalization, that during his second trip, in spite of what he called "the sluggishness of the Bolivian *compañeros*," they had initiated the contacts that would be crucial for his first steps toward Che's epic Latin American struggle.

My appearance, particularly my dark skin color and my hair, drew the attention of the Czechs, whether they were employees or customers at restaurants where we occasionally ate. I was jeopardizing Che's clandestine presence in Prague and he decided at the end of March to send me back to Havana. Ariel temporarily replaced me in Czechoslovakia for several days until Carlos Coello (alias Tuma or Tumaini)[3] took over. I did not know about it beforehand, but when I arrived in Havana I was immediately appointed head of the VMT department that would organize actions of the Cuban Revolution in solidarity with national liberation movements in Africa.

Following Piñeiro's instructions, during the third week of April

1966, Diosdado traveled to Prague again to carry out work related to Che's disguise and subsequent clandestine journey to Havana. Diosdado describes this time as one in which he had "the great honor of belonging to the small group of *compañeros* who participated in the support work that the [Cuban] revolutionary government gave to Che Guevara."

During his stay in Prague, Che asked Diosdado on more than one occasion for his expert opinion on Tania's situation. This was particularly the case in the beginning of April after José Luis Ojalvo moved him from the operations apartment that we had initially occupied to the same operations house located on the outskirts of Prague that Diosdado and Tania had lived in for almost six months in 1964.

Diosdado still remembers the moment when he was introduced to Tuma and Harry Villegas Tamayo (alias Pombo),[4] who had just arrived in Prague a few days earlier. When they had dinner together, Che asked him to step outside to talk because there might be a listening device hidden in the house. In spite of the fact that Che was known to be suspicious and always on the alert as a guerrilla fighter, this precaution surprised Diosdado because these subtleties of conspiracy would never have crossed his mind, particularly given that he was in a socialist country.

As it was the first time that he had talked to Che, although Diosdado did everything he could to remain calm, he acknowledges that he was struck by Che's strong personality and by the numerous stories he had heard about his outstanding political background. Nevertheless, Che was very natural and relaxed. Behaving as if he had known him for years, Che placed his hand on Diosdado's shoulder and invited him to go for a stroll. After a while he suggested they sit on the grass, under some pine trees, where they talked for almost two hours.

During this conversation, without going into detail, Che told him that about a month before he had been informed of a clandestine contact that Tania had made in Bolivia and he asked Diosdado if he had any more recent news about her. Diosdado shared what he knew about the outcome of the contact Tania had recently made with Ariel and Adolfito in Mexico City. When he was told about the change of her passport and the reasons behind it, Che seemed satisfied and agreed that this would help her obtain Bolivian citizenship. He also said that this had been a major step forward on the part of the *ramiritos*, which was what he usually called MININT officers.[5]

Immediately afterwards, he said that no order should be given to Tania that might lead to her being detected—what is known in technical language as *quemar* [to be burned].[6] Che also said that she should be given clear guidance and allowed to take all the steps required for her residency papers to be entirely in order because, as he pointed out, all the signs indicated that what had been planned for a long time was now bearing fruit. Likewise, Che inquired after Tania's physical and mental health and insisted on learning how she had dealt with loneliness, whether we communicated regularly with her, and if Diosdado knew how her parents in the GDR were.

Che was satisfied by the answers that Diosdado gave him. He ended the discussion by reiterating that we were to look after her, not to put pressure on her to move ahead too fast, as he had important work for her to do. Such was his concern that whenever he was alone with Diosdado, Che raised the issue of Tania again, as if he was thinking about the missions that he was going to assign her.

Diosdado told Che some stories about the time when he and Tania had shared the operations house, which they called *la finca* or the ranch. Che would laugh about these stories and show his satisfaction with how Tania had acted during her stay there, how she had proven her ability for self control, her patience, and daily discipline in carrying out practice work and exercise, such as the hikes she had gone on in the surrounding countryside. Che told Diosdado a number of his own stories and stressed the importance of combating lethargy and routine which often took over if demoralization set in when someone suspected that they were doing nothing useful or apparently important.

At different times, Che asked Diosdado if he was certain that the Czech security services were unaware of which country Tania was residing in, as he did not discount infiltration by Western security services of what he called "the Czech apparatus." Che also insisted that his presence in Prague should not be revealed to any functionary or official belonging to Czech security. To assuage his concerns, Diosdado explained all the details of the support given by *compañeros* in the Czech security services and the compartmentalization principles that were applied. He also mentioned that in spite of their knowledge of the name in the passport Tania was carrying, her destination was never mentioned and they never asked.

During all the conversations that he held with Che, Diosdado commented, "I noticed very clearly that Che was always concerned that Tania should not be given any work that could lead to her detection. She needed to be ready for the major responsibility that she would have to assume. Similarly, he was worried about her health and state of mind as she was alone in a hostile environment and subjected to strong psychological pressure."

As a consequence, the meeting that Tania had been expecting for a number of months took place in April 1966 when she met with a Cuban officer (Ariel). Although she was not aware of it, at this same time Che again had become involved in the plans for the revolutionary struggle in Latin America that, since 1963, had been behind Tania's recruitment, her training in Havana and Prague, and her clandestine arrival in Bolivia. Che's involvement in Operation Fantasma determined the following years of Tania's life, her sacrifice, and her transformation into Tania the Guerrilla.

REUNION WITH CHE

Just as Ariel had instructed, in the third week of April 1966, Tania tested her new Argentine passport on her return flight to Bolivia from Mexico City. She was to wait in La Paz with the patience and astuteness she had already demonstrated, not undertaking any work that could compromise her safety. Mexico City was the site of the next clandestine contact, scheduled to take place with a "Cuban *compañero*" whose identity was unknown to her.

This *compañero*, as Ariel had explained, would be responsible for directing all the political-operational work she would have to undertake in the near future. He did not tell her then that his instructions had come personally from Che. This *compañero* would deal with Tania's future involvement in support work for the international guerrilla movement that Che had begun to organize from Prague with the crucial support of the top ranks of the government and the PCC. Ariel updated Tania on the telephonic signs and countersigns the *compañero* would use to inform her of his arrival in La Paz. They also went over the way in which both would make themselves known to each other, as well as the time and place where, at the right moment, they would have their first personal contact.

To Tania's surprise and satisfaction, she went to the scheduled place of contact in early May 1966, after having received the signal by telephone and having completed countersurveillance measures.

Her joy was complete when on arriving she saw that the Cuban *compañero* Ariel had informed her of was none other than Papi. Tania had a long-standing professional relationship and friendship with Papi, and she deeply admired him in spite of the occasional arguments they had in Havana about Cuban machismo.

After greeting each other and sharing memories and news, Papi reiterated to Tania that she must not get involved in any illegal activity in the immediate future, although he did not mention the exact origin of this order to her. She would have to take advantage of the relations she had established which included people in Bolivian official, cultural, and political circles as well as journalists. Her assignment was to obtain information that could help to analyze the political and military situation in the country.

According to Diosdado, Che reiterated his instructions for Tania on many occasions, especially during the first of two trips Diosdado had made to Prague in mid-June and mid-July to help prepare Che's itinerary and cover. Diosdado worked on Che's disguise and the passport with which, between July 19 and 21, 1966, he would enter Cuba clandestinely under the name of Ramón Benítez Fernández, after having stopped in Moscow and several Western European cities.

During the first trip, Diosdado recalls that as soon as he met with Alberto Fernández Montes de Oca (alias Pacho or Pachungo)[1] and Che in the operations house on the outskirts of Prague, Che, while strolling outside, inquired about Tania's situation after Ariel had made contact with her in Mexico. Diosdado told him that as far as he had been informed, Tania was fine and had established contact with Papi in La Paz.

Diosdado also recalls Che's insistence on finding out whether Tania's marriage to the Bolivian student Mario Martínez Álvarez had been her own initiative or whether it was an order by the VMT officers of MININT responsible for her. Learning from Diosdado that Tania had made this decision of her own free will (see appendix 9), and that the marriage to Mario increased her chances of receiving

Bolivian citizenship, Che was satisfied. Nonetheless, he stressed that regardless of the operational use that a decision of this nature might have, it was always important to take into account "the will of *compañeros* and never to force things upon them, particularly in such delicate matters."

On another day in mid-June, after discussing several matters of interest, Che repeated the importance of not involving Tania in any activity that could affect the work he planned to assign her in the future and pointed out that he had already given express instructions on the matter. Even though I had no direct contact with Tania or with the operation in Bolivia, I subsequently learned that Diosdado's version coincided with the instructions Che had sent Papi on July 10, 1966.

Furthermore, Pombo, today a general in the Cuban armed forces, has confirmed that some days after this event, that is, on July 25, he arrived clandestinely in Bolivia together with Tuma. Under Che's orders, he gave Papi a number of instructions concerning Tania: Papi, as well as Tuma and Pombo, should avoid clandestine contacts with her in order to reduce the risk of her being detected and sabotaging all the patient and meticulous work she had performed over two years.

Pombo went on to explain that Che told them Tania was not to take part in any of the operational assignments linked to the organization of their guerrilla movement. They were, for example, looking for a ranch that could later be used by members of the guerrilla movement, and seeking to purchase weapons, uniforms, and other provisions. She was not to be linked with political contacts who were engaged in the selection of future Bolivian combatants or to be associated with the PCB led by Mario Monje. She also had to keep away from the Bolivian mediator Julio Dagnino Pacheco (alias Sánchez)[2] and the party's dissident group, known as the Peking Line and headed by Moisés Guevara.[3]

Throughout July and August 1966, in line with these orders, the numerous contacts between Papi and Tania were limited to passing on the information she had obtained through her relations with people in Bolivian political circles. Pombo restricted himself to indirect contact with Tania. For the first of these contacts, all three went to a restaurant known as the Confitería Malí, where they sat at separate tables with the sole aim of mutually recognizing each other. For Pombo, this step, as well as identifying the house where Tania was living and the means of entering into contact with her, was vital to ensure there was an emergency location available where they could hide, should this be necessary.

With a similar goal in mind, Papi introduced Tania to Renán when he arrived in Bolivia in mid-October 1966. According to Renán, he met her in an operations house that Tania and Papi had made available in La Paz. During this and sporadic future contacts that he had with Tania, they did not work closely together. On the contrary, Renán recalls that Che personally instructed him at the San Andrés ranch in Pinar del Río (where the Cuban *compañeros* headed for Bolivia were completing military training) to concentrate on obtaining legal status. He was ordered to welcome Cuban *compañeros* who, over the following weeks, would begin to arrive clandestinely. Renán recalls that Tania was not supposed to participate directly in this assignment.

Nevertheless, this situation began to change after August 1966 because of what Renán calls the weakness of the urban clandestine apparatus that Papi was organizing in conjunction with the PCB. There were not enough people to fulfill all the duties, so Tania began to participate in the preliminary work creating the material and security conditions for receiving members of the guerrilla movement. As Pombo recalls, part of this work involved renting houses and other buildings that could be used for receiving personnel or as storage spaces for the provisions they were acquiring. There was also a "secret compartment to be prepared for sending a message to Havana" that was assigned to Tania. She helped to rent the "reserve house in La Paz for the possible arrival of Ramón [Che]," although she was not aware of the plans for his arrival.

With her characteristic discipline and efficiency, Tania accomplished each of the assignments given to her. At the same time, she continued with the process to obtain Bolivian citizenship, which she gained in 1966, according to information provided by the former Bolivian government minister Antonio Arguedas Mendieta.[4] She then formalized her divorce from the Bolivian student Mario Martínez Álvarez as discreetly as she had married him (see appendix 9). With the support of Papi and with the unwitting assistance of the general secretary of the PCB Mario Monje, Tania helped Martínez continue his engineering studies in Bulgaria, a country which at that time belonged to the bloc of Eastern European socialist countries.[5]

As is apparent from Antonio Arguedas's testimony, obtaining Bolivian citizenship helped strengthen the cover story Tania had been using since she arrived in Bolivia at the end of 1964. With this in mind, and also to enrich her knowledge of anthropology, she continued her studies of ceramics in the workshop that her friend Yolanda Rivas de Plaskonska had in La Paz. Similarly, Tania continued her meticulous research into the rich folklore of the Bolivian high plateau.

In Salta, Argentina, she held an exhibition of a display of typical costumes from the different ethnic communities of this Andean region.[6] As a member of the research committee, she also registered with the Department of Folklore in the Ministry of Education, continued compiling and recording a range of musical pieces representative of the culture of the indigenous population in the area. Such was her determination that, according to the Cuban historian Adys Cupull, some Bolivian intellectuals considered Tania as the author of one of the most valuable collections of folk music in the country to date.[7]

While Tania was working under Papi's orders in all this legal and clandestine work, the Cuban combatant Pacho arrived together with

Che in La Paz on November 3, 1966. Che was carefully disguised and used the Uruguayan passport and identity of a business person, Adolfo Mena González. According to Renán, in line with the Communications Plan sent from headquarters, at lunchtime on that day he went to the restaurant El Prado, which had been established as the contact place to meet two incoming Cuban *compañeros* whose precise identity he did not know. At the restaurant, he met Pacho, whom he had known from Cuba, and they agreed to a new clandestine meeting that evening with Che, most likely at the operations house rented by Tania and Papi. Renán recalls that Tania was not present during this meeting, but according to historians Adys Cupull and Froilán González, Che met with her later (probably with Papi) on November 4.[8]

Although none of the few survivors of these heroic events have been able to confirm whether this meeting went ahead, historical research has verified that, at Che's request, Tania made available to him the letter of presentation allowing him to travel throughout Bolivia. The letter was signed by the director of Information Services for the Bolivian presidency, Gonzalo López Muñoz, although he has never acknowledged writing it. Tania developed even closer ties with him after returning from Mexico. Such was the nature of the friendship between them that, according to López Muñoz, she sometimes slept over at his house, because she had not only made friends with him but also with his wife and the rest of the family, including his eldest daughter, Amelia, who for a long time kept a bracelet Tania had given her.[9]

The letter presents "Sr. Adolfo Mena" as "a special envoy of the OAS who is carrying out research and gathering information on the economic and social situation in the Bolivian countryside." López Muñoz requested from "national authorities" and "private individuals and institutions" that they provide the bearer of the letter "all possible cooperation for his research."[10]

This same day, thanks to the steps taken by Tania, Che also received other letters from the director of the Institute of Colonization and Development of Rural Communities in Bolivia in which "civil and military authorities" were requested to give Sr. Adolfo Mena "all the necessary cooperation regarding the provision of relevant information and data" for research on socioeconomic conditions in Bolivia that he was undertaking for the Economic Department of the OAS.[11]

Between November 5 and 6, 1966, Che, bearing both documents and accompanied by Pombo, Pacho, and Tuma, as well as the Bolivian combatant Jorge Vázquez Viaña (alias Loro or Bigotes),[12] undertook a reconnaissance by land that ended at midnight on November 7 at the Ñacaguazu[13] ranch. The ranch had been purchased beforehand by Roberto Peredo Liegue (alias Coco) to be used as one of the places for gathering and training the combatants of the guerrilla movement, later called the Bolivian ELN.[14]

According to Pombo's testimony, because there were not enough trustworthy *compañeros* in La Paz, Papi was obliged to "directly use Tania" to help the Cuban combatants when they arrived separately and clandestinely in La Paz. She had to bring them to the Ñacaguazu ranch between November 20 and December 19, 1966, even though she was not supposed to be involved in that job. For this reason, "she was not the one who met *compañeros* at the airport. Instead she mainly bought food and cooked, or acquired whatever else was needed in terms of clothes." All things considered, "she helped them directly." Pombo went on to say that, "as they arrived, Tania visited them and took some men around La Paz to show them the city." That is why all the Cuban fighters were pleased when Tania, following Che's instructions, arrived for the first time in the early hours of the morning of December 31 at the newly established camp. She was accompanied by Papi, Mario Monje, the leader of the PCB, and another Bolivian, Antonio Jiménez Tardío (alias Pan Divino).[15]

The atmosphere was tense because of Monje's arrival at the guerrilla camp and, above all, by his speech in which he gave PCB activists an ultimatum: to "stay [in the guerrilla movement] or support the party."[16] Pombo describes the atmosphere that surrounded Tania:

On her arrival in the guerrilla camp, Tania was very jubilant. In spite of having walked some eight or nine kilometers, she was physically in good shape. She shook hands with everyone and embraced all of us, and jumped up and down with spontaneous happiness. She knew almost all the *compañeros*, men whom she had welcomed to the country with affection and kindness. The *compañeros* who had gone with Che to meet her on the way were Tuma, Inti, Urbano,[17] and Arturo.[18]

Che devoted a substantial amount of time to talking to her first, and then to Monje. For the remainder of the night there were New Year's and Cuban Revolution anniversary celebrations.[19] We spent a lot of time talking to her, being with her; for us, Tania's arrival was very important. She brought recordings of Cuban songs from Radio Havana that she had taped on a small cassette recorder. She also brought Argentine folk songs by Atahualpa Yupanki,[20] small gifts for everyone, colored handkerchiefs, candy, flashlights, and small lanterns. We sang and drank, and Tania was the life of the New Year's party.[21]

Tania was there when Che gave a speech to bring in the New Year. In memory of the Bolivian patriot Pedro Domingo Murillo, leader of the first declaration of independence of a Latin American colony from Spanish control, Che compared the international struggle in Bolivia with the famous *Grito de Murillo* of the continental revolution.[22] The next day (January 1, 1967), she witnessed Che's response to Monje's treachery, when Che predicted "difficult times and days of moral anguish for the Bolivians" and announced his decision to work for "the unity of all those who want a revolution."[23] Che had decided to include in the guerrilla movement all those activists of other Bolivian political organizations, including the so-called Peking Line of the PCB, as well as activists from other countries who wanted to join the struggle for the liberation of Latin America.

Tania's profound identification with this revolutionary initiative was once again made apparent later that afternoon. After having helped Papi and Pombo write and code a message sent to the top ranks of the Cuban government and the PCC and after developing some photos taken during her stay in the guerrilla camp, she had another meeting with Che. According to his diary, on that occasion Tania agreed to undertake the crucially important and dangerous mission of traveling to Argentina in order to set up a secret meeting for Che with Ciro Roberto Bustos (alias Carlos or Pelao)[24] and with the former Argentine Communist Party activist, journalist, and lawyer, Eduardo Jozami, who had expressed his support for the revolutionary armed struggle.

Having accepted this mission, Tania left the guerrilla camp in the company of the Bolivians Coco and Sánchez, both of whom were also entrusted with building up the urban support network. She left, very moved, after listening to a speech given by Fidel Castro to celebrate the eighth anniversary of the Cuban Revolution. Tania was not aware of it, but her parents, Erich Bunke and Nadia Bunke Bíder, were included among the special guests at this event in Cuba.

Tania's death and the limited contact that she had with Renán—as well as the impossibility of obtaining for this book the accounts by Loyola Guzman and other survivors from the urban network operating in La Paz—prevented me from reconstructing the details of all the activities that Tania was involved in between January 2 and March 19, 1967. During this time she was directly following Che's orders because Papi had remained in the guerrilla camp from the end of December 1966.

According to the versions Loyola has given to other Cuban authors, everything seems to indicate that during this period Tania was teaching conspiracy strategies to inexperienced members of the recently established urban network.[25] As is apparent from Che's diary on January 21 of the same year, Tania left for Argentina to meet with Ciro Roberto Bustos and Eduardo Jozami. She successfully carried out this mission in spite of the fact that Jozami was not able to make contact later with Che. Thanks to Tania's persistence (according to Bustos, she made another trip to Argentina in February of the same year), Jozami twice went to La Paz, but on neither occasion did he have the time available to go with Tania to the camp at the Ñacaguazu ranch.

In his diary, Che wrote that on March 19, when he was returning to the camp after having undertaken a long reconnaissance of the operations zone, he was surprised to discover Tania there. She had arrived with the Peruvians Juan Pablo Chang Navarro (alias Chino),[26] Dr. Restituto José Cabrera Flores (alias Negro),[27] and Lucio Edilberto Galván Hidalgo (alias Eustaquio)[28] at the beginning of March. A few days later she returned to the ranch with Ciro Roberto Bustos and the French intellectual Regís Debray, both of whom now "regret" the commitments they made to revolutionary causes during those years.

According to Pombo's account, in spite of the fact that everyone was happy with Tania's arrival, the news and a meeting with her on the following day upset Che "in view of the fact that he had given her instructions not to return to the guerrilla camp and to make every effort not to get involved with this kind of activity so as to avoid being detected."[29] Pombo went on to say that Che did not want her to "directly participate in supplying the guerrilla force or in any of its military actions. Instead, she was to exploit her ties with high-ranking government circles and other sectors where strategic and tactically important information could be obtained; she was to devote herself entirely to this kind of work and stay there in case the guerrillas needed help from the city. From an operational perspective, in case it was necessary to use a person who was not under suspicion, the guerrillas needed someone who was in the right place, someone trustworthy enough to hide a *compañero* or to receive a messenger carrying something very important."[30]

After Che greeted Tania at the meeting on March 21, he criticized her for being there. The situation at the camp had become difficult due to the desertion of the two Bolivians: Pastor Barrera and Vicente Rocabado,[31] both of whom belonged to the group that Moisés Guevara had brought to the Ñacaguazu camp. Furthermore, there were numerous signs that the Bolivian armed forces had already discovered the existence of a guerrilla movement. A Bolivian military detachment had just raided the *casa de calamina* [zinc house[32]] and the Bolivian Salustio Choque Choque had been captured on March 17.[33] Because of this, Che ordered measures immediately be taken to guarantee the departure of Bustos, Debray, and Tania from the guerrilla camp.

Tania explained to Che she had disobeyed orders because, since no one in La Paz knew the way to the guerrilla camp, she had volunteered to bring out the three Peruvian *compañeros* and later, Debray and Bustos. If she had not done so, "the *compañeros* would have had to wait even longer" in the Bolivian capital. Years later, this information was corroborated by Loyola Guzmán in her account to Adys Cupull and Froilán González. She said that the weakness and lack of organizational experience in the urban network in La Paz was such that its few members were overwhelmed by the amount of work Che had given them when they went to the guerrilla camp at the end of January.

In Pombo's view, Tania's response to this situation demonstrated "her determination to act and to carry out plans even though they were not assigned to her." In taking "these *compañeros* to the heart of the zone where the operations base was located," she also proved her willingness to give priority to the needs of the guerrilla over her own safety and the safety of the mission, which required her to remain in the city as the strategic reserve for the guerrilla movement.

In any case, an assessment of Tania's supposed lack of discipline should take into account that she did not know Che would take so many days to return to Ñacaguazu, because the column's vanguard was already there on March 13, a few days after her arrival with Debray and Bustos. In my view, whatever conclusion can be reached retrospectively regarding Tania's actions, it should always be acknowledged that an immense number of chance circumstances influenced the development of events, which she was not in a position to foresee at the time she decided to take Chino and his *compañeros*, as well as Debray and Bustos, to the guerrilla headquarters. This was particularly the case, in my opinion, because Tania's way of seeing things undoubtedly influenced her view that a meeting between these people and Che was essential to the success of the regional expansion of guerrilla warfare.

Whether or not one agrees with my assessment, it is clear that all these circumstances and others allowed Tania to finally fulfill her dream of directly participating in the armed revolutionary struggle in Latin America. In 1962 she had told Carlos Fonseca, the founder of the FSLN, that she was ready to fight. She told us too, in all sincerity, during our first meeting, in the final days of March 1963, in the library of Manuel Piñeiro's historic home.

CHAPTER **1 2 |**

TANIA THE GUERRILLA

On March 23, 1967, two days after the meeting between Che and Tania in the Ñacaguazu Central Camp, the international guerrilla movement engaged the enemy in combat. According to Che's campaign diary, "A few minutes past eight in the morning, Coco arrived in a hurry to inform them that a section of the armed forces had been caught in an ambush" that had been prepared the previous day under the leadership of the Cuban internationalist combatant Olo Pantoja.[1]

The outcome of this armed encounter was seven dead (including a lieutenant) and 14 prisoners, including a major, a captain, and five wounded soldiers, all belonging to the Bolivian army.[2] As Che indicated in his Bolivian diary, his men captured three 60-mm mortars with 64 rockets; 16 Mauser rifles with 2,000 rounds; two BZ sub-machine guns; three USIS rifles, each with two loaders; two radios; and other provisions (uniforms and boots) useful for warfare. They also captured the Bolivian army's operational plan to reach the zone where the guerrilla encampment was located by converging with other units of the Fourth Division of the Bolivian army deployed in the region.[3]

After tending to the wounded "to the best of the ability" of the guerrilla's medical services, Che freed all prisoners after they had been given "an explanation of the movement's ideals." The Bolivian army was offered a truce so that they could recover the bodies of the men who died in combat.[4] On March 25, Che sent three of his men to the mountain lookout point to keep watch over the Ñacaguazu River's two entrances, while he prepared the rest of the guerrillas to defend the camp.

As no further confrontations took place that day, at 6:30 p.m. Che held a meeting in which he critically examined both himself and the majority of the 43 Bolivian, Cuban, and Peruvian combatants who attended. Also during the meeting, among other things, a decision was made to officially name the guerrilla movement the Bolivian ELN and to prepare for the first stage of the war. Several weeks afterwards, they would announce the goals of this new political-military organization and the details of the recent military engagements would be made public, nationally and internationally.[5]

Tania took part in this meeting, even though Che considered her a "visitor" to the guerrilla camp. According to Pombo, at this time the plan was for her to leave the operations zone "once it became clear how much the enemy knew about her."[6] The situation, however, began to change rapidly after March 27 because the Bolivian government launched an intensive propaganda campaign and began to spread information that led Che to conclude, "everything seems to suggest that Tania has been identified, meaning two years of good and patient work have been lost..."[7]

Subsequent events confirmed these conclusions. According to the government minister in the Bolivian dictatorship, Antonio Arguedas:

> The first reports on Tania were prepared when intelligence service agents examined the suitcases found in a jeep parked in a garage in Camiri. The suitcases contained civilian women's clothing, along with a notebook of telephone numbers and addresses that belonged to Laura Gutiérrez Bauer. But it was not known that this person was Tania. The addresses were only of people who were above suspicion, so a raid was carried out on Yolanda Rivas's house. This woman told them about Laura...
>
> Laura's house was searched. She lived modestly. The head of intelligence told me that he had confiscated personal photos of Laura and others in which she appeared with people prominent in the social and political life in Bolivia... They even gave me a photo where she appears

in between President Barrientos and the head of the armed forces, General Ovando, during a farmers' event. There were also personal letters, one from the man who was her husband, but nothing that linked her to the guerrilla fighters. They [had] also requisitioned an enormous quantity of tapes that had been used for recordings. Later they told me that the people from the CIA who were responsible for going through her belongings spent a day and a half listening to all the recordings in search of something suspicious. But all the recordings were of folk songs and music, particularly from the high plains area… That search produced no clues for the time being.

The image of Tania as a member of the guerrilla force began to emerge when the Bolivian guerrilla fighters Vicente Rocabado and Pastor Barrera deserted; they said that they would only talk to me. Both deserters explained how they had been recruited and taken to Camiri… Later they said that after Tania arrived in Camiri… she became a different woman, that is to say, a guerrilla…[8]

Although Che never found out about all of this, his constant vigilance and innate distrust of the enemy made him decide immediately to abandon the central camp at the Ñacaguazu ranch. He incorporated all the "visitors" (Tania, Debray, Bustos, and Chino), as well as a "Bolivian refugee" (Serapio Aquino Tudela),[9] into the guerrilla column. On March 31, Tania joined the unit that Pombo called the central platoon—in other words, the group led directly by Che. Pombo said, "I believe that one of the most important moments for her was when Che decided she was to be one more combatant and gave her an M-1 rifle."[10]

Tania belonged to the central platoon until April 17, when Che ordered that she, together with another 12 combatants (4 of whom were sick) and the 4 Bolivians known as the "leftover group"—Julio Velazco Montana (alias Pepe), José Castillo Chávez (alias Paco), Eusebio Tapia, and Hugo Choque (alias Chingolo)[11]—would remain in the rearguard of the guerrilla column, under the command of the Cuban internationalist combatant Juan Vitalio "Vilo" Acuña Núñez (alias Joaquín).[12]

According to my research, Che's decision was influenced by Tania's high fever (over 102.2 degrees Fahrenheit). She was also confronting difficulties (like the other sick *compañeros*) during the constant traveling of the guerrilla column. At the same time, she was in pain from an injury to her leg, the cause of which was unknown.[13] Also, according to Pombo, and this has been confirmed by other sources, the military boots given to her caused her problems because they were "a little big for her, which is why she was uncomfortable for a while."[14]

Pombo went on to say that for the 18 days she remained with the central platoon, "We saw that she was stoic, because she was not used to our long hikes, but she still held out. On many occasions she refused to be given special treatment as a woman; on the contrary, she wanted to be treated like the rest of the *compañeros* in the guerrilla army." Such was her determination that "she did not want anyone to tell Che that she was sick."[15]

It was decided that Tania "should do something useful during the time she was with us. The first job she was given was to sew clothes... The second job she was given was to assume responsibility for compiling information together with Papi; she kept a chronology of all the news broadcast from Bolivia and other foreign stations. She listened to Radio Havana, Radio Balmaceda, and other Argentine stations... Tania was in charge of tuning into and selecting the news, what we called 'information analysis.' Moreover, she began to cipher messages and collaborate with Papi on this kind of work." She also helped in the distribution and control of food.[16]

Tania kept up a positive attitude during the four months (between April 17 and August 31, 1967) she remained with Joaquín's column. Historical research has not yet established all the details of movements and attacks undertaken by these experienced combatants. However, through the work carried out by the Cuban historians Adys Cupull and Froilán González, I have discovered that the 17 members of the guerrilla group remained almost three months (April, May, and June) near the area known as Bella Vista, located in the Serranía del Incahuasí.[17] They were following the instructions Che personally gave to Joaquín when they separated on April 17.

During the column's relatively prolonged stay in this area, there were no encounters with the Bolivian army. Their ability to avoid detection by the enemy forces was decisive, as well as the support they received from some peasants in the region. At first, the Bolivian army lacked the will to engage in direct ground combat. The army restricted itself to patrolling the outlying areas of the zone (particularly, the pathways and the farms) and to bombing the region where they presumed the guerrilla group was located, but without undertaking any land-based attack on them. Nevertheless, at the end of April, the Bolivian army's siege intensified in the area and this managed to sabotage Che's first attempt to locate Joaquín's column.[18]

The Bolivian army's brutal repression of peasants was growing, and Joaquín's column suffered the desertion of the Bolivian Pepe. During combat on June 2, 1967, Antonio Sánchez Díaz (alias Marcos)[19] and Casildo Condori Vargas (alias Víctor)[20] both fell. At the end of the month, the group decided to leave the Bella Vista zone. They started on a slow and dangerous route that led to additional deaths (the Bolivian combatants Serafín and Pan Divino) and desertions (the Bolivians Chingolo and Eusebio Tapia) as well as intense sieges by the Bolivian army. They managed, however, little by little, through a series of maneuvers, difficult marches, and reverses, to get close to the Río Grande, where Che's guerrilla detachment was engaged in combat.

The betrayal by the Bolivian peasant Honorato Rojas led to an ambush by the Bolivian army at the ford at Puerto Mauricio, situated in the zigzagging bank of the river. The two detachments of the guerrilla movement were prevented from finding each other in the beginning of September 1967, as they had hoped. Before narrating the terrible events of those days, however, I want to highlight Tania's behavior along the challenging trail between the Serranía del Incahuasí and the Río Grande.

According to the version given by the Bolivian deserter Eusebio Tapia, when Tania recovered from the worst of the injuries that had led to her inclusion in the rearguard of the guerrilla column, "she walked as well as any of us. Although we all tried to help her because men are always sensitive to women… she [said that] she didn't need help and [that] she did not want it; she was just one more member." He added, "I felt she was like a mother. She tried to help me and make me see the mistakes that I had made. She had a little blue bag that she wore on her shoulder, and she liked to collect pretty and colorful little stones…"[21] These details were confirmed in the research carried out by Adys Cupull and Froilán González on what they called the "fifth stage" of Che's life.[22]

Years later, this information was supported when some of Tania's belongings were located (including the little blue bag),[23] and the account of what happened to Joaquín's column was analyzed. According to the Bolivian Paco (the only survivor of the ambush at Puerto Mauricio), at different stages along the dangerous march between Bella Vista and Río Grande, Tania took responsibility for important work. For example, at a certain point, she was left almost on her own to protect the belongings of the guerrilla group. This was at the beginning of August when, after breaking through the siege laid by the army, its members left to look for food and to engage the enemy in a village called Taperillas. According to Froilán González, from this position Tania also took part in hard-fought combat.[24]

A few days later, Tania, armed temporarily with a 30-caliber machine gun, was left in charge of the guerrilla camp while the detachment went to get supplies at the village of Chuyuhaucu, located in the Serranía de Iñao. At that point, Paco said, "Tania was fine; the only problem she had was *chigoes*, which were causing her pain."[25] At the same time, he added, "her boots were not the right size for her."[26] These remarks, made in passing, categorically refute another of the fallacies of the Uruguayan writer José Friedl Zapata, who claimed that Tania, prior to her death in combat, was suffering from intense pain in the lower abdomen caused by "terminal cancer of the cervix."[27]

At the same time, the accounts by Eusebio and Paco confirm the version Pombo told me in 1969 when we were working together with Marta Rojas and Mirta Rodríguez Calderón, on the first edition of *Tania the Unforgettable Guerrilla*. In this book, he said, "We knew that in all the activities carried out by Joaquín's column she was stoic, her attitude strengthened the morale of the group, which was facing a very difficult situation, as it included recruits who were potential deserters, who refused to continue with the guerrillas and had practically betrayed the ideals of the revolution. Her presence in the group was an incentive, proving that she could rise above the conditions that had so affected those pathetic men. In spite of everything, she remained committed. Put another way, we considered her as one of the elements boosting the morale of the men to fight in a group that suffered much more hardship than ours."[28]

There are accounts of Tania's distinguished role during combat and the demoralizing impact she had on the Bolivian soldiers by calling out to them to surrender during battles.[29] Her ability to strengthen other guerrillas' will to fight was probably one of her greatest contributions to the entire guerrilla column. She motivated the fighters both at the camp in Ñacaguazu and during the dangerous trek undertaken by Joaquín's column before they were ambushed by a reinforcement of the Machengo regiment of the Eighth Division of the Bolivian army at the ford at Puerto Mauricio.

The reconstruction that I have been able to create out of different accounts was that one day before this massacre, the 10 guerrilla fighters belonging to Joaquín's column drew near Honorato Rojas's house near the Río Grande. Two of its members attempted to make contact with him, but they returned to where the group had made camp when they heard shots being fired from the other side of the river. A few hours later, another dispatch left, led this time by Gustavo Machín Hoed de Beche (alias Alejandro),[30] and managed to meet with Honorato.

When Alejandro and his companion left Honorato's house, one of the two soldiers who had been hiding in his house (with Honorato's knowledge) departed at full speed to inform the military chief of the arrival of the guerrilla group. Unaware of this situation, that very evening Joaquín and other combatants visited the traitor's home to give him money so he could buy the provisions they needed. They also discussed with him the details of the support he had promised Alejandro and the possibility of giving shelter to Tania and Alejandro, both of whom were still sick. The rest of the men would continue to try to locate Che's column and Honorato would be needed to guide the entire group to a ford where they could safely cross the deep and turbulent waters of the Río Grande. The operation was scheduled to take place in the afternoon of the following day.

The Bolivian army had subjected Honorato's family to brutal pressure and had virtually taken his wife and daughter hostage. The Bolivian army surreptitiously occupied advantageous positions on both sides of the ford at Puerto Mauricio, where Honorato was to lead the guerrilla group on August 31. The group arrived in the area late in the afternoon of August 31 and when they received the agreed signal from Honorato, the guerrilla fighters entered the river in single file. The army, lying in ambush on both banks of the river, opened fire on them from positions that had been previously selected and fortified.

The army's extraordinary advantage, together with the difficult conditions and the precarious health of the guerrillas since their departure from the Bella Vista zone, explains the swiftness with which the 35 members of the Bolivian army were able to kill 7 of the 10 members of Joaquín's column, including Tania.

According to Antonio Arguedas, when Tania emerged from the undergrowth to enter the water, the soldiers crouched in hiding saw for the first time the woman whose defiant voice they already knew. "A blond woman... thin from the privations of combat... who was extremely beautiful. She wore camouflage pants, soldiers' boots, and a very faded blouse with green and white stripes. She carried a backpack and a machine gun. When the first shots from the enemy were heard, Tania raised her arms to reach for the machine gun hanging from her neck and fire it. It is not known whether she managed to fire. But one of the soldiers, Vargas, opened fire on her and shot her though the lung..."[31] Then she fell into the water and was carried downstream by the current. Seven days later, the army found her and her backpack with the help of tracking dogs.[32]

Arguedas's account of these terrible events coincides with that given by Paco, the only member of Joaquin's group who survived the ambush. According to what Paco told Adys Cupull and Froilán González, he was crossing the river in front of Tania. Joaquín walked behind her, as he always marched close by her. After seeing the distinguished Cuban guerrilla Israel Reyes Zayas (alias Braulio)[33] fall, and hearing the number of shots increase, Braulio ducked into the water, with an instinct for self-preservation. When he raised his head, he saw that Joaquín had managed to get out of the river and that he was walking with difficulty. Then he saw Joaquín collapse on the banks of the river. When the guerrilla group ceased resisting, the soldiers emerged from both sides of the river. They had been shooting at the guerrilla column from both sides of the river.[34]

When the attack had ceased and Paco was taken captive by enemy troops, he noticed that the Bolivian combatant Freddy Maymura Hurtado (alias Ernesto) had also been taken prisoner.[35] After being tortured, Ernesto was brutally assassinated that same night. Tania and Negro were not among the dead or captured.[36] Negro was taken prisoner on September 4, 1967, at the Palmarito River, a tributary of the Ñacaguazu. He was then taken to the village of Camiri, where he was beaten to death by the Bolivian army. Three days later, Tania's body was found.

Because different stories circulated after September 3 about the annihilation of Joaquín's column, the news about Tania's death in combat was not made official until September 7. That day, filled with incredulity, Che wrote in his diary, "Radio la Cruz del Sur has announced the discovery of Tania's body on the banks of the Río Grande. It does not ring true, like the news about Negro. According to this radio station her body was taken to Santa Cruz."[37]

In addition to this circumstantial evidence, different elements must have influenced Che's conclusion. For example, on the night of September 1 (24 hours after the ambush), the vanguard of his column had gone to Honorato Rojas's house without noticing anything out of the ordinary. Furthermore, on the following day, another of his combatants had taken prisoner four mule drivers who had no information about the event either. They said that Honorato's wife had complained about the army because the soldiers had beaten her husband and eaten all the food they had.

Che had met Honorato earlier in the year on February 10 and had described him as "a potentially dangerous man."[38] On the night of September 2, Che went back to the traitor's house, where he found a few signs (such as a lit fire) indicating that someone had been there recently. Perhaps because of that, he decided to continue with the march, cross the river and set up camp in what he called a "cowpath" until dawn. In the early hours of the morning of September 3 he received news about the "annihilation of a group of 10 men led by a Cuban called Joaquín in the Camiri region." Nevertheless, he wrote in his diary, "…the news was broadcast by the Voice of America and local radio stations have said nothing."[39]

Che's skepticism about the news of the annihilation of Joaquín's column partially dissipated over subsequent days. He then heard about the September 26 ambush of the guerrilla detachment in which Coco, Manuel Hernández Osorio (alias Miguel),[40] and Mario Gutiérrez Ardaya (alias Julio)[41] lost their lives. At the same time, the tactical siege by the Bolivian army was being strengthened and fear was growing among the peasant population; in Che's summary of the month of September he pointed out:

> It should have been a month of recovery and it almost was, but the ambush in which Miguel, Coco, and Julio died sabotaged everything and we are now in a dangerous position… On the other hand, it seems that some of the news is true about deaths in the other group which we have to presume has been liquidated, although it is possible that a small group of them is wandering around fleeing from the clutches of the army. The news of the seven deaths could be false or, at least, exaggerated…The most important task is to get away and find more suitable areas, then work on the contacts, in spite of the fact that the entire urban apparatus in La Paz is in shambles, as they have also been hit very hard…[42]

While Che pursued this tenacious search for the best routes that would allow him to continue with his project to transform Bolivia into one of the centers of the Latin American anti-imperialist struggle, the doomed combat at the Quebrada del Yuro pass took place. In the early afternoon of October 8, 1967, he was taken prisoner together with the Bolivian combatant Simón Cuba Saravia (alias Willy).[43] He was suffering terrible wounds in one leg, and could not shoot because his rifle had been damaged by enemy gunfire and he had no remaining bullets for his pistol.

The next day, following the instructions of the US government and its Bolivian puppets, Che and his heroic *compañeros* in the struggle, Willy and Chino, were assassinated by nervous, trembling mercenaries of the Bolivian army in the little school at La Higuera. His death, however, and that of the majority of the 49 Bolivians, Cubans, and Peruvians who accompanied him in the epic Latin American struggle—including Tania—did not signify the end of the myriad of revolutionary, democratic, and anti-imperialist struggles throughout the world, particularly in Latin America and the Caribbean.

In his famous "Message to the Tricontinental," where he appealed for the creation of "two, three, many Vietnams,"[44] Che had foreseen that for the coming years, throughout the length and breadth of Latin America, his "battle cry against imperialism" and his "call for the unity of peoples," would gradually reach new "receptive ears." Other hands continue to "reach out to take up our weapons," other men and women are ready, as was Haydée Tamara Bunke Bíder, to chant a "funeral dirge with the rattling of machine guns and with new cries of battle and victory."[45]

CHAPTER 13

RETURN TO CUBA

Official confirmation of Tania's death in combat was given in a communiqué issued by the Bolivian armed forces on September 7, 1967, published on the following day by the newspaper *Última Hora*. According to this brief, vague document, her body was found on the banks of the Río Grande and would be moved to Santa Cruz."[1] Nevertheless, the Bolivian press reported that Tania's body had been transported by helicopter to the small mountain village of Vallegrande where, on September 3, the remains of all the other guerrilla fighters killed during or immediately after the cruel ambush at the ford at Puerto Mauricio were taken.

Apparently, Tania "was treated differently."[2] The bodies of the others had initially been abandoned in a nearby ravine (an insult to the religious beliefs of the local population). But when Tania's corpse arrived in Vallegrande on September 8, some women led by the teacher Dora Cárdenas took the initiative of talking to the head of the Engineers Regiment of the Eighth Division of the Bolivian army, Colonel Andrés Sélich, to ask that Tania's remains not be treated in the same merciless way as the others. The rest of the guerrilla fighters were buried, practically without identification, in a pit near this picturesque village.

Sélich was unmoved. He behaved in the same criminal and abusive way he had behaved throughout his military career. He told them that the army did not have a budget to buy a coffin, sheets, or candles to give Tania a "Christian burial." So the women of Vallegrande organized a collection to purchase these objects and particularly to buy and embroider a shroud, all of which created a difficult scenario for the army.[3]

In order to control this situation, the Bolivian dictator René Barrientos arrived in the area on September 8 and in a storm of publicity was photographed with Tania's corpse. He stated that he had decided to bury, with "military honors" and in accordance with the rites of a Catholic funeral service, "the body of Laura Gutiérrez Bauer, the Argentine woman who belonged to Joaquín's column under the alias of Tania."[4]

According to reports of this publicity stunt in the La Paz newspaper *Presencia,* the ceremony was held on September 10 and officiated by the chaplain Mario Laredo. In addition to a "military platoon," several local people attended. A group of women surrounded "the wooden box where Tania's body had been laid to rest wrapped in a white sheet" that was bought "thanks to a collection organized by the women of Vallegrande."[5]

This information is supported by an account by the Cuban historian Dr. María del Carmen Ariet. From March 1996, she belonged to the multidisciplinary team of professionals including Cuban geophysicists, geologists, archaeologists, anthropologists, and specialists in forensic photography who, under the leadership of Dr. Jorge González Pérez (alias Popy), participated in the search for the remains of all the members of the international guerrilla movement led by Che.

María del Carmen Ariet was able to determine in her interviews with the women who lived in Vallegrande that when Tania's body arrived, they "fought for the right to talk to the army and forced them to give Tania a Christian burial, as she was the only woman in the guerrilla unit." Moreover, it was they who collected "the funds to buy the white shroud in which Tania was buried." The army, under pressure from the women of Vallegrande, was compelled to give her a coffin.

In spite of the supposedly "humanitarian" and "Christian" gesture, Barrientos, the top ranks of the Bolivian armed forces and intelligence services in Vallegrande (advised by the CIA and other US government agencies) immediately stepped up their efforts to denigrate Tania's memory. They violently interrogated Paco in an attempt to get him to "confirm" Tania's sexual relationship with Che and other members of the guerrilla movement.[6] They also tried to prevent the inhabitants of Vallegrande and the press from discovering the exact location of her grave.

According to María del Carmen Ariet, Tania's remains were taken to the Third Military Tactical Unit of the Eighth Division, across from the Vallegrande airport. The local people were forbidden to enter the confines of this military base and, in the late afternoon, they watched what was happening from a distance of approximately 500 meters. At the same time, some locals noticed that soldiers were digging a grave in the cemetery on the immediate periphery of the town. During the night, from a distance, they watched as military vehicles arrived, presumably to bury Tania's body.

No one, not even a peasant who had hidden himself in order to watch the burial, was able to identify the exact site of her grave. This uncertainty enabled the version spread by the armed forces that Tania's body was buried on their base to go unchallenged for a long time. Some people even said that the army had spitefully placed Tania's remains with those of a Bolivian soldier named Benítez, who was killed while fighting against the guerrilla forces.

Other versions suggested that Tania had been buried in a grave marked with a simple wooden cross where, for some time, the people of Vallegrande left flowers in honor of Tania's memory. María del Carmen Ariet states, "When the dictatorship of General Hugo Banzer (1971–78) came to an end, some young people opened the graves, but they could find no evidence that Tania's remains had been there." This discovery pointed to the theory that after Tania's remains had been "officially" buried in the cemetery, a group of soldiers from the army, under orders from Colonel Sélich, had surreptitiously removed them and buried them elsewhere, at an unidentified site.[7] When the Cuban interdisciplinary team arrived in Bolivia, the view that prevailed was that Tania's body had been buried at an unidentified site in the cemetery at Vallegrande.

The practice of burying bodies in unidentified graves had previously been adopted by the Bolivian repressive groups to deal with the remains of guerrilla fighters, among others. They did the same to the bodies of Che and all his *compañeros* killed by the Bolivian army. María del Carmen Ariet argues that the disinformation campaign linked to the location of Tania's body formed part of the plans consciously put into practice by "the Bolivian intelligence, the army, the CIA, and all those who had something to do with the burial of these compatriots."

The aim was to "prevent people who sympathized with the guerrilla forces from paying tribute to them and thereby prolonging the memory of their images and example." The murderers wanted to "definitively bury the history of the guerrilla struggle led by Che," but they have never accomplished this goal. In fact, the village of Vallegrande, particularly the laundry room of the Señor de Malta hospital where Che's body had been on display, and the village of La Higuera, have become places of pilgrimage for all those who want to pay homage to Che and his *compañeros* in the struggle. It is certain that his murderers concealed the site where his remains were buried for almost 30 years.

These well-kept secrets of those Bolivian soldiers implicated in the sadistic practice of "disappearing" their victims were influenced by the political instability characterizing Bolivia and were the result of the systematic repression of the people by most of the military, narco-military, or civilian-military governments that ruled the country from the end of 1964 until August 1993. Bolivia's situation is typical of the so-called "national security dictatorships" that devastated Latin America between 1964 and 1990.

The top ranks of the Cuban government and the PCC never gave up hope that one day they would recover the remains of all the

Cuban, Bolivian, and Argentine guerrilla fighters, including Tania, who had participated in Che's epic Latin American struggle. They were sure that they would be able to pay tribute to these heroic combatants, just as they had done with the Cuban international fighters killed in Grenada and Africa.[8]

The political conditions conducive to achieving this goal, however, did not evolve until the end of November 1995, when the retired general Mario Vargas Salina revealed to the US journalist Jon Lee Anderson that Che's body had not been incinerated, as the official version claimed in October 1967. Salina said that it had, in fact, been buried together with the other guerrilla fighters on the runway of the old Vallegrande military airport. This revelation was soon made public by different news agencies. Thanks to persistent local and international pressure, including that of the Bolivian Association of Disappeared Relatives and Martyrs (ASOFAMD), the constitutional Bolivian president Gonzalo Sánchez Lozada (1993–97) had no choice but to allow an investigation into the whereabouts of the remains of these *compañeros*.

With this objective, a group of Argentine forensic experts traveled to Bolivia four days after receiving permission and immediately began searching in a 2,000 square meter area of the runway. Popy joined the group as a representative of Che's Cuban relatives and of Tania's mother, Nadia. A few weeks later, Nadia formally requested Fidel Castro's support for the work related to the search, exhumation, and identification of her daughter's remains (see appendices 14 and 15).

On December 12, 13, and 17, 1995, thanks to information given to ASOFAMD by a peasant named Vicente Sabala, who had witnessed the burial, the remains were found in Cañada del Arroyo of all those who were killed or captured in the combat at Cajones on October 12, 1967, three days after Che's assassination. These included the Bolivian Jaime Arana Campero (alias Chapaco),[9] the Cuban Octavio de la Concepción y de la Pedraja (alias Moro),[10] and the Peruvian Lucio Edilberto Galván Hidalgo (alias Eustaquio). After this discovery, the Argentine forensic experts had to discontinue their work due to a lack of resources. The Cuban government then solicited the Bolivian government for authorization to continue the search for the remains of the other guerrilla fighters. Once authorization was granted, the Cuban multidisciplinary team traveled to Bolivia.

This decision gave new impetus to the search for the remains of the dead heroes, particularly after March 15, 1996, when the remains of the Bolivian Francisco Huanca Flores (alias Pablito) were located.[11] Three months later, on the outskirts of Vallegrande, the remains of the Cuban Carlos Coello (alias Tuma or Tumaini), who died in combat at Alto Seco, on June 26, 1967, were discovered. Despite more arduous work in subsequent months, new finds were not made. As María del Carmen Ariet explains, the next step was to conduct a patient sociohistorical review aimed at corroborating the different versions of events, before undertaking the search for Tania's body. Work at the Vallegrande cemetery was not making progress, and in addition, haphazard digging might lead the local people to accuse them of violating one or several graves in the cemetery.

The team devoted its energy to geological explorations and to excavations on the landing strip and property that had belonged to the Eighth Division of the Bolivian army. By pure historical coincidence, their efforts bore fruit at the time when in different countries throughout the world—mainly Argentina, Bolivia, and Cuba—preparations were being made to commemorate the 30th anniversary of the death of Che and his *compañeros* in the struggle.

To the immense satisfaction of the Cuban multidisciplinary team, on June 28, 1997, Che's remains were discovered, together with those of Juan Pablo Chang Navarro (alias Chino), Simón Cuba (alias Willy), René Martínez Tamayo (alias Arturo), Alberto Fernández Montes de Oca (alias Pacho or Pachungo), Aniceto Reinaga Gordillo,[12] and Orlando Pantoja Tamayo (alias Olo). The first three had been assassinated in La Higuera and the other four were killed at the Quebrada del Yuro pass, when they were outnumbered on October 8, 1967.

The discovery of Che's remains and those of his Bolivian, Cuban, and Peruvian *compañeros* led to a series of exciting events. Emotions ran high during the memorable journey by the cortege on October 8, 1997. The impressive Che Guevara Memorial, designed by the Cuban sculptor José Ramón de Lázaro Bencomo (alias Delarra), was built in the historic city of Santa Clara, and the remains were laid to rest with a moving speech by Fidel Castro (see appendix 16). Subsequently, the First International Che Guevara Conference was hosted in Vallegrande. All of this undoubtedly gave new impetus to the Cuban multidisciplinary team to continue the formidable task of locating the remains of the other guerrilla fighters.

Thanks to the team's systematic efforts, on February 11, 1998, the remains were discovered of Roberto Peredo Liegue (alias Coco), Manuel Hernández Osorio (alias Miguel), and Mario Gutiérrez Ardaya (alias Julio). Two days later at a site that had not previously been investigated, where Noel Pérez (an engineer belonging to the Cuban team) was carrying out a geophysical study, the body of the Bolivian combatant Julio Luis Méndez Korne (alias Ñato)[13] was found. He had been killed on November 15, 1967, in the final combat between the Bolivian army and the sole surviving group of guerrilla fighters from the detachment commanded by Che.[14]

At the same time, the Cuban team received information indicating that Tania's remains were not in the cemetery at Vallegrande. According to María del Carmen Ariet:

After Che had been found with some of his *compañeros*, people began to speak more freely and some soldiers sent us messages saying that Tania was not in the cemetery, that she had been buried outside it. There were even people who said they had information about Tania and would pass it on to us if we were prepared to pay. Then, unexpectedly, a German appeared who had a restaurant in Vallegrande, and told the Cuban anthropologist Héctor Soto that Tania was buried outside the cemetery. We knew that this German was conspiring with the Bolivian army, which is why we thought that the truth was being withheld. What they really wanted was for us to give them money, and if we did, then they would give us the information.

We had to find out which version was truthful. There were many different stories about the burial of the other guerrilla fighters who had not yet been found and the search for Tania's remains was part of this work. Then, in the city of Santa Cruz, a soldier met with Popy to talk about Papi's burial site. The soldier said that he knew nothing about Papi, but he did know something about Tania. His version coincided with the one claiming that she was buried outside the cemetery. For my part, I interviewed the German who had spoken to Soto. We compared both versions with the information obtained in Santa Cruz and Vallegrande affirming that Tania's burial had taken place outside the cemetery.

At that time, work on recovering the remains was concentrated in the zone of the former army command where the bodies of Coco, Julio, and Miguel had appeared. But the discovery of Ñato's body next to the fence of the former military base gave credibility to the accounts indicating that Tania had been buried next to a group of trees at the back of the wall adjoining the defense perimeter of the command of the Eighth Division. (This site is now the Rotary Club, but in 1967 it belonged to the ranch of a woman named Eufronia.)

According to these versions, the burial was conducted at night and people were kept at a considerable distance, so the military managed to take Tania's body, undetected, to a small hole by the fence that had previously been dug. In this way, they could avoid using the digging equipment they had used for the other burials in places where the population had no access.

Acting on this information, on September 17, the Cuban team decided to perform new geophysical studies of the area by the fence. And it was there that Noel Pérez was relieved to discover, on the morning of September 19, 1998, the first signs of Tania's burial. According to María del Carmen Ariet, when new excavations were undertaken on the site of these remains, there was no doubt that they belonged to her:

> The remains of small rubber boots, as well as fibers from women's underwear and pants were found in the pit. There were traces from the coffin, such as metal rings and glass. Even for those who knew nothing

of anthropology, it was clear that this was a woman because female bones are different from those of a man: the hips are different. At first glance you could see that the bones were robust, that they belonged to a woman who was physically in very good shape due to exercising her whole life. The shape of the skull was "European." Finally, according to the account given by General Vargas Salina, Tania had been killed by a machine-gun bullet that, after piercing her arm, penetrated her lung and caused internal hemorrhaging. The only bullet mark found in these remains was in the arm.

In addition to this evidence, a range of tests carried out by experts at the Señor de Malta hospital in Vallegrande confirmed beyond doubt that Tania's remains had been found.

The area where Tania's remains were discovered allowed the Cuban team to confirm that all the burials of the guerrilla fighters had taken place either on property belonging to the Bolivian army, such as the Vallegrande airstrip and the interior perimeter of the Pando regiment where the command post of the Eighth Division was located in 1967, or on the land of individuals linked to the army. This was the case of the ranch that belonged to a former member of the armed forces at Cañada del Arroyo, where, as has been indicated, the remains were found of Jaime Arana Campero (alias Chapaco), Octavio de la Concepción de la Pedraja, Lucio Edilberto Galván Hidalgo (alias Eustaquio), and Francisco Huanca Flores (alias Pablito).

Over subsequent months, this conclusion facilitated the discovery of the remains of Juan Vitalio Acuña Nuñez (alias Joaquín), Israel Reyes Zayas (alias Braulio), Gustavo Machín Hoed de Beche (alias Alejandro), Walter Arancibia Ayala (alias Walter),[15] Moisés Guevara Rodríguez, Apolinar Aquino Quispe (alias Apolo),[16] and Freddy Maymura Hurtado (alias Ernesto) on June 7, 1999. The majority of those belonging to Joaquin's group had been found, and this allowed Cuban researchers to focus their efforts on the search for *compañeros* who had been buried by the army or the guerrilla fighters themselves in different sites throughout the Camiri area.

It was in Camiri in March 2000 that the Cuban team came across the remains of the last member of Joaquín's column, the Peruvian Dr. Restituto Cabrera Flores (alias Negro), who was brutally beaten to death by the Bolivian army. Later, the skeleton of José María Martínez Tamayo (alias Papi) appeared, who was killed in combat at the Rosita River on July 30, 1967. Several months later, on July 9, the remains were found of Serapio Aquino Tudela (alias Serafín), killed during the battle at Iquira; Antonio Sánchez Díaz (alias Marcos) and Casildo Condori Vargas (alias Víctor), killed in combat at Bella Vista on June 2, 1967; Eliseo Reyes Rodríguez (alias Rolando),[17] killed fighting at El Mesón on April 25, 1967; and Antonio Jiménez Tardío (alias Pan Divino) killed in the confrontation near Monteagudo on August 9 of the same year.

At the time of writing in October 2004, the only bodies not yet found are those of Jesús Suárez Gayol (alias Rubio), who died in combat at Iripití on April 10, 1967;[18] Jorge Vázquez Viaña (alias Loro or Bigotes), who was killed at Camiri on April 29, 1967; Raúl Quispaya,[19] killed in combat at the Rosita River on July 30, 1967; as well as Benjamín Coronado Córdova,[20] and Lorgio Vaca Marchetti (alias Carlos)[21] who, in spite of all efforts to rescue them, accidentally drowned in the Río Grande on February 26 and March 16, 1967, respectively.

More than one book will one day have to be written about the scientific feats and human endeavors surrounding these events. But for now I only wish to highlight that all of this has been possible thanks to the tenacity and professionalism of our experts. Once initial resistance had been overcome, the Bolivian people and, in particular the inhabitants of Vallegrande, gave us their invaluable collaboration. Without a doubt, it was their hospitality and solidarity that facilitated the discovery and return of Tania's body to her beloved Cuba.

According to María del Carmen Ariet, the people of Vallegrande helped enormously, particularly two of the women, Dora and Edith, who had taken part in the negotiations with the armed forces to request that Tania be given a Christian burial. They asked María del Carmen Ariet if they could organize a farewell to Tania's remains in the small cathedral in the city, where a young Polish priest said a beautiful and eloquent farewell mass recalling all the guerrilla fighters killed in 1967, especially Che. In a tradition among the people of La Higuera, Che has also become known as Saint Ernesto de la Higuera.

After this mass, many people of Vallegrande joined the procession carrying Tania's ossuary to the pit where her remains had been discovered. After recalling how 31 years before they had confronted the disgraceful Bolivian army, the women officially handed the ossuary to Dr. Jorge González (alias Popy), who was representing Tania's family. Immediately afterwards, those present sang "La Cacharpalla," a Quechuan song that, in addition to being a farewell, expressed their wish that the ossuary would have a "happy end" after leaving Vallegrande.[22]

Once this moving ceremony had finished, and in the midst of resounding shouts of "Viva Tania!" and "Glory to the guerrilla struggle!" her ossuary was taken by car along the dusty, zigzagging dirt road that crossed rivers, valleys, mountains, and villages, reaching an altitude of 2,000 meters in the steep Andean foothills. They continued on to the tropical plains where, bordered by the Piray River, the 400-year-old city of Santa Cruz de la Sierra is located.

After circling the main square and the cathedral, the motorcade went to the small clinic belonging to Dr. Chato Peredo (Coco and Inti's brother), where dozens of local people waited. Tania's remains were then taken by air to La Paz, and were then transferred to Havana after the necessary paperwork.

Almost 34 years after arriving for the first time in Bolivia, Tania, as she had so often dreamed, returned to Cuba, her "third homeland." This time, she did not leave the El Alto airport under the clandestine Argentine-German name of Laura Gutiérrez Bauer, but under the name of the renowned internationalist fighter Haydée

Tamara Bunke Bíder, or rather, as Tania, who fully accomplished her life's mission.[23] She had earned the right to be embraced by immortality, to enter the history of the peoples' democratic, anti-imperialist, and revolutionary struggles throughout the world, especially the unfinished struggle of the peoples of Latin America and the Caribbean for their true and definitive independence.

CHAPTER **1 4** |

"MY LITTLE ITA"

During the second week of December 1998, I went to the Varadero international airport to wait for Nadia Bunke to arrive in Cuba. When she arrived, I saw that it was with mixed emotions, happiness and pain. The news that had officially been sent to Germany about the discovery of her daughter's remains in Vallegrande and their return to Havana had brought Nadia face to face with the undeniable evidence of her beloved daughter's death. Still, she was consoled that, finally, her daughter's remains would now rest permanently in Cuba, the island she loved so much and considered to be her homeland. It is here that Tania's memory is forever preserved in the names of schools, CDRs, FMC delegations, health clinics, and other workplaces.

These same emotions surfaced on the day that Commander Ramiro Valdés drove us to the Ministry of the Revolutionary Armed Forces. Popy opened the ossuary so we could see and touch her remains before they were taken, along with the remains of nine other internationalist guerrillas killed in combat in Bolivia, to the Che Guevara Memorial, erected one year previously in Santa Clara. After showing Nadia some of Tania's belongings found in Vallegrande, Ramiro Valdés asked her what flag her daughter's remains should be transported under. Without hesitation, Nadia answered, "Under the Cuban flag, the flag of her other homeland for which she fought and which honored her by accepting her into the Cuban Communist Party." (See appendix 17.)

Tania's sense that she belonged to the deepest roots of José Martí's nation was reinforced for Nadia and me when once again we observed in silence, and with tears in our eyes, the very moving tribute given to her by the Cuban people. Tens of thousands of people from Havana, Matanzas, Cienfuegos, and Villa Clara lined the route between the cities of Havana and Santa Clara to pay homage to the solemn cortege taking the fallen to Santa Clara on the morning of December 29.

During the afternoon, night, and early morning of the following day, countless men, women, elderly people, and children kept vigil over Tania's remains, and those of the Bolivians Roberto Peredo Liegue (alias Coco), Mario Gutiérrez Ardaya (alias Julio), Aniceto Reinaga Gordillo, Jaime Arana Campero (alias Chapaco), Francisco Huanca Flores (alias Pablito), and Julio Luis Méndez Korne (alias Ñato); the Peruvian Lucio Edilberto Galván Hidalgo (alias Eustaquio); and the Cubans Manuel Hernández Osorio (alias Miguel), and Moro. On December 30, in a ceremonial caravan with military honors and under their respective national flags, they were driven to the Che Guevara Memorial and placed in alcoves. There, bathed in the eternal light of a bright flame and symbolically surrounded by jungle vegetation, everlasting homage is paid to them.

Earlier, our emotions had been sorely tested when Ramiro Valdés, in a heartfelt and profound speech, recalled several episodes from the life of "that brave, intelligent, and thoughtful young woman" who had devoted her life "to the cause of our country. As a clandestine combatant she provided invaluable service to the Latin American revolutionary movement" before filling, as a guerrilla fighter, "a glorious page in the history of Che's actions in Bolivia." Ramiro Valdés, paraphrasing parts of Fidel's speech for Che and those who died in Bolivia, included Tania and other *compañeros* in the "reinforcement of invincible combatants" that had come to support the Cuban people in their "difficult battle… against the Yankee enemy that is trying to destroy us… and in the

defense of the ideas of the revolution, solidarity and socialism."
(See appendices 16 and 17.)

On the morning of the last day of that year, this speech and other
thoughts were in our minds and hearts as we returned to Havana.
We were traveling the road from Santa Clara to Havana, along which
Che and Camilo, surrounded by the Cuban people, had traveled to
occupy the last bastions of Batista's overthrown dictatorship 40 years
before.[1] On the journey, memories surfaced of that sad moment at
the end of October 1967, when Nadia and Erich Bunke were officially
informed in Havana of the death of their daughter while she was
with the ELN in Bolivia.

I also recalled how both, in spite of the pain that the news caused
them, had immediately understood Tania's decision to join the
struggle for the national and social liberation of Latin America. They
understood why we had, with Tania's consent, kept the delicate and
risky work she had been undertaking in Bolivia since the end of 1964
secret from them during their visit to Cuba in 1966. Undoubtedly,
as parents, their grief was inconsolable, but as communists, they
expressed their deep satisfaction that she had died as she would
have wanted to in her dreams: fulfilling her revolutionary duty and
giving her life for her most deeply felt political ideals.

For many years, both of them—proud of their daughter—dedicated their lives to remembering Tania, to making her life and her
feats public, to telling the true story of her sacrifice, as opposed
to the lies being spread about her in the media, ensuring that her
example would live on for new generations. Erich's death meant that
Nadia had to continue with this work on her own, and so she did.
She did not even give up when the GDR disappeared in 1990. On
the contrary, she redoubled her efforts to preserve her daughter's
memory.

This was difficult because, as Nadia described, our ideological
enemies took advantage of the political-ideological confusion gener-
ated by the disintegration of the Soviet Union and the disappearance
of European socialism. Sooner or later they were bound to besmirch

Tania's memory. That is what happened in 1997, when the well-known publisher Aufbau Verlag, of West Germany, decided to publish the libel written by the Uruguayan writer José A. Friedl Zapata under the title (in German) *Tania, the Woman Che Guevara Loved*. The book revives lies about Tania's life that since the beginning of the 1970s have been circulated by the CIA through the deserter and corrupt former officer of the East German security services, Günter Männel.

Nadia, despite being 81 years old, initiated a brave and successful legal battle against this book from the time the publication of this insult was announced. A Berlin court banned its publication in Germany, forcing the publisher to withdraw unsold copies of the book in March 1998. Even more important was the ruling that prohibited 14 specific defamations of Tania from ever being published again, setting a fine of 500,000 German marks or a six-month prison sentence if anyone ever does so (see appendix 13).

I believe it was when Nadia and I were discussing this subject that I mentioned my plan to write this book. Little by little, I managed to convince her to discuss the matter. Finally, in 2001, I asked for her account of events, which she gave to me for this book. Since Nadia died in February 2003, I am leaving her version, intact, open to readers for posterity, to be captivated by her deepest feelings toward her daughter Haydée Tamara, her "little Ita":

> In 1935, Erich, a German communist, and I, a Russian Jew, were forced to leave Germany because of fascist repression. We planned to go to Moscow, but the paperwork took so long that we decided to go to Argentina, where we had relatives.
> Erich and I immediately joined the Argentine Communist Party. We held clandestine meetings in our house, hid publications and sometimes weapons too. Olaf and Tamara[2] grew up in a communist environment. They knew about our activities, the letters we received from Germany, and how terrible the fascist repression was.
> When we moved to Argentina we wanted to have a little girl, but in the beginning Erich earned only 200 pesos as a physical education teacher and this was not enough to live on and to have [another] child.
> One day Erich was a given a raise of 20 pesos and we immediately

decided to have a baby. We had it in our minds that it would be a girl and we had even chosen her name; she would be called Tamara, which had been my mother's name. My mother died when I was nine-and-a-half years old.

One of Erich's pupils was blond and very pretty and he wanted our daughter to have the same name as her: Haydée. I said, okay, Tamara will be her second name.

When she was born Erich said, "I have a beautiful little girl with dark hair and blue eyes." I replied, "Okay, her name will be Haydée Tamara."

It was a difficult struggle to raise two children; we wanted them to have a good education and to live in an environment free of hardship. All the responsibility fell on my husband's shoulders. He taught German classes, physical education, and mathematics; he tried as hard as he could to increase his salary of 220 pesos.

We had joined an antifascist organization composed of German workers living in Argentina. This political institution had a ranch on the outskirts of Buenos Aires that was also a recreation area where different sports were played; that's where we went with Olaf and Tamara.

She was very singled-minded. At four years old she was already climbing trees and at seven she could climb over a five-meter high fence that surrounded the house. She climbed ropes and rode horses. She was a good rider: at 12 years old she rode bareback and without reins. She learned how to swim and cycle at a very young age.

She was very well proportioned as a child, tending to be a little chubby. When she was born we were all surprised because she had long black hair and her complexion was quite dark. After three or four months, she totally changed color; she became very fair-skinned and blond. She had blue eyes right from the start. She was strong; she weighed four kilos at birth. Everyone who saw her thought she was two or three months old. She started walking when she was one year and one month old and was able to say "mommy" when she was seven months old.

Tamara was gentle, affectionate, and calm; she did not cause problems and she was not afraid of anything. She loved the water, particularly because she had seen how her parents enjoyed it. At the age of two, when she had not yet learned how to talk properly, she would say, "Ita is going into the water tomorrow."

She loved dolls and had quite a few. She could spend hours with them, playing like little girls do. From a very young age, at about a year old, she would go to sleep with a little doll in her arms; she looked like a little mother. Her favorite doll was called Cuca.

When she started growing up, she began to practice sports. She also liked to read a lot apart from her school textbooks. When we left for the GDR, she gave her books away to a classmate, Nélida, who was her best friend.

At primary school, she studied Spanish, English, German, and French and took piano lessons. Later she studied the accordion and painting. We bought the accordion for Olaf, who took 10 classes that came free with the purchase of the instrument. Olaf taught Tamara but in the end she played better than him.

From the time she was little we called her "Tamarita," but she was only able to pronounce the last syllable. This was the reason why we always called her "Ita." In letters she wrote to us, she always signed them like that: Ita.

When fascism was defeated we returned to Germany. Tamara was fourteen and a half. She didn't want to leave Argentina—it was really her country. She asked us to let her return there one day, and we promised we would when she was an adult.

German socialism was a revelation for her. It was what she really wanted and that was why she immediately became involved in the political events of the country. After she attended her first meeting of the FGY, she returned home very enthusiastic. She had seen that socialism gave her the possibility of freely expressing her thoughts and political concerns.

Tamara felt a very strong bond with Latin America. When we returned to Germany, she told her friends about her preference for Argentine, Peruvian, and Uruguayan folk music. She liked Argentine folk dances and her companions were surprised at how many Latin American songs she knew, although they were aware that she also liked classical music.

She was in love with life. She was happy, very optimistic, energetic, tireless, very open, pleasant, and she also had her romantic dreams, like any other girl of her age. She wanted to get married and have children, but her main priority was her revolutionary duty, participation in the Latin American revolutionary struggle.

In 1957, when she traveled to the Soviet Union to take part in the fifth World Festival of Youth and Students, she made contact with some Cubans. They told her about the struggle by Fidel Castro in the

Sierra Maestra and how there was an Argentine with him named Che Guevara, who was considered to be a communist.

From that point onward, Che became a special figure for her in the continent's revolutionary struggle because he was Argentine and, above all, because he was a communist.

Her final two years in the GDR were spent organizing a trip to Latin America. She got her passport and obtained authorization from the party, which was very understanding of Tania's determination to return to Latin America.

On one occasion, *compañeros* from the GUWSP said to her, "We know you well; we trust you completely, and we know that wherever you go, whether it be a socialist or capitalist country, you will continue with the struggle in the ranks of the working class in the revolutionary movement."

She was certain that being in Cuba would allow her to fully learn everything there was to know about the revolution and that this would be useful for the work she planned to carry out in Argentina. Yes, that was the way she thought and she was convinced that her duty was to fight in Latin America. We, as parents, had no right to deny her this.

When we learned about her decision to go to Cuba we were pleased because she would have run a lot of risks in Argentina. The communist party was illegal there and she would have undoubtedly worked with them. She could have been arrested, tortured, and even killed. We never thought that in Cuba she would be given such a mission, which she successfully accomplished.

She knew how to keep secrets from us and from her friends in Cuba concerning the important mission that Che had assigned her. She told us in telephone calls and letters in 1964 that she would visit us. We waited for the arrival of our daughter who we had not seen in several years and we were really happy waiting for her visit. That visit never occurred and we were deeply saddened by this because we would have been overjoyed to see her after so many years.

On October 15, 1964, she wrote us a letter in Spanish:

My dear old compañeros,
In the first place, HAPPY BIRTHDAY, Compañera *Mama! I hoped to give you a surprise and to be there for the 25th but as you can see, it wasn't possible. But our "old lady" is still a young student at the university, an athlete with a gold* Sportleistungsabzeichen *[medal], and an eternal traveler, etc.*
You must be surprised that I have written in Spanish. I haven't forgotten

German and neither is it because of faulheit *[laziness]. I'm sure you'll understand that when working on a job of a military nature, writing in a foreign language might generate distrust… In any case, it is good practice for you to read and write in Spanish.*

I still can't say when I will be able to get there, possibly soon, for Christmas or New Year's. I have the opportunity to take a special course but no definite decision has been made yet. If I'm accepted, I hope that I'll be able to visit you first.

Kisses and ein bisschen drucken *[hug me a little] against your hearts*
Ita

Our "Ita" had become Tamara, then "Tania the Guerrilla" with Che in Bolivia. History records her name as Tania and she was finally buried at the Che Guevara Memorial in Santa Clara, together with Che and his *compañeros*. This is a very great honor for my dear daughter Tamara-Tania, and an immense source of pride for me, as the mother of my dear Ita. I have lost a daughter, but I have many, many children among the Cuban people.

Reading what Nadia wrote about the years of Tania's life before I met her, thinking about everything that has been written in these pages, and recognizing the exceptional talent that some human beings are endowed with, I would like to paraphrase what Fidel Castro said about our brilliant guerrilla commander Camilo Cienfuegos, "There are many Tanias among our people!"[3]

I have seen some of them, with different names and different faces, among Algerian, Argentine, Chilean, Cuban, Dominican, Ecuadorian, Guatemalan, Nicaraguan, Palestinian, Puerto Rican, El Salvadoran, and Saharan women, who, without losing their tenderness or their love of life, have committed themselves, body and soul, to humanity's many different struggles to save the "wretched of the earth."

That is why I would like to finish this book by saying to Nadia and Erich that Tania is and will always be alive among us. Her example lives on in the steadfast spirit of the people of Our America who keep the flame of rebellion burning bright in the continuing struggle for the rights of women, children, the elderly, people of all colors, the indigenous, and the landless. The struggle continues for healthcare and education systems that cover all needs—without discriminating against anyone, whether it be for social, economic, gender, ethnic, or religious reasons.

The example of Tania—Tamara—lives on in Cuba where her socialist dreams are increasingly becoming realities that cannot be reversed. Her example lives on in the struggles in Argentina, Ecuador, and Bolivia, where the power of the working class has forced corrupt and weak governments to resign; in Colombia, where armed struggles are still being waged against imperialism; in Venezuela, where the power of the people overcame the coup d'état in April 2002 against President Hugo Chávez—a coup that was organized by economically powerful groups and US imperialism because Chávez had committed the "crime" of putting into practice the Bolivarian ideal of leading the dispossessed toward a better future.

Nadia and Erich, rest in peace in the certainty that Tamara's example has not only endured and will always endure, but has multiplied and will continue to multiply...

APPENDICES

PERSONAL RECORDS PREPARED FOR THE TANIA CASE

*Tamara Bunke wrote this autobiographical note
in preparation for her new identity as Tania.*

SECRET

Tania's name is Haydée Tamara Bunke Bíder and her nickname is Ita. She was born on November 19, 1937, in Buenos Aires, the federal capital, as her parents were forced to flee from Germany two years previously due to fascist persecution. They fled for two main reasons: political and racial. The political reason was because her father had been a communist party activist since 1928 and the racial reason was her mother's Russian Jewish origin.

Tania spent the early years of her life in Saavedra, a Buenos Aires neighborhood, with her brother and parents. Subsequently, they moved to Corrientes and Pasteur and later to Sarmiento, all of which are in Buenos Aires. During this period she frequently traveled to Altagracia, in the Córdoba region, and to Quequén, in Necocha, to the south of Buenos Aires.

Tania went to primary school in Argentina, the same school where her father worked as a teacher, and then later she studied a year in a teachers' college. She also studied piano, some guitar, and more seriously, the accordion. She attended a course on painting and drawing and enrolled in ballet classes during her final year in Buenos Aires. From a very young age, Tania enjoyed sports and practiced them extensively, although her favorite events were track and field.

From the very outset Tania's life developed in the context of a militant and revolutionary family. Her parents were members of the Argentine Communist Party and worked tirelessly against fascism;

they also helped Jewish refugees, hosted party meetings, stowed weapons, etc. From her very early years, Tania became involved in this struggle, delivered messages, distributed clandestine information, and handed out newspapers.

In 1952, Tania's parents decided to return to Germany. They traveled by boat to Hamburg and from there to Berlin. While they were looking for work they lived in Potsdam-Babelsberg, in the home of an old friend of Tania's father, a colleague from work and a member of the East German Communist Party.

In November of that same year, Tania's parents settled in the age-old city of Stalinstadt while Tania and her brother lived in the boarding school in Fürstenberg-Oder, where they studied for their baccalaureate. In October 1952, Tania joined the FGY and took part in a range of activities organized by that group.

Once she had finished high school, Tania rejoined her parents while her brother moved to Berlin to continue his studies. During the period from 1954 to 1956, she worked as an activist in the leadership of the FGY in Stalinstadt, as a member by then of the GUWSP. At the same time, Tania took part in several equestrian courses and a number of shooting competitions.

In 1956, Tania decided to move to Berlin, where she lived alone until her parents moved to the city the following year. During this period she undertook a number of journeys into the interior part of the country accompanying delegations and organizing international events. On her arrival in Berlin, Tania began to work for the Ministry of Foreign Affairs, where she was active at a grassroots level in the FGY in different posts (information and finance). In 1957, in response to an appeal by the movement, she began to work in the leadership of the Pioneers organization of central Berlin after attending a preparatory course. Meanwhile, Tania had already started work in the International Relations Department of the Central Council of the FGY. This job allowed her to put her language skills into practice, as she spoke German and Spanish fluently, in addition to some knowledge of French and English.

In 1958, Tania began to study philosophy at Humboldt University. She finished her first year at the university while remaining active in the FGY, mostly distributing information. During those years, Tania focused her energies on the FGY International Relations Department, promoting relations with Latin America.

Tania took several trips abroad, to Moscow and then to Prague. In 1959, she worked on preparations for the seventh World Festival of Youth and Students.[1] She carried out work within the Latin American Bureau, forming part of the Argentine delegation, and living in Vienna during the time she held this post. Her activities in the Bureau gave Tania the opportunity to develop ongoing contacts with delegates from Latin America and other countries.

During this period she became increasingly involved with the progress of the Cuban Revolution. This involvement began prior to the success of the revolution, a process to which she was widely and strongly committed, by giving conferences, organizing solidarity campaigns, and writing press articles in support of the cause.

In 1957, while at the festival in Moscow, Tania made contact with Cuban delegates, representatives of the World Federation of Democratic Youth.[2] A short time later, she met a Cuban *compañero* who arrived in her country with a cerebral blood clot as a consequence of torture suffered at the hands of Batista's police.[3] On a trip to Prague, she met with other Cubans residing in that city. This relationship with the Cuban Revolution intensified with its victory. When numerous Cubans began to arrive in Europe, Tania had access to material providing information on the revolution. The importance of these activities should not be underestimated, even though in these early years in Europe, Tania did not fully understand the path taken by the Cuban Revolution or the magnitude of its repercussions for Latin America, meaning that there were some inconsistencies in her political position.

In July 1959, Tania worked with the first official Cuban delegation to arrive in the GDR, made up of representatives that included Antonio Núñez Jiménez, Orlando Borrego, and others.[4] In December of that same year Tania made contact with another official Cuban delegation, led by Che Guevara. Later, during her last weeks in Germany, she worked in the Cuban provisional mission.

In 1961, having made all the preparations to return to her native country, Tania received an invitation to travel to Cuba; she arrived on May 12 that same year. Shortly after her arrival, Tania became involved in the International Student Union Preparatory Commission.[5] Subsequently, she began to work in ICAP, accompanying delegations on trips to the interior of the island. She became directly involved in revolutionary activities, collaborating with the UJC and the trade union coordinating body, as well as the Federation of University Students and the FMC. Upon moving to the Translations Department at the Ministry of Education, Tania continued with her activities in such grassroots organizations as the UJC and joined the militia.

Tania became acquainted with a number of Nicaraguan *compañeros* who were active in the United Nicaraguan Front, known today as the FSLN, and began to collaborate with them.[6] She began to meet with Carlos Fonseca, the leader of the FSLN and the Nicaraguan guerrilla forces, at the Radio Havana station and other places in Havana. Fonseca discussed with Tania the possibility of her traveling to Nicaragua and joining the armed struggle in his country. They began to concretize plans that, for various reasons, were never realized.

Tania's personal relationships can be spoken of in some depth. Her relations with her family have always been good and were once described by her in the following way:

> My relationship with my parents has always been good, as parents and even more so as *compañeros* in revolutionary ideals. My mother, in particular, is a woman with boundless energy and is infinitely dynamic, and I deeply admire her. My relationship with my brother is similar, although our different interests have distanced us from each other to some extent; he has opted for science and purely intellectual work, while I have gone for politics and revolutionary activities.

TANIA'S OPERATIONAL PLAN FOR THE CIENFUEGOS PRACTICAL EXERCISE

Havana, February 12, 1964
Year of the Economy

SECRET

1. OBJECTIVES: This Practical Operational Plan includes the following goals:
  a. Test the knowledge acquired in the course of the Tania Case, as part of Operation Fantasma in the following fields: radiotelegraphy, radio transmission, codes, secret messages, dead drops, personal contacts, photography, secret compartments, use of communication plans, and all security and clandestine measures.
  b. Ensure that Tania acquires all the necessary confidence in the technical measures that she has been instructed in, given that during the 11 days of this Practical Operational Plan, the agent will be operating clandestinely in our country as if she had infiltrated the enemy. Therefore, she will have to outwit revolutionary vigilance forces, which will give her confidence in the work she will carry out abroad in the future.
  c. Develop habits and experience in terms of the different security measures that she must follow to keep her cover during the course of her work.

2. PRACTICAL OPERATIONAL PLAN TO BE FULFILLED:
1. Tuesday 2/18/1964:
  a. Depart from Havana for Santa Clara Province, where she will carry out her Practical Operational Plan.

b. Operational study and familiarization with people she will be in proximity with and the city itself.

2. Wednesday 2/19/1964:
   a. Reconnaissance of the town with the aim of studying it from an operational perspective and locating the best sites for dead drops.
   b. Inform us of her operational situation and of her possibilities of fulfilling her Practical Operational Plan; this will be done through a secret script and code.
   c. Mail the letter containing the message.
   d. Take half a roll of film of photos of documents.
   e. Develop these photos.

3. Thursday 2/20/1964:
   a. Reconnaissance of the town with the aim of locating dead drops.
   b. Purchase an appropriate object, to be turned into a secret container, the interior of which can be used to store the photos of documents.
   c. Prepare the container, in which the photos of documents will be sent to us.
   d. Mail the container with the photos.

4. Friday 2/21/1964:
   a. Install antennae for the transmitter.
   b. Study the area surrounding her dead drop.
   c. Test her radio equipment.

5. Saturday 2/22/1964:
   a. Stroll around the town and take half a roll of film of photos during this stroll.
   b. Make a complete sketch of her dead drop.
   c. Receive a message from Point 3, at ____.[1]
   d. Decipher the message received from Point 3.

e. Prepare a message for Point 1.

f. The message will be transmitted to Point 1, at ____with the CIA equipment.

6. Sunday 2/23/1964:

a. Take half a roll of film of photos of documents.

b. Make personal contact at 20:00 to hand over the sketch of her dead drop (completed).

c. Prepare this roll of undeveloped film, to be placed in her dead drop.

d. Send a transmission from Point 1, at ____.

7. Monday 2/24/1964:

a. Decipher the message received from Point 1.

b. Place the roll of undeveloped film in her dead drop.

c. Inform us of her operational situation and fulfillment of her Practical Operational Plan through the secret script and the code.

8. Tuesday 2/25/1964:

a. Prepare a message of some 80 groups for Point 1.

b. Establish two-way contact with Point 1, at ____ receive the message from Point 1 and send him the message that she has for him with the CIA equipment.

c. Decipher the message received from Point 1.

d. Prepare a message for Point 4 (Havana), and include in this message the same information that was contained in the previous message of the secret script and the code.

e. Make two-way contact with Point 4 (Havana) at ____ transmit the message for Point 4 and receive hers with the EICO equipment.[2]

9. Wednesday 2/26/1964:

a. Decipher the message from Point 4.

b. Check her dead drop to see if there is something in it for her.

c. Prepare a message of some 70 groups for Point 4.

10. Thursday 2/27/1964:
   a. Receive a message from Point 1, at _____.
   b. Retransmit the message received from Point 1 to Point 3, at _____ using the CIA equipment.
   c. Receive a message from Point 3, at _____.
   d. Retransmit the message received from Point 3, to Point 1, at _____ using the CIA equipment.

11. Friday 2/28/1964:
   a. Gather up all the materials.
   b. Depart for Havana.

3. MATERIALS NECESSARY IN ORDER TO ACCOMPLISH THIS PRACTICAL OPERATIONAL PLAN:
   1. CIA equipment.
   2. EICO transmitter.
   3. All the parts that our workshop deem to be necessary for our agent during the period she will be fulfilling the Practical Operational Plan, along with tools and material for setting up antennae.
   4. Prepare the Communication and Frequency Plans to be used by her in her work.
   5. A 35-mm Reflex camera.
   6. Liquid developers and film fixative.
   7. A bottle for developing 35-mm film.
   8. Lead-gray colored and black paper on which to prepare undeveloped film.
   9. Four rolls of 35-mm film appropriate for taking both regular photos and photos of documents, each roll having 36 exposures.
   10. An extension for taking photos of documents.
   11. A magnifying glass with which to read her plans and to determine the quality of her negatives.

12. All materials that the agent will require to work with the secret script.
13. All materials required to decipher our messages.
14. Photographs of the Communication and Practical Operational Plans.
15. Prepare secret container with negatives of the photos of these plans.
16. Have access to a man from Group 1 who will contact her and collect and store items in the dead drop.
17. See what possibilities there are during the course of our agent's work to assign a countersurveillance team to her for two or three days.
18. Minox camera with accessories.

Revolutionary greetings,

Ulises Teobaldo
Operative Official
Technical Instruction Manager

Aldo
Head of Technical Division MI
COPIES

O = Operative Official.
C = Technical File.
C-F = TANIA.
Meca = Teobaldo.

TANIA'S REPORT ON THE CIENFUEGOS
PRACTICAL EXERCISE

ONLY COPY
SECRET

To: Ulises
From: Tania
Subject: Tania's report on work from February 21, 1964, to March 1, 1964

A. GENERAL ACTIVITIES REPORT

I arrived in Cienfuegos on the night of Friday, February 21, at 02:00. A minor problem arose immediately when I registered at the reception desk of the hotel. Not only was the room booked by the Ministry of Industry but it was also booked in the name of Tania Lorenzo. Furthermore, my identification in the name of Tamara Lorenzo was written incorrectly, which drew attention to me. Nonetheless, I believe that from the conversation and my behavior then and subsequently, I was able to effectively minimize the confusion and there were no further problems in this respect.

On that occasion I let it be known that I worked as a translator for different organizations, that I had recently been working for the Ministry of Foreign Trade, and that I had been given my identity card at the last minute. The *compañero* who made the reservation for the room worked in the Ministry of Industry and was not well informed; my colleagues at work called me Tania and for this reason the room was reserved in that name. I was resting and waiting for a call to begin work with a delegation of foreign technicians; in this way I was establishing a possible motive for a change of hotel or an unplanned trip and convenient explanations in case I should have visits from people who know me, etc.

In relation to my cover as a tourist, I have to say that I was barely able to sustain my cover in the early days, later it was almost impossible on account of the numerous tasks that I had to fulfill in the time frame established by my Practical Operational Plan. So I decided to justify my absences from the hotel by mentioning places I had visited (Laguna del Tesoro, Trinidad), sites I had been to on another occasion, and by talking about my interest in photography and journalism. The pretext of an interest in photography would have been useful in the case of an emergency but also as a cover for my visits and stays in the operations house, considering that it is a very small city and that one constantly meets up with the same people (in relation to the operations house I could have argued that my friends or relatives also had the materials required for developing film).

In terms of a cover, this should be given special consideration in the case of a woman, who needs a certain amount of time to get ready and get dressed, etc. Once again, in this respect I was only able to fulfill my task in a very limited way. With regard to the rest, I had no major problems in handling myself, using my cover in accordance with the requirements and situations that arose. In general, people thought I was Russian or Czech, which could be useful in the city (to take photos, etc.). In the hotel it was best to make things as clear as possible so that no doubts would arise.

At the outset I said only that I was Cuban, according to what was planned, and my identification, etc. Later I added that my mother was German and that I had spent a number of years abroad. Insofar as people who arrived at the hotel or in the city knew my real identity, I said I worked for the Ministry of the Revolutionary Armed Forces, etc. I saw some people who knew me, but I had not spoken to them for a long time. I think that some of them recognized me but I pretended that I hadn't noticed them or didn't recognize them. On the other hand, some people appeared whose presence could have complicated matters for me. For example, an ICAP delegation with some of its officials arrived. I saw their vehicle in the city and later in the hotel parking lot from the window of my bus just in time, so I decided to return to the hotel later.

In another case, I saw some *compañeros* I know from the Ministry of Education while I was leaving the hotel and they were just arriving with their suitcases. I immediately walked over and greeted them; they asked me what I was doing there and where I was working and I told them I was working in the Ministry of the Revolutionary Armed Forces (taking into account that they were close friends of a *compañero* to whom I had disclosed this information a few weeks previously). I added, however, that in recent weeks I had been working with the Ministry of Foreign Trade, but that work had been held up because some technicians had not yet arrived and that was why I was resting in Cienfuegos. I also gave them my room number to prevent them asking at the reception desk.

In relation to my cover and my story, I think I should have been acquainted with some details of the house whose address was registered in my identity card. (For example, Sixth Street is between which two streets?) Moreover, I should have known, for example, some names of people who work in the Ministry of Foreign Trade, particularly in the department mentioned in the identity card.

ACTIVITIES IN THE FIRST THREE DAYS:

First, after having studied the Practical Operational Plan, I had to look for the most appropriate means (dead drop, false lining, conventional notes, etc.) to conceal the notes and material that I always had to have at hand. This was a problem that I resolved in the following way: there were no adequate places for a dead drop in the proximity of the hotel, so I destroyed the Practical Operational Plan and wrote in its place a diary that apparently had been written a few weeks previously (on my life in general, work, friendships, walks, activities, etc.) from which I could extract at any given moment the instructions they gave me in the Practical Operational Plan.

I made a secret compartment in the tube of toothpaste I was using in the hotel for the instructions concerning the emergency code, signs, and countersigns for personal contacts, etc. Over the following days I also found a dead drop in which to conceal larger size material by opening up some windows that gave access to a loft space. In the operations house I concealed the photographed material that had been delivered to me (Practical Operational Plan, Communications Plan, etc.) in a groove in a window in the room I used for my work. I kept some notes I was making there and thought that if I continued working in that location I could also keep deciphered messages there, data on the operational situation, etc., (photographing the material). I had a brilliantine container, lipstick, and a film case in which to transport small notes or photographed material. I also had a book that I handed to my contact on Sunday, February 23.

The first day began with a study of the operational situation of the city and I started taking some photos. Furthermore, I had to become familiar with the zone where the operations house was located, and get to know the house, my cousin, etc. At the same time, I reviewed the working material that was already in the house, thereby discovering that some things were missing: an eyedropper and a heater. The light bulbs were 40-watt (and my film was 160 ASA).[1] Later I discovered that cable and insulators, etc., were also missing.

From the first day I began to search for material that could be used as secret compartments (dead drops and contact material) as well as those missing things that were necessary for my work. I also discovered that conditions in the house for some of my work were poor: a lack of water and no spirit stove. I initially decided to carry out some of the work, for example, to expose film in the hotel, but then a shortage of time did not allow me to efficiently coordinate the different tasks, the cover that I had to sustain, etc.

I decided to do these jobs in the operations house. I had until Sunday to resolve the problem of the dead drop and of the container to hand over the sketch of the dead drop during the personal contact.

Moreover, there were photos of documents to be deposited in the dead drop. For this latter task, first I had to carry out a photograph test given that the light bulbs were 40-watt and the film speed was 160 ASA, as well as the corresponding exposure before making the definitive photos of documents which had to be deposited undeveloped in the dead drop.

Another problem arose: there were no sample documents with which to practice taking photos. This is why I tried to obtain the local newspaper *La correspondencia*, which, as I found out later, had been closed just at that time. The same Saturday I also had to acquire a container or material that could be used as a secret compartment to send half a roll of developed operative photos by post. That same day, in addition to taking photos and making contact with individuals in the city (an activity that I was also engaged in during the following days), I had to study and have the reserve zone and Emergency Plan ready.

I made the relevant inquiries in several hotels, taxi stands, and bus and train stations. That day I had to dedicate four (!) hours to activities related to my cover (hairdressers). Later a downpour that lasted for several hours took me by surprise and prevented me from completing the preparation of the dead drop, sketches, etc. I finished those tasks on Sunday, together with some studies and photos of the operational situation in the city and then I spent an hour and a half on countersurveillance. Furthermore, I had to meet the radio technician in the operations house and begin technical preparations; that was when we both discovered that we still could not prepare the antenna, as we did not have the Communications Plan. In any case we decided to prepare the conditions, study the possibilities on the roof of the house, etc.

I was surprised by the indiscreet way in which the technician behaved. He spoke loudly in front of other *compañeros* in the house about the problems with the radio, about the equipment itself (even mentioning the CIA on one occasion, etc.) The *compañero* whose home we were in told him several times that he understood nothing of the matter or about the problems at hand. Later I spoke to the technician about the incident and he said that I was right to object but that in any case the *compañero* who lived in the house should know something about these problems and, besides, he had to help find the second house. I told him that the only thing that the *compañero* had to know was that an antenna had to be placed on the house and, at the very most, the size of the roof.

Furthermore, they were talking about a series of technical questions and contradicted each other continually, whether that was to test me or due to a lack of knowledge, I do not know. I decided to avoid any argument and asked only that he place the antenna in whatever direction it had to be placed, etc. The *compañero* became upset and agitated by the problems and the delay, and it seemed that he did not understand that in addition to technical training, I also had to have a convincing cover and to accomplish set tasks. Right up until the last minute, he insisted that the conditions were not right for a series of matters, insinuating that for this reason he could not do a good job. For example, he had trouble in placing the dipole antenna, which, facing in the right direction with the corresponding extension, would entail crossing wires, cables, and television aerials. He insisted until the last minute that it had to be placed another way, that the cables prevented transmission, etc.

We had just begun to place the antenna on Monday when the Communications Plan was handed to me; it was delivered on Sunday at 19:30 (the scheduled time of the appointment) during the contact. It was not possible for me to arrive at 17:00 because, as I have already mentioned, on that same day I completed my studies of the conditions of the dead drop and took photos. After that I had to make the sketches and photograph the documents to deposit them undeveloped in the dead drop. I was working on such a tight schedule that I hardly had time to make the 17:00 appointment. Then an unforeseen difficulty arose, and I couldn't get into the house because my cousin had gone out (this problem did not arise again because they gave me the key to the house).

I finished the sketches and went to meet the contact, first performing a preliminary half-hour countersurveillance measure in the area. I handed over the package with the sketch inside and was given a package which held photographs of the Communications and the Practical Operations plans, descriptions, a message, etc. I was not given a magnifying glass; I asked my *compañero* to try to read the material with the camera lens. We agreed with the *compañero* who had made the contact that another contact would be made on the following Sunday.

We also talked about the dead drop and the contact we had just made. We decided that in relation to the dead drop, the place was not ideal; I think that only two regular buses passed by and then if the agent had to be there for 10 to 15 minutes and several buses passed the spot, it would bring attention to the agent. There were better, more appropriate places, for example, outside a movie theater, bookshop, store, etc. We decided upon another contact for the following day, prior to returning to Havana. The fact that my *compañero* made notes of many of the details on large sheets of paper caught my attention because he had to move around, stay in hotels, and travel from one place to another. For my part, when I returned to the house, I immediately prepared a small note with the signs, countersigns, time, etc., of the next contact and I concealed it inside the brilliantine container.

The following day I took the note to the hotel and placed it inside the toothpaste tube. That same Sunday evening I finished developing the first roll of operational photos of the city (for the package to be sent as a present through the mail service) and I took some proofs and also a photo of the documents explaining the rest of the photos (Series 1) that I sent by mail. I started organizing the initial information I had gathered on the operational situation, contacts, etc.

First, I read the material that I had been given during the contact. I made the mistake of not copying the Communications Plan meticulously; I was exhausted and all I did was quickly read over the main parts: frequencies for placing the antennae and the message with new instructions. Even though I had agreed with the contact on depositing the package containing a secret compartment in the dead drop the following day, I gave up this idea when I read the instructions because the message told me explicitly that I had to deposit it only on Saturday, February 29. In addition, that night I began the letter that I had to send by mail (it was already a day late), although I still did not have an eyedropper for preparing the ink. (I was finally able to dispatch this letter on Friday or Saturday, although the coded message was already behind in terms of its content. I thought that it would be of some use in practice.)

On Monday, my time was divided between technical preparations and the transmission and preparation of messages (ciphering and deciphering), etc. I barely had time to prepare the package with a secret compartment, and the letter and other gifts that were going with the package, and take it to the post office. In addition, I met up with the contact again and accompanied him to the airport—was that the correct thing to do? Once again, I arrived late because we were involved in placing antennae in both houses; at the second one I went up (or rather, I climbed up) to the roof and, of course, I got dirty in the process. Looking like that, I could hardly walk around the city and make the contact. I had to go to the hotel first and tidy up.

In the second house, we encountered a new set of problems in placing the antenna. There was only one way in which we could install the antenna because there was no other means of tying down the poles we had to use. In any case, we decided to put it in place and change its direction on the following day to the opposite way (pointing toward the correspondent). I have to explain that the house is in a location that faces a street which is used by tourist buses, and which leads right to the National Institute of the Tourism Industry (INIT). A substantial number of people who stay at the Jagua hotel often visit this place for dinner and to stroll around, etc.

I think that it was a mistake on my part to have placed the antenna there and to have used this house, although I had been given instructions to do so for two main reasons: to avoid having two antennae in one house and to better hide the radio base. I was able to accomplish the second of these objectives, but the first was, in any case, ineffective, since we did not have a relay antenna, I was forced to put together a reception antenna that would have served perfectly well for the small CIA equipment, employing it in the same house. At the same time, the problem of the cable was finally resolved in that we were able to procure one on Tuesday, allowing the *compañero* whose home we were using to install the EICO reception antenna.

I insisted that the technician make the appropriate calculations when he placed the extension on the last antenna and to try to place it in a way that would allow that antenna to be used by the CIA equipment. (I did not want to keep climbing up to the roof as this drew attention to us.) I do not know whether the *compañero* did not understand me at that time or was very upset by the difficulties, the rush, etc. Besides, I insisted on several occasions that the downward cable could be fed into the interior of the building through a window in the workroom. This way, only nearby neighbors would see it, and they could easily be misled about its purpose. If we used the other window, then many passersby on the street would see it. The technician ignored me and said that the perfect place was through the other window, where there was a table on which the apparatus could be placed and that was where he put it. I think that it was a serious mistake on my part, and even more so given that I myself could have changed the location of the cable in the following days.

On Tuesday, I planned to establish the first communication with the small CIA device (according to the plan, I had to make contact with Point 4). We finished installing the antenna very late (we could not locate the cable and the insulators until noon on Tuesday); I had to prepare a message and cipher it, and then I could not get a taxi. The bus did not arrive, and I had to walk there (some 18 blocks), arriving just in time for the transmission. Without having prepared the equipment, I could not send any communication. The technician and I decided to carry out a test on the following day between the two apparatuses (two minutes VVV GA, VVVK response).

The test was performed on the following day and the EICO unit worked perfectly, but that was not the case with the other one. A few minutes later, we discovered that one *cristal*[2] was not working and we could not insert the other one as planned. We had decided by then to stick with the other apparatus but the *cristales* were not working and the antenna did not function at this frequency. That is why we agreed with Ulises to enter into communication on the frequency established for the EICO antenna on Wednesday at 17:30. This was the first communication in which I transmitted a brief message.

A small problem persisted that made the transmissions difficult: the on/off switch was broken and had to be constantly repaired before and during transmissions. My time was almost entirely spent on radio transmissions. I copied all the messages but one, where I think I stopped in the middle because of interference in the reception. I had no problems copying the numbers. Communication with Point 3 could not be concluded as there was a lot of interference. Point 4 repeated the entire contents of the message although I had only missed the last two numbers. I found it difficult to copy letters of the alphabet, which is why I believe it is essential for me to practice transmitting and receiving letters.[3]

I had some problems deciphering some messages; in one case that could have been because it was not copied properly as it involved a communication between two points, but in the other case I think the reason was because the message was not ciphered properly (something that should be checked). I noticed how communications between different points were very prolonged and that sometimes two points crossed over, for example Points 3 and Point 5, in spite of the fact that Point 4 continuously transmitted the signal AS, instructing me to wait. Point 4 transmitted the times and frequencies of the next communication to me, even though they were identical to those set out in the plan; this could have led to the discovery of the base. I think that this could be included perfectly well in the printed descriptions in which the blanks and numbers could be used to mark times, etc.

I managed to establish contact with all points; I only sent two short messages and planned to send my first long message with information on the operational situation in the transmission that had been requested for Friday at 17:00. I later asked for this time to be pushed back 20 minutes, because when I started the transmission I again had problems with the on/off switch. I began to transmit at precisely 20 minutes past, in accordance with the time Point 4 had indicated to me, but no one replied. I also used the reserve frequency but there was no response on that either.

The message was long and consisted of operational information on the city and contacts that I had established. Some of the data I had already included in the secret compartment package containing the sketch, undeveloped film with photos of documents, and explanations of the Series 2 photographs. I had deposited the package on Saturday, February 29 in the dead drop. (The package contained other photographs for Series 2, as well.)

In addition to some tourist contacts in the hotel (a Czech, hotel employees, etc.), I planned to use the following contacts for my study and reports on the operational situation: a hotel employee named Carmelo; a member of Battalion 320 in the People's Defense Militia (see Series 2 photographs), Miguel Angel Medina, who fought at Girón; an organizer of the PURSC branch at the cigar factory on Floor 2B-7, between 60th and 51st avenues, by the Red Cross. This *compañero* invited me to visit the factory (I met him at the Casa del Bon on 320 19th Street between 54th and 56th streets).

In addition, I made contact with a very poor family that lives in front of the Cayo Coco naval base. I also established contact with secondary school students (from the school formerly named San Lorenzo, on 4828 21st Street), including a girl, a second year student named Caridad Lara. Over these past few days I have met one of the *compañeros* who worked in the INIT provincial delegation, Isaac Torres, who took me to the Diesel Motor factory on Saturday, and to the new School of Technology, and the building that housed the new jetties for loading sugar in bulk.

That same day I prepared the undeveloped film with photos of the documents (sketches with operational reports, maps of the city, and explanations of the Series 2 photos) and I placed them together with the Series 2 photos in the container and headed for the dead drop. I believed by then that I was under surveillance and the operations house had been detected (with its two visible antennae), but I wasn't absolutely certain.

I have to mention that in relation to the countersurveillance measures, I had all but ignored this aspect of my work. I was only able to carry out my tasks as well as I possibly could, particularly the transmission, preparation, ciphering, and deciphering of messages, etc. I sustained my cover as well as possible, justifying my comings and goings from the hotel, talking about excursions I had made and my interest in photography, justifying my presence in the cousin's house to the neighbors, misleading the individuals with whom I had established contact.

I did not take any countersurveillance measures in the real sense of the word (preparing a plan, carrying out certain activities with the established goal of double-checking myself). I was restricted to double-checking myself in the midst of the rest of my work; my Practical Operational Plan gave me neither the time nor the conditions in which to fulfill security measures. Besides, there was so much emphasis on the technical aspect—to transmit and to communicate with the other points—that when the time came to undertake real countersurveillance measures, sometimes I thought that I had been completely detected, but sometimes I was not quite sure.

I could have been detected by someone from the Ch. Brigade[4] opposite my cousin's house. When the car broke down that belonged to the *compañero* who was helping move the apparatus, my attention was caught by a man who was close to the house. (The man appeared out of the darkness in a place where no one was around.) I also noticed that there were two men at the exit of the Diesel Motor factory. One of them was Afro-Cuban and was next to the wire fence; the other seemed to be taking photographs.

At INIT, where my dead drop was, I made the following observation: I left the cafeteria and noticed that there was a man and an

Afro-Cuban woman in the small wooden building, near the window that overlooked the sea. I headed for the quay. I did not get as far as the dead drop before I returned to the cafeteria with the aim of having lunch. When I returned, I saw the two people I had been observing were sitting close to the door. I had lunch. Once again I headed toward the dead drop. The two people were now sitting on the sea wall: a tall, slim Afro-Cuban woman wearing glasses and a man of the same origin, who was shorter. He seemed to be the same one I had noticed at the Diesel Motor factory.

I reached the dead drop, deposited what I had there, and returned to the cafeteria where I waited for a while. I saw a bus coming, but I still had to place the signal. I met two *compañeros* from INIT and made it look as if I were leaving INIT for the day but I returned by a side route to another smaller sea front road. I saw how the two people headed off in the direction of the site of the dead drop, but they only took two steps and when they saw me they pretended to head in another direction. For my part, I continued with my stroll and headed to the site where I had planned to place the signal. I saw a gray-haired man there sitting next to the tree that had been indicated. I returned to the cafeteria again and saw how the two people whom I had been observing walked off in the direction of the dead drop.

After analyzing the situation as best I could under the circumstances, it seemed that the obvious thing to do was to not place the signal in order to protect the agent or collaborator who was going to collect the secret compartment package. I returned to the operations house. I went with my "cousin" to have a manicure in a nearby house and a blue and white car that stopped in front of us while we were crossing the street caught my attention; it did a U-turn. I thought that was an ideal moment to take a photograph of the car. In the house I began to assess the situation again, but I was still uncertain; I thought that because of the way in which I had been working over the past few days it was logical that I could have been detected and my activities uncovered.

First, I decided not to make contact that night, given that the first thing I should do in a situation like this is to break off all contact with other individuals related to our activities. I wanted to undertake an in-depth and well-planned countersurveillance exercise to see whether the conditions were right for returning to the site of the dead drop, to collect what had been deposited there or place the signal (is that right?).

Meanwhile, I prepared a small container with a message that I planned to deliver to the contact. I had not yet decided what I was going to do. I left at 20:00, planning to take a taxi, something quite difficult to do on a Saturday evening. Two people standing at the taxi stand caught my eye, and after a short while, a vehicle pulled up. I thought that the same taxi could be a surveillance team. I took the taxi to the Jagua hotel. Just when I was getting out, another taxi that was white and blue, which I had noticed on another occasion, stopped a few meters away and a man got out who appeared to be the same man I had noticed at INIT. I also immediately saw the two Afro-Cubans whom I had seen at INIT; the man got up and went to the bar. I went up to my room. There was hardly any time to think; I should not try to make contact at this point, at most, I ought to try to become acquainted with the person with whom I had to meet, but not give the countersign. The following day I would organize my things and leave for Santa Clara.

On the other hand, I thought that I was imagining things, that in any case the Practical Operational Plan would not allow me to take the countersurveillance measures required, that it was best to make the contact and see what the *compañero* had to say. Besides, I was not entirely certain that the surveillance operation had been detected, or whether I was constantly crossing paths with the same people, as had occurred on other occasions due to the layout of the city and especially because people in general and tourists in particular tend to visit the same places. On going down to the lobby, I thought I caught a fleeting glimpse of one of the men who had been near the operations house. It is difficult to describe him; in this respect I have substantial difficulty, it is one of the things that I must practice (memorizing and describing people's appearances, faces, distinguishing features, etc.)

At 21:00, the contact approached me when I was sitting in the bar. "Would you mind if I asked you a question? Are you Talia?" I replied, "Don't you mean Tania?" He said, "I remember…" He did not say the rest of what he was supposed to say. We sat down at a table, and I waited and told him what I was supposed to say. The *compañero* asked me if I smoked and I told him I did not. He insisted, saying that I should and that he would give me the cigarettes as a gift (strongly implying that a secret compartment was inside the packet).

For my part, I was very worried; I thought that for a mission of this nature, I was getting it wrong in practice. I should not have made the contact. I thought that if I were really accomplishing a mission of this kind in another country, I would have to suspect that the man talking to me may well have been a member of enemy counterintelligence, that had intercepted communications and had a series of data in its possession. The data, for example, could have come from a collaborator who had fallen into enemy hands and who had revealed everything he or she knew, or from one of its agents who had infiltrated our ranks, etc.

At the outset, I avoided conversation. While making gestures toward the bar, the *compañero* began to ask me questions about the work I was involved in, the transmissions, my messages, etc. He also asked me why I had not placed the signal. I told him that it was not possible, that someone was on the scene, and that I suspected I was being followed. I added that I was not planning to make the contact that evening and that I was unclear as to how I should carry out the Emergency Plan, knowing that the surveillance team was in the hotel itself and had compromising information in its hands (the dead drop, operations house, etc.). At the same time, I noticed that at a nearby table there were what appeared to be some members of the team, but it was too dark to see; I also thought that the situation was ideal for a tape recorder and for recording our conversation.

I told the *compañero* that I had not eaten and asked if he would accompany me. He went with me to the dining room; at the same time, he constantly insisted that the operation was a success, that I was handling things very well, and that he had seen me with the INIT man. He said that he had not expected to meet someone like me, and that we could go dancing at the club since our work for the day had finished, etc. (I don't know whether this was the *compañero's* mission, or whether he was pursuing me on his own initiative.) When he realized that he was not getting anywhere with me, and that I wanted to go to sleep early, he excused himself for a moment and returned to the bar. (I thought that he was acting this way because I was a woman, but he also could have been part of the surveillance team.)

The following day I went to the house. I developed the photos that I had found in the secret compartment. I returned to the hotel. During lunch, I saw the Afro-Cuban woman again together with another woman with eyeglasses, who was a little shorter than average height. In the cafeteria opposite the hotel, I once again saw one or two of the men that I had already spotted. I went up to my room and began to prepare a countersurveillance plan. This was when *compañero* Ulises called to say that he would meet me at my cousin's house. While I was waiting for a taxi, a young man began to talk to me and invited me to go out with him. He got in the same taxi. I thought that he could also be a member of the team that was trying to blow my cover. I arrived at the house and met with *compañero* Ulises. (Above all, my attention was caught by a gray-haired man, two young men of medium height, an Afro-Cuban man, and the two women I have already mentioned: one was Afro-Cuban and the other was quite short and wore eyeglasses.)

I think that this practical exercise has been highly useful in allowing me to develop my knowledge in different aspects of our work and to test it through practical experience, such as recognizing the need to learn more about a number of elements (see the summary).

In addition, I have to organize my work better and respond more quickly; I should have taken more initiative and made decisions rapidly when the circumstances required me to do so.

B. SUMMARY

I. WORK ACCOMPLISHED

Communications by radiotelegraphy for three days. Contact with the four points. Four messages copied. Transmission of two short messages, both ciphered and deciphered. (I was unable to transmit the third message that had been prepared.)

Technical preparation carried out for the operation of two radio bases.

A letter with legal text and a message ciphered in invisible ink.

A container with a secret compartment (photographs developed of the operational situation and the dead drop) sent as a gift through the post office mail service.

A dead drop. Photographs and corresponding sketches. Container with a secret compartment containing undeveloped film and a photo to be deposited in the dead drop.

Two contacts. Handover of material by me to one of them.

Containers and dead drops in which to conceal instructions and information, etc.

Study (begun) of the operational situation of the city and of the contacts made.

Two series of developed photographs of documents explaining the operational situation.

Undeveloped film for a series of photos of documents.

Activities crucial to sustaining the cover of a tourist. The same applies to justifying the operations house and staying there as a cousin.

II. DEFICIENCIES, ERRORS, ETC.

Preparatory phase: The Practical Operational Plan is too wide ranging. It was impossible to fulfill all the tasks, especially given that the work started one or two days behind schedule.

The Communications and Practical Operational plans with their corresponding instructions were handed over at the last minute.

Identification was poorly planned. Details, for example, in relation to the home address and workplace that appeared on my identity card were unknown to me.

There was a lack of material: insulators (particularly a large insulator for the dipole antenna); an antenna cable; a relay antenna; an eyedropper for preparing ink; a heater (in accordance with the conditions of the house or workplace); 40-watt light bulbs for photos of documents; and a magnifying glass to read photographed material.

There was indiscretion and lack of experience on the part of the technician.

The times and frequencies of the next transmissions were broadcast by radio (the descriptions may be included). Transmissions lasted too long and arrived late.

Mistakes in my work:

I should have moved the dipole antenna and used camouflage for the downward cable.

Installation of the second radio base should not have been in another house, given the need to place, in any case, the two antennae in the main operations house.

Unpunctuality. (Although in many cases this was justified by the problems that arose.)

I did not take enough countersurveillance measures, particularly in the final days, or make necessary or appropriate decisions fast enough when I realized (although on a superficial level) what the case was. (For example, I should not have made the contact on Saturday, February 29.)

The sites of the dead drop's signs and countersigns should be located farther apart.

III. DOUBTS, SKILLS TO DEVELOP

I have doubts regarding the Emergency Plan and its application in different circumstances.

Learn the Morse code for radiotelegraphy.

Clarify a series of matters in relation to communication through radio and with regard to the antennae.

Study the equipment, weapons, etc., of regular armies to be able to orient myself in regard to military information.

In relation to countersurveillance: I should learn how to memorize and describe people.

TANIA

TANIA'S MESSAGE FROM PRAGUE AFTER HER FIRST TRIP TO WESTERN EUROPE

To: MOE
From: Bolívar

SECRET
MESSAGE 3

Point. Start. On my departure on Monday, April 13, I met a delegation from the GDR in the airport. Included among them was a *compañero* who had been a translator in the GDR embassy in Havana and with whom I had a close friendship, as I did with other members of the said delegation. It appears that my hair color and hairstyle, eyeglasses, and the "tactic of not getting to know anyone" worked for the 45 minutes that this test lasted.

A heavily pregnant Argentine woman was among the passengers traveling with me, and I avoided all conversation with her thinking that she could be a revolutionary because, like me, she came from a socialist country. She was on her way to rejoin her husband.

It was difficult for me on that trip to have to constantly adopt my temporary cover as Marta. Finally, I worked out the basics about her, Marta, in relation to the data initially agreed. I am Argentine, a gymnastics teacher; I teach private classes to women and children, and my father is a salesperson and travels all the time with my mother and my sister. I don't have a good relationship with my family and that is why I live alone or with friends in Buenos Aires. Right now I am taking a tour of Europe on which I have to do a few favors for Argentine friends who helped me out with the costs. Lastly, I have some friends in Germany whom I have to meet so that we can continue traveling in a car they have; that is the reason why I am on my own during this stage of the journey.

A difficult problem to resolve in Europe, especially for a woman who is a tourist and on her own, is the matter of friends. In some countries, while traveling by train for example, you can converse in a relaxed way with a man without running the risk that within a question of minutes he will start flirting with you, while in others this is the first thing a man will do once you start talking to him. For the information that I needed I was interested in people of a middle-class background, getting to know their family, their problems, how they live, study, work, and the places they go to in accordance with their economic resources.

Students or young unemployed people, in addition to the marginalized, always tended to hang around in the areas of travel agencies that organize city tours. The latter, of course, are likely to be collaborating with the police. Their lack of money, language skills, and contact with foreigners, along with other factors, makes them attractive to police services. As I was constantly under siege by different people, I decided to "make a move" before they started making a move on me. In this way I got to know Pacífico, some of his friends, and later his family members, with whom I spent some time and obtained the information I needed on the life of the family nucleus.

Through Pacífico I learned numerous things that interested me: how to become involved in other middle-class families and how to resolve the problem of inner-city transport with one's own motorbike. Pacífico studies graphic art, drawing, and painting in a night school, together with his inseparable friend Alberto.

In this context, I was effectively able to carry out a strategy for maintaining an identity over a number of days in which it became necessary to recount anecdotes of my life, my family problems, and my aspirations, to the point that I even managed to convince myself that I was talking about my own life. Generally speaking, I came across as someone who was not interested in politics but instead in their profession and work, who did not discriminate on the basis of race or religion, but was somewhat anticommunist. An anti-German, anti-fascist position was convenient for me, above all, because in

Seven-year-old Tamara in
Buenos Aires, Argentina.

Tamara, 18 years old,
in Bebelsberg Park,
East Germany,
practicing gymnastics.

Tamara playing the accordion.

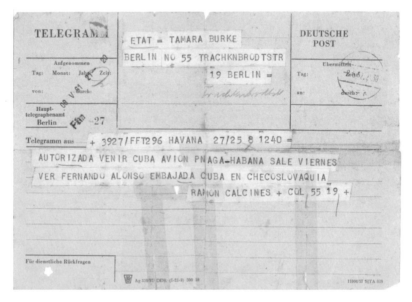

Above: Tamara with Anita Prestes (daughter of Luis Prestes and Olga Benario), and members of the East German army. German Democratic Republic, 1960–61. Below: Telegram authorizing Tania to come to Cuba in 1961.

Tamara giving accordion lessons to Cuban prima ballerina, Alicia Alonso.
Tamara served as an interpreter for Alonso when the Cuban National Ballet
toured East Germany in 1960.

Interpreting for a delegation of young German
writers and journalists in Cuba.

Portrait of Tamara.

Above and below:
Tamara at a political meeting
in Havana, Cuba.

Tamara with friends in Havana.

Santiago de Cuba. Tamara with Vilma Espín,
president of the Federation of Cuban Women (FMC).

Tamara (third from left) and Che Guevara (second from right) in a group of volunteers constructing a school in Havana.

Tamara in Cuba,
in her militia uniform.

Tamara, on the Malecón, Havana's famous seaside boulevard.

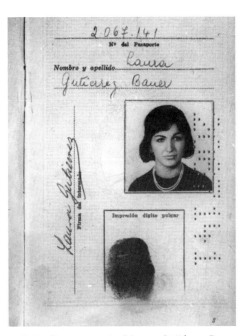

Argentine passport of Laura Gutiérrez Bauer
used by Tania in Bolivia 1964–67.

Tania as Marta Iriarte in Berlin.

Tania as Laura Gutiérrez Bauer
in Bolivia.

Tania as Haydée González in Europe.

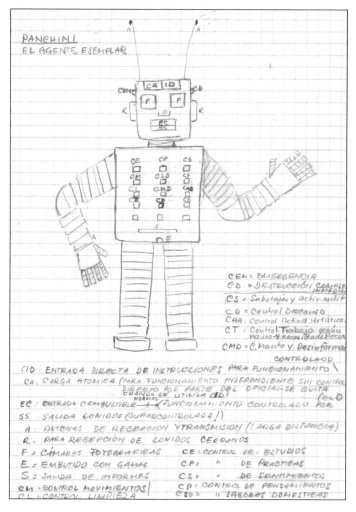

Tania drew this picture of "Panchini: The Exemplary Agent" for her Cuban friends while in Prague. It was accompanied by the following note:

Dear *compañeros*,

Now that I must go out and put my "Homeland or Death" to the test, and with all that I have learned during this time, and always being aware of my weaknesses, defects, shortcomings, and bad habits, etc. And so that you don't give up hope in one day creating better International Agents (IAs) that are more perfect than this "lost cause," and considering the needs of our work and also the wishes, comforts, and plans of the "O," I send with this note a project-proposal for the creation of an ideal IA. A candidate for the model IA of the vanguard.

A big revolutionary hug,

Tania

Above and below left: Tania as Marta Iriarte in Northern Italy, with the Italian policeman Tomasso. Below right: Tania as Marta Iriarte with Pacífico in Europe.

Tania, at left, with Che Guevara at the guerrilla camp in Bolivia.

Bolivian General René Barrientos (second from left in front row) observing Tania's cadaver, September 9, 1967.

Tania's mother, Nadia Bunke, in her home in Germany.

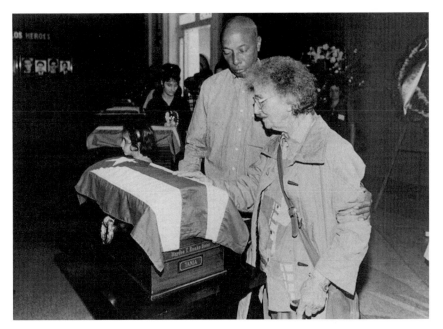

Author Ulises Estrada and Nadia Bunke, with Tania's remains, Cuba, 1998.

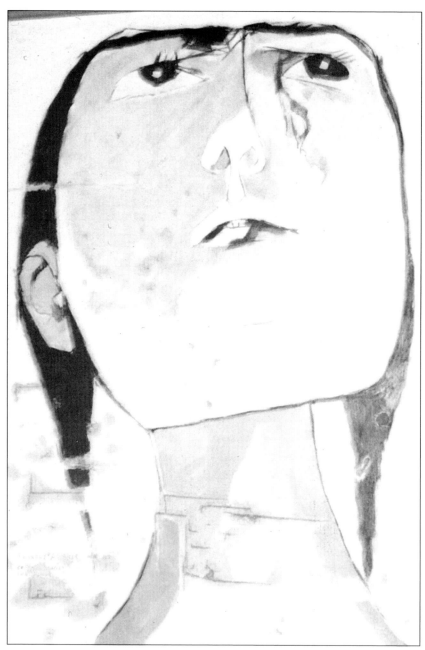

Painting of Tania by the Ecuadorean artist Oswaldo Guayasamín. Guayasamín gifted this painting to the socialist Chilean President Salvador Allende. It was in Allende's office at the time of the 1973 coup d'état. The slashes at the bottom of the canvas were caused by gunfire during the coup, in which Allende was killed.

Europe anyone who speaks German is suspected of being an agent working for fascist circles. This group of young people with whom I had become involved had a political viewpoint, although at times they adopted an "official democratic" position that was sometimes partly progressive, which concerned me because it wouldn't have helped me to be linked to people with revolutionary tendencies, much less pro-communist ones.

Later, while I was traveling by train, a rather strange man entered my compartment. He spoke to me in Spanish about something I couldn't understand. I asked him to speak in Italian and he answered in Spanish that was so poor and with such a strong accent that I asked him if he were North American. Then he spoke incoherently in German about things that were related to a trip he was supposed to make to Cuba as a journalist. At the same time, he seemed to be telling me that he was a guerrilla fighter, gesturing with his hands in a way that suggested he had a rifle.

I aggressively asked him if he was communist and told him to identify himself as a journalist, to which he replied that his work was political and therefore he was forbidden to identify himself. Some Germans entered our compartment and the same man continued to say absurd things in his unintelligible Spanish. When a priest passed by in the corridor the man said offensive things about the church and it was then that I discovered for the first time how hard it was for me, how difficult it was, to go against the principles I have defended throughout my life. I became furious with the man and raged against communism to the extent that the Germans who were in the compartment came to my defense and forced the man to leave. I never discovered whether that provocateur believed me or not, but I am sure that his mission failed to achieve the expected results. End. Point. Bolívar.

APPENDIX 5

TANIA'S MESSAGE FROM PRAGUE BEFORE HER SECOND TRIP TO WEST GERMANY

Although this message is addressed to the MOE, Tania wrote this letter to the author, Ulises Estrada.

SECRET
TO: MOE

Message 6. Point. Start. Here I am sitting in front of the typewriter in the middle of my final preparations, with your letters in my hand and in my head, "a product of the cinema," my mind buzzing with thoughts, having to make an effort not to confuse my "identities."

Where do I begin? The truth is that I have had a lot of time and have left this until the last minute. It is not that I forget; on the contrary, sometimes I devote too much time to memories. I think you know "a little" about my emotional and romantic tendencies. There are those who consider this to be an obstacle or a weakness; for me it has always provided support and encouragement, particularly in the most difficult moments.

Well, *compañeros*, I'll move on to the "diary," or rather, to the extract from the diary. Of course, it isn't easy but I'll try to tell you a little about my life at this point. You will recall my last set of worries. In fact, they weren't new, they had been discussed again and again, but this uneasiness has arisen that I think anyone who is facing a challenge would experience. Yes, I was sure that I could face it, but I was impatient to "get to work." Remember that we mentioned that it was the first time in years that I would live in the "free world" and in this particular set of circumstances it would be something very new for me, even more so, taking into account the kind of life I would be leading. In the meantime I have taken my first small steps, I have had my first experiences and, even though I am more conscious of the problems and difficulties that have to be faced, I feel more confident.

At the beginning when I first experienced these "moments" I asked myself in wonder, "How can you be so relaxed, as if this were really you, as if this were true, as if everything were legitimate?" On one hand the least important problems concern me; I think nonstop, discovering thousands of things that could expose me and ruin our work, and at the same time, I search for the best way of dealing with them, answers, etc., although sometimes it is very difficult to come up with them, either that or they don't exist.

What if I get nervous and feel afraid? Why shouldn't I? I think that one of the things that has given me more peace of mind and confidence is thinking through all of the problems that could arise, about our shortcomings, about the tiny "details," precisely because then, at the decisive moment, everything will be easier. In this way I feel better prepared.

On one hand, I take the necessary precautions, sometimes being too calm and collected, and I begin to feel "modest satisfaction"... I observe the "ignorant puppets" and I feel pity for them and want to laugh at them and say, "You are all stupid. Where is your strength?" And when I "circulate" among people with my new "identity" making them believe that I am just one more of them, my "hidden me" observes and takes notes like a journalist with an invisible cloak who encounters men and women who have found the path of struggle, some of the time it is not the most correct one and other times it is our path. But they struggle and in deep silence my heart salutes them, sings with them, and would like to be with them; and then there are thousands of human beings who simply live, or perhaps don't live...

What else? It is a pity that I cannot take notes at the very time when things are happening, but in any case I could talk to you for hours on end, going into detail. Something else that gives me great peace of mind is to have the opportunity to "misinform," to talk on and on about "my life."

I have discovered that I have an "actor's talent" and I interpret my role perfectly. I hear the voice of your thoughts: I have now realized... Hmm... Well... You know, sometimes I think that it won't be long before I myself begin to believe the story and if someone comes up to me and says the opposite, I would think them mad. But moving on to more specific things, as you are aware I have had a lot of opportunities on this first trip to practice the matter of our work. The best part is that they think "I am a bit stupid and crazy." They are right, aren't they? And so then, they would never even imagine that I am up to something. Of course, I am referring to the male of the species in this country. I have begun to loathe them, particularly because of the way they go after you. Well, I'll let DD2[1] tell you the whole story as I have talked to him a lot about it, besides some very "interesting" photos are heading your way...

I don't want to repeat here things you have learned from other reports, mistakes that have been made, for example, in terms of contacts, which in any case have been useful experiences for me.

Do I feel lonely? Yes, a lot of the time; then it helps me most to "dream" a little, remember, dream... and simply return to reality, think about work, about responsibilities. It helps a lot to have a good radio. Over here I can tune to stations from this continent in languages that I understand, but I can also hear our own stations. And although I listen to it every day, I always feel the same when I switch on the small speakers and hear "Onward Cubans..."[2] Sometimes we hear it so loud and clear that we almost believe we are in Havana. We have discovered that this was a very worthwhile purchase; with its fold-up transistors and aerials we can hear perfectly well.

At certain times I have also been able to tune to regular radio stations from our continent, which are more wide-ranging than those that are broadcast especially for these regions. Here, the Radio Havana program makes every day into a small "festival of the spirit." First political information and then emotional moments—we take down our sign, "Silence, genius at work," and put up another, "Club Saudades," to create an atmosphere for listening to our music.

A few days ago a complete program was broadcast with Portillo de la Luz's songs: "So Far Away and Yet I Love You," "Things of the Soul," "Strange Spell," "Reality and Fantasy," etc., etc.[3]

And how are things with Tarzan,[4] the runner, who currently lives in my house? Ask him if he measured his strength by trying to rip into any of the books that I have left around the place, or does he still specialize in telephone directories. And how is "life as a couple" working out for him? Remind him about the letters that might arrive in my name, mainly those from my parents. Ah, in relation to my parents, I have spoken to them two or three times by telephone and I have written. Imagine how they have insisted that I pay them a visit or that they visit me, and they have asked about my boyfriend, saying that we will be separated for so long and why we don't get married. Well, in short, these are the kinds of things they talk about… If they knew just how close I am to them, hardly a few hundred meters from where they work, from where they live. I have even seen the buildings.[5]

It is true that the revolution puts you in unusual situations. How could I ever have imagined returning to see this area, to these places that, at the end of the day, hold so many memories for me? I have been just a few hundred meters away from places where I used to work and study. I have seen people I know, but unfortunately they have either "fallen by the wayside" or "are working like me."

Well, I am going to stop here because I have been incredibly indiscreet. The "censor"[6] says that there are no problems up to a certain point, but anyhow… I am sending you a letter for my parents in Spanish to try to get them to answer in the same language so you can read what they write. I have given them news of the course of study I am going to pursue in one letter and I am sending you another in which I tell them that I am now studying. In any case, if they become impatient when some time has gone by and begin to cause problems, it might be better to be straight with them about the Party mission. They will have to understand that more information cannot be disclosed and tell them that they should explain this to the others. Well, you can think about it and decide the best way to resolve the problem… there is always a way out, isn't there? Recruit them… Don't laugh; I am being serious.

Don't forget to send the package. Also try to get a recording of the Second Declaration of Havana. You might also send them other publications. I hope that my mother is there when the pianist's mother arrives. She had some business trips arranged to Lenin's homeland. Some day I will meet my mother when I have on my disguise. It would be interesting to see if she recognizes me.

There are still so many things to write, but I will have to stop now; it is 6 a.m. and dawn is breaking over a sad, ugly, cold, and desolate day. It makes you even more eager to be on our little island, where everything is so full of color, the palm trees, the sea, the moon… the brave hearts of its people.

Today I am moving elsewhere for a few days; I will continue this little letter before I start on the trip. End. Point. Bolívar.

THE LAURA GUTIÉRREZ BAUER COVER STORY

July 25, 1964
Top Secret
TO: M1 Copy 1
FROM: MOE Page 1

Re: Definitive cover for Tania sent by Diosdado from Prague.

1. Name: Laura Gutiérrez Bauer

2. Parents' names: Antonio Gutiérrez Sáenz and Hilda Bauer Bergmann.

3. Place and date of birth: Buenos Aires, federal capital, republic of Argentina.

4. Biography:

I, Laura Gutiérrez, was born on January 15, 1938, in Buenos Aires, in the Saavedra District of the federal capital.

My mother, Hilda Bauer, was born on October 13, 1915, in Berlin. Her parents were Otto Bauer and Rosa Bergmann; the latter took her husband's last name after getting married, as is the tradition in that country.

They lived on Krausen Street, in the central area of Berlin. My grandfather was a radio-electronics technician and had a shop in which he repaired electrical equipment. My grandmother was a homemaker, and had another daughter, named Rosa Bauer, who was a year older than my mother and worked as a language teacher.

My grandparents were interested in their daughters' professional and cultural development. My mother used to speak a lot about how her parents helped her with her studies and how my grandfather always said that a happy woman should be capable of independently meeting her own economic needs. He also often took them to the theater and to concerts.

My mother, like her sister, achieved a level of education at school known in Germany as the "intermediate level." Both of them went on to study languages and secretarial skills. This course was useful to my mother when she married my father, allowing her to help him with the administrative side of his work.

My grandfather had belonged to an evangelical religion and my grandmother was Jewish, but neither of them practiced their faith. Nor were they interested in politics.

In 1934, when the fascists began to attack Jews, my grandparents decided to immigrate to America, but my grandmother, who was ill at the time, died toward the end of that same year. My grandfather then decided to travel with my mother to Latin America at the beginning of 1935.

My aunt had insisted on remaining in Germany as she planned to get married soon. In Argentina, my grandfather settled in a house with my mother in Quilmes. They had German acquaintances there and my grandfather began working straightaway in his profession as a technician specializing in radio repairs. My mother was 19 or 20 years old at that time and took care of the house.

In the middle of 1936, my mother met my father, Antonio Gutiér-rez Sáenz, at a barbeque on the beach at Quilmes.

My father was born on August 19, 1904, in Buenos Aires. His father had the same name and was a Creole from the Córdoba Province. He worked in cattle farming. His mother, María Sáenz, was of Spanish origin; her family lived in Quilmes.

From a very young age my father showed an interest in technical things, mainly those related to electricity and radio, but he was also interested in business.

After primary school, and following a year in secondary school, my father studied at a technical school. Later, while working, he studied business.

My father's family was not interested in political affairs, but they were very religious. They belonged to the Catholic Church.

I only met one cousin from my father's family. They lived in Córdoba when I was 8 or 9 years old.

My father met my mother's father, Otto, through work, at the beginning of 1936. My father, who was 32 at the time, was trying to become independent and set up a business with a partner. He achieved this around the end of 1936 and from then on devoted himself to importing electrical devices and components.

In the meantime my parents had got to know each other and became engaged some months later. This relationship met with fierce resistance on the part of my father's family on account of my mother's origin, given that she was not Catholic and had different ideas and traditions. My mother had been educated in the European style of the period, which was very much in contrast to the prejudices prevailing in my father's family, and in him too.

In early 1937, my paternal grandfather died and my mother moved to Córdoba to live there with my grandfather's relatives. My father, influenced by this situation, decided to get married in 1938, in spite of the unresolved disagreements. My mother's father was not entirely happy with this situation but he let my mother decide. Finally, my parents got married on March 21, 1938, and shortly afterwards settled in the Saavedra District of Buenos Aires, where they rented part of a house belonging to another family on Republiquetas Street.

My grandfather Otto lived with us until he died in 1942.

During the first few months of their marriage, my parents argued a lot. I learned about these problems some years ago while I was living in Europe. After a serious argument with my father, my mother told me about the problems she faced. This was a period when they were about to separate and my father, using work as an excuse, went away for a while. He traveled to Córdoba and returned even more heavily influenced by his family. Shortly after I was born, the situation between my parents improved.

I do not have any specific memories of the period when we lived in Saavedra; all I recall is that the house had a garden where I played with other children, and there were chickens and a dog. My grand-mother often played with us; I remember that she wore glasses. Then she fell ill and I got used to being by her bed, entertaining her. But these memories have become confused with others and with photographs my mother later showed me.

In 1934, after my grandfather's death, we moved to 2109 Sarmiento Street, in the 11th District of Buenos Aires. My parents rented an apartment there in a modern building constructed a short time before. The apartment was on the second floor and had three bed-rooms, a bathroom, a kitchen, and a service room. For many years, a woman named Carmen worked in our home; she also took care of me when my mother was too busy. Carmen was hardworking and very kind; I have a lot of nice memories of her.

During 1943, I attended kindergarten at the Cangallo School, a private German school, and the following year I enrolled in first grade at that school. In addition to the required curriculum, the school gave classes in German, English, and French. I remember some of my classmates, such as "know-it-all María" (reference: María from the teachers' college);[1] the two blond sisters of German origin (reference: the Sauers); and Alfredo, "the most handsome in the class" (reference: Castelar). My best friend was Norma Vidal, who lived on Cangallo Street (reference: Nélida). I remember our teachers: Beer, Meyer, Jimez, Troche, Trongee, and the principal: Williams (reference to authentic data).

I remember many cultural activities at the school and the New Year's parties for which we prepared dance and song recitals that were directed mainly by Miss Williams, who was a kindergarten teacher. I was quite a good pupil in the early years, but then my parents began to travel frequently to the interior part of the country for work and they often took me with them. That was in 1947, while I was in third grade, which I did not pass and had to repeat. My mother then decided to leave me in the care of a dressmaker friend named Doña Ana so that my studies would not be interrupted. Doña Ana lived on Cangallo Street, on the corner of Junín Street. She was an elderly, gray-haired, short woman.

That was how I spent the following years. I stayed for long periods with Doña Ana and at times, particularly during vacations, my parents took me with them on their travels. During this time they had serious arguments and even separated for a while.

In 1952, while I was in sixth grade, I became ill with tonsillitis, which meant that I could not finish elementary school. Toward the end of 1953, my tonsils were removed. The surgery was performed by Dr. Lehmann, in his private clinic. In general though, my mother took me to the children's hospital located at the junction of Galio and Paraguay streets, in the Norte neighborhood. My mother began to become very worried about my nervous condition, possibly because of the situation prevailing in our family.

I have many memories of our neighborhood. I remember the businesses located on our street, such as the Cuyo pharmacy on the corner beside the Presbítero Alberti School. Farther up, on the same side of the street, there was a tenement building, but as a rule I was not allowed to play with the children who lived there. On the corner of Sarmiento and Uriburu streets there was a public mailbox; on our side of the street there was a bakery; on the other side of Uriburu was the Martona dairy and beside it a Jewish synagogue. Along Sarmiento Street, there was a small fabric store, and after that a Jewish sports club called Macabí, and farther, the local market. On the other side of the street, there was a small shop where children bought sweets and candies.

On Junín Street, almost on the corner of Corrientes, there were a number of grocery stores belonging to Jews of Russian and Polish descent. On Corrientes Street, between Junín and Ayacucho streets, there was the Cataluña cinema with 1,200 seats and other restaurants and businesses. On Junín Street there was a huge ice cream parlor called Laponia. On the corner of Junín and Bartolomé Mitre streets there were two bookshops, and the largest was on the left. I also recall the San José convent, where we were taught religion classes and prepared for our first Communion. The church was at the side of the convent, surrounded by four streets: Cangallo, Bartolomé Mitre, Azcuenaga, and Larrea.

We were also used to going to Congreso Square; there were no squares close to our home, which is why we tended to play in the street. Some of my childhood friends were Lotti, Elvira, and Mario. During vacations my parents took me with them or left me in summer camps, for example, in Córdoba, in a German summer camp in Calamuchita. As I was often sick during that time, I stayed home or my parents sent me to Córdoba to the house of a German family whose last name was Beil (reference: Byl family). Their children were Enrique, who was the same age as me (reference: Hinni), and an older boy who was studying in Buenos Aires. Mr. Beil was a teacher. This family also grew fruit and had been living in the region close to Altagracia for a number of years. When I was in good health, Mr. Beil gave me some lessons. The rest of the time we went on hikes, rode horses, and helped in the orchard.

At the beginning of 1953, my father had to travel to Europe on business, purchasing and selling for different import and export businesses. He decided to move there with the entire family. Business forced my parents to travel often, mainly within West Germany, but also to other European countries, such as Austria, France, etc.

For the first few years there, we generally traveled altogether, or my mother and I would stay in a city in West Germany such as Frankfurt or Munich. We lived in hotels or guesthouses. Problems with the language prevented me from continuing with my formal schooling. I studied German at home and read textbooks on history, geography, etc., which I had brought with me from my secondary school in Argentina. Also, my family's lifestyle and the constant upheaval made it difficult for me to attend school regularly. My mother tutored me and was always concerned about me progressing in my studies, about making me into the woman that her parents wanted her to be. This was the cause of new quarrels between my parents. My father did not want me to work when I grew up; he was mainly interested in marrying me off to Jorge Ramírez, the son of a well-off business person (reference: Omar).

The Ramírez family was in Europe for reasons similar to those of my parents; they had two children: Jorge, three years older than me, and Elena, who was my age. The Ramírez family lived on the outskirts of Frankfurt. During those years my parents had heated arguments about these matters, which brought to the surface problems from the early years of their marriage, etc. I was raised in a tense family environment and I began to look for ways to become independent. My mother always supported me in this regard. She got me some translation work, and helped me with it; she also taught me how to teach Spanish to Germans and German to Latin Americans.

One of my mother's friends who lived in Berlin was a language teacher named Mrs. Sauer, who also helped me. She lived in the Berlin-Zehlendorf neighborhood and when I began to work, I often visited her in her little apartment to get advice on questions related to translations.

In 1961, I moved to 146 Kant Street in Berlin-Charlottenburg, with a friend, Kristina Becker, a music student who specialized in the piano and the violin. Until then I had lived in guesthouses. I met Kristina at a party where she gave a small concert. She was from Frankfurt but was thinking about continuing her studies in Berlin. She was already living on Kant Street but preferred to share her room with someone. The room is in an old building right in the city center; at some stage in the past wealthy families must have lived in these apartments since they have many rooms. The Hase family has a guesthouse here and also rents out rooms. We had a room that was furnished for two people; we were provided with bed linen. Some of our laundry was sent to the drycleaner's and some of it was washed there. There were a shared kitchen and two bathrooms. Each of us paid an average of 150 marks per month.

In the beginning, I earned just enough to survive on (and sometimes a little more) from the translations, around 400 or 500 marks. Later on, I earned more: up to 1,200 marks per month. During the last few years, I generally did translations for private individuals and for other translators who had an official license but did not have time to do all their work. This is not legal, but it is a widespread practice. They charge clients between 15 and 20 marks per page, and then pay the translator who works for them, and whose work they later revise, 10 to 12 marks. For example, I did translations for a Mrs. Schmidt, who lived on Pestalozzi Street. The work mainly consisted of creative writing, travel reports, stories, and literary commentaries. In addition, I also worked for a Mr. Müller, who lived on the outskirts of Berlin. We had to communicate by telephone. I did technical translations for him. At the same time, my mother continued to send me work from West Germany.

Kristina had some friends we would meet up with on a regular basis; they included two sisters, Helga and Marianne Richter, who were also music students (reference: Helga Eichler, Marianne Grossmann). Kristina had a boyfriend, Peter Neuberg (reference: Pedro S.) who was an art student. He had a friend named Rolando (reference: Roland Bisand). We went out a lot together to the movies, the theater, and other places. On Saturdays and Sundays, we went to the Wannsee lakes. The Richert sisters borrowed a Volkswagen from their cousin. Kristina was born in the south of West Germany, close to Frankfurt, on August 13, 1940. Her father died in the war, and her mother died some years ago. She has relatives at 5 Barning Street, in Berlin.

In 1962, I met Carlos Federico Tabú, born on December 8, 1932, in eastern Prussia. He had lived in Latin America for many years with his mother, before the war started. After a short time, the friendship developed into a relationship. He did journalistic and literary work and that was why he traveled a lot, which was the cause of arguments between us. I thought that it would be better for him to settle down somewhere and to study at the university.

In 1963, however, I decided to travel to Latin America and carry out research in folklore and ethnology, etc. At first, he was going to travel there too and do some writing, but later he changed his mind and stayed in Germany. He had relatives in Berlin-Schöneberg: an aunt who had a son named Rudolf, who was a philosophy student (reference: Rudolf). Some more friends include Kurt Vogt, a former boyfriend of mine, and Werner Lehmann, who had been in Latin America and who, like my boyfriend, worked as a journalist. I also knew some Latin Americans, but only superficially since, as a rule, my boyfriend did not want me to make friends with them; he did not trust them because he was very jealous. I remember a Colombian named Carlos (reference: Luis); a Peruvian, Belisario (reference: Benjamín); a Brazilian, Danton (reference: Milton); and two Chileans, Celia and Jorge (reference: Celia and Jorge). I saw them at a cultural event held in the Ibero-American library in the Lankwitz neighborhood in the Americas House.

In the meantime, my parents were still having problems. My mother visited me in Berlin several times, when her failing health allowed her to, but she got worse over the final years; she was suffering from cancer. I visited my parents in Frankfurt, Munich, or wherever they happened to be at the time, but there were always serious arguments and angry scenes. In addition to the problems that already existed, they were not happy about my friends and my boyfriend. My mother wanted me to study and urged me to travel to Latin America to continue my education there.

At the end of 1963, my parents insisted that I travel first to Argentina, if only for a few months. They paid for my ticket and sorted out the issue of lodging in Buenos Aires. I could stay in the apartment of a German family who was in Europe at the time, also on business. The family was named Kuhn.

On Wednesday March 19, 1964, I departed on a Lufthansa flight from Frankfurt at 9:15 p.m. and I arrived at the Ezeiza airport at 3:15 p.m., via Zurcí, Dakar, Rio de Janeiro, São Paulo, and Montevideo. My friend Elena Ramírez, Jorge's sister, was waiting for me there. In spite of all the time that had passed, my father still had it in his head that I would marry Jorge. She borrowed a car and kept me company during my stay in Buenos Aires. The apartment was at

1900 Cabildo Street. There was a Minimax close by at Belgrano Square, which is at the junction of Obligado and Echevarría streets. Otherwise, my recollections of Argentina are quite hazy, and it had changed a lot during the time I was away.

A few weeks after my arrival, my father wrote to tell me that my mother was seriously ill and he advised me to return to Europe. On April 20, I received a new Argentine passport; the previous one had been issued and renewed in Europe. It was the end of May when my father asked me to return. Receiving my Italian visa on May 18, I returned to Europe on May 23 on an Alitalia flight, and I arrived in Rome on May 24. My father went to San Remo, where my mother had been living in a rented apartment for a few months. A few days later, on May 30, she died.

Before she died, my mother advised me to return to Latin America and study. She gave me $2,000, a watch, and a ring that she had bought a short while before, along with a few other things.

Other details about my parents:

My father is a tall, strong, gray-haired man who wears glasses (reference: María Rosa's father). He devotes all his time to work. My mother, a delicately built woman, has dark brown hair (reference: Lidia's mother). In addition to speaking German and Spanish, my mother also spoke English and French. She was an avid reader and liked the opera and concerts.

After my mother's death, I continued traveling through Italy. I first went to Rome; afterwards I returned to the Riviera, and then on July 23, I arrived in Nice on July 23. I planned to spend some time relaxing there, but once I determined my financial situation, I decided to go back to Berlin as quickly as possible to deal with some outstanding matters I had there. I planned to travel to Latin America at the end of October, preferably to Peru and Bolivia. But I wanted to go to Austria first to say good-bye to Kristina, and then to France by train to catch an Air France flight.

I spent about $1,500 of my savings on the trip to Argentina and my subsequent stay in Europe. I sold some things in Berlin before I departed to raise $500 more. In this way, with the money my mother gave me, plus what I had left, I was able to put together around $3,200 and leave Berlin on October 13 from the airport at Tempelhof. From there, I went to Frankfurt and Munich, and then by train to Austria. (Note: When I left Berlin on October 13, 1964, I headed for Frankfurt, where they do not use an entry stamp or have a list of passengers traveling by train. I spent 20 days in Austria, since there are no restrictions because I went by train. No one stamped my passport during the time I was in Frankfurt.)

Note: While I was putting the finishing touches on my travel arrangements, my father was busy going through the legal procedures to transport my mother's body to Berlin. The name of the cemetery where my father planned to bury her is Columbia Damm, and it is close to the airport.

Arguments with my father continued even after the death of my mother, which is why I decided to go directly to Latin America. I wanted to open up new horizons for myself and to try to break off all contact with my father, particularly since I had discovered that during the years my mother was sick, he was involved with another woman. This had made my mother even more depressed. My father continued with his work in West Germany, mainly in Frankfurt, and I left for Peru and Bolivia, where I will take up residence and devote myself to researching folklore and ethnology and try to leave behind my family and its past.

Conclusions:

Tania's cover story tends to convey an image of psychological conflict due to the poor relationship between her parents, the constant abandonment she was subjected to as a child, and the need to become independent as a consequence of that situation. This will help justify in her personality the need for an isolated lifestyle in Bolivia and her refusal to talk much about her past.

Diosdado

The elements within the cover, in terms of the names of people, places, and the course of her life, appear to us to have been devised in a way that makes them as close as possible to reality.

The family life is marked by problems that Tania observed in the real lives of her friends, which will help her to forget her own reality of a happy home and to adopt one of a household filled with conflict and a dependent and unhappy childhood.

In general, we believe that with these elements, Tania will be able to control, expand, and polish her cover story under any circumstances.

MOE

MESSAGE TO MERCY FROM HEADQUARTERS, REGARDING FUTURE CONTACT WITH TANIA IN BOLIVIA

Mercy. Message 5. November, 1965. Start.

During this period of waiting, something we very much hoped for happened that will cheer you up. Among other things, it will facilitate the work assigned to you. We received news from Tania that could be processed perfectly. She says she has decided to change the existing form of contact, as the places chosen that you are acquainted with do not provide security right now. Study this new contact plan. In addition, at the next contact you will be handed material that you should take to exchange for that which Tania has and review with her the direct communication system she has with us.

New contact plan with Tania: On your arrival in La Paz, you should organize a detailed check on Tania over a period of several days in order to find out whether she is under enemy surveillance. Once the required check has been completed, you will telephone her at 23696, between 13:00 and 14:00, local time, and you will initiate the following dialogue:

Mercy: You will ask for the German teacher and you will say that you would like to take some business German classes.

Tania: If she answers in the affirmative it will mean that you have to call back until she says that she does not teach business German.

Note: A man might answer the telephone; he is the owner of the house Tania lives in. Regardless of this, you should ask for the German teacher because she is, actually, giving German classes right now.

How to make contact: The day after the call during which she states that she does not teach business German, at 19:30 local time, Tania will be at the kiosk in front of the Lanza market, drinking a milkshake, and from there she will walk in the following direction: Zagárnaga Street to Linares, Grau, Héroes del Acre, Landaeta, up to the library; during this route or at the kiosk you can make contact.

Visible signs of identification: Tania will wear a dark gray coat and a yellow scarf.

Signs of danger: Tania will carry a black handbag in her right hand. If she has detected surveillance, she will switch the handbag to her left hand.

Note: See the appendix with information on the Lanza market.

Site of reserve contact: On the following day, if contact as arranged has not been made, at 20:00 the meeting will take place in the national library using the same signals already indicated.

Visible signs: When the meeting takes place you must use the key words that you know in order to identify Tania. We are sending you the address of where she lives in La Paz and other places she goes to so that you can locate her at any time.

Her usual address is 2521 Presbítero Medina Street, Sopocachi. You can also find her in the Helena Rubinstein beauty parlor. End.

MOE

MERCY'S REPORT ON CONTACT WITH TANIA IN BOLIVIA AND BRAZIL

*Report on the various contacts made between January 7
and the last days of March 1966.*

TO: MOE
FROM: MERCY

Start. On January 1, 1966, I arrived in La Paz and stayed at a hotel of the same name, in order to get to know, initially, the situation in the city as best as possible and especially to become acquainted with the places that Tania frequented (the Department of Folklore in the Ministry of Education and the Maritza beauty parlor).

At the first place I went, I showed an interest in books about folklore, particularly in the book, *La Diablada*. The head of the department of the aforementioned ministry sold it to me for 30 Bolivian pesos even though it is normally free of charge. In this way, I took advantage of the time to visit the museum and I toured practically the whole building trying to locate Tania, but I was not able to find her. Later I was told that Tania did not work in the Ministry, as I had been informed; instead, she belonged to the Folklore Research Committee, which works directly for the Ministry on a voluntary basis, without receiving any salary.

I arrived at the hairdressing salon with a business card and a copy of the note of introduction that I had sent through the mail, offering the products of the companies I represent. I did not see Tania there either; that was why I chose to follow her when she left home. I sat waiting in Montículo Park, which is in front of the house where she lived (I was there from 07:00 until 08:30 on January 5, 1966.) Tania left her home at 08:30 on that day wearing a dark gray coat and a scarf on her head; she left in a hurry and when I left

Montículo Park to follow her, she was ahead of me by two blocks. Precisely at the moment when I caught a glimpse of her, she was boarding a public taxi[1] that was heading in the direction of Isabel la Católica Park, and for that reason, I lost sight of her and didn't see her again.

That day I telephoned her house and asked for the German teacher, they told me that she was not in; in the evening, I carried out surveillance on her house and I observed her return after 19:00. I remained close by until almost 22:00, but she did not leave. On the following day, January 6, I returned to her house, but on that occasion I changed my observation point, placing myself in the entrance of the Caja de Ahorros bank that is on the corner by her house and I blended in with the people who were waiting.

At almost half past eight she left her house wearing a gray plastic waterproof coat. She crossed a park opposite the Ministry of Defense and continued on foot to the San Pedro neighborhood. She entered a house that is also a ceramics workshop and spent the whole morning there. Knowing that she would return home at noon I returned to my place at the Caja de Ahorros bank. At approximately 13:20, I saw that she was arriving with her shoes and clothes covered with clay; she took a taxi and I went to a pharmacy that is close to the Monje Campero cinema. I called and asked for the German teacher, and they told me to hold on, after a short time I heard a voice saying, "But, don't you realize that it is for me? Hang up please." Then she said, "Can I help you?" I asked if she was the German teacher and she said she was, so I asked, "Señorita, do you teach business German classes?" She answered, "I really don't teach business German." I apologized and hung up. Later I returned to the corner of her house.

At 13:55 she left. She looked happy. When I saw her I caught up with her and then waited until she passed by and went ahead of me for two blocks to where she had taken the public taxi on the previous day. When she boarded the taxi, so did I, and when she got out of the taxi, I followed her. I walked in the opposite direction from her and I saw that she entered a house and a boy greeted her. She spent three hours there. (Tania subsequently told me that this was a pupil's home.) She then walked to the San Pedro neighborhood and entered a hardware shop. A little while later, she left and walked to the city center. At the corner of the university, she greeted some young people and went with two of them to her home. (Later she told me that these were her boyfriend and his brother, both of whom were students.) I stayed in Montículo Park and after 20:00, she left with a young man and they went to the Monje Campero cinema. I had something to eat in a nearby Chinese restaurant and subsequently I saw them leave the cinema when the film was over and go to her house on foot. During the walk, she took the lead.

On January 7 at 08:30, she left her home, took the same route as the day before, and ended up in the ceramics workshop. At noon, once again, she waited for her pupils and then went with her boyfriend to a restaurant that is on Seis de Agosto Street; afterwards she went home. She changed clothes and left, took a public taxi and got out at the same spot. She walked and entered the same house that she had gone to on the previous day. I took advantage of this to follow the route that had been set up for the contact. I orientated myself in relation to the places that I would check out at night and I went to the hotel to move to my new address.

At 19:15 on January 7, while waiting for Tania to arrive, I sat in a small park opposite the stand where milkshakes are sold at the Lanza market and to find out whether she was under surveillance. So, just as any other citizen would do, I sat there waiting, until Tania arrived, which was at approximately at 19:30. After arriving, she drank a milkshake, got up, and walked the route agreed to beforehand to make contact. I followed her for two blocks, and then I took a taxi and waited for her to go past the Murillo cinema.

Once she had passed it and I saw that nobody was following her, I walked along Linares Street and stopped on a corner. I saw her pass by again, and then I walked along a route parallel to hers. At every corner I watched her pass. I continued like this until the corner of Landaeta and Ecuador streets (one block before the library) where I waited for her, but she did not finish the route. Instead, she turned onto Ecuador Street. I then followed her three blocks down a dark street.

After I was sure that she was not being followed, I walked up to her and asked, "Señorita, can you tell me where Bolívar cinema is?" She replied, "It is on Simón Street." So I added, "Close to Sucre?" She smiled and held out her hand. I greeted her and invited her to go somewhere that we could talk undisturbed. She said, "We can talk in a cafeteria that is opposite the Seis de Agosto cinema." We took a taxi and went there. I relayed to her the greetings that all the *compañeros* had sent. I told her that I had mail for her, but not on me at that time, and that we would have to meet in a safer place where we could work, given that we would have to work for quite some time. I asked her if she could look for an apartment and she said, "I have a friend who has a little room in Calacoto and she always lends me the key when I need it. But we will have to wait until Monday or Tuesday, because I will have to ask for the key since the owner spends Sundays in the room." I told her that we didn't have much time and that we had to use it as best we could, and that we would have to meet before Monday.

Then we left the cafeteria and walked a few blocks to a small street stand. There we agreed to meet on Sunday at 09:00 on the corner of Landeta and Héroes del Arco streets to go on a trip and also to collect the secret codes she had hidden in a remote place outside of the city. At the same time we decided that, if at any point, we lost touch with each other, we would meet at the milkshake stand at 20:00.

I left my home on Sunday at 08:00, took a taxi and went to the place where we had arranged to meet. Then I walked a few streets to see if I was being followed or watched. At 08:30 I arrived at Montículo Park and I saw her leave; I followed her a few blocks without her knowing it. When I saw that she was approaching the meeting point, I went around to the other end of the street. She was sitting in a doorway. I greeted her and we took a public taxi to the Tembladerani neighborhood. We got out at the terminal and walked among the hills taking photos.

About six miles from there she told me to wait a moment, she was going to collect the secret codes. She went to a creek in the mountains and after a while she returned with a little bone that had the secret codes hidden inside it. I told her it was a mistake to have hidden them in such a remote and quiet place as every time she had to use them she would have to take a long trip, and she could make people suspicious if they saw her alone in this area. She told me that she had been taught to hide them well away from her home. I advised her to hide them somewhere close by or inside a piece of furniture; I recommended a broom.

We sat down in a small wooded valley and there we destroyed the secret codes she had collected. I handed over the others that had been sent to her. I warned her how important it was to meet soon to begin the training and that she should try to devote at least three hours daily to it. She replied that it was impossible at the moment—since she had to attend ceramics class in the morning, and in the afternoon had to give German lessons to a number of pupils—but that these were coming to an end and I should wait for a few days. We had some bread and sardines for lunch and at 16:00 we started our descent from the hills. We then took a public taxi and agreed to meet on Tuesday morning at 09:00 at the exit from La Paz for Calacoto, from where we would travel to the house that she visited there. On our arrival in the city, she got out first and I continued to the center.

On Tuesday morning at 08:00, I arrived at Montículo Park and saw her leave her house at 08:30. I followed her, always using streets parallel to the streets she used. Then I took a taxi and went to the designated meeting place. I watched the place and entered a service station opposite to use the bathroom. When I came out I watched her for a while. At 09:15, I approached her and without speaking, we took the same public taxi to Calacoto. We got out and greeted each other. While she went to the place and opened the door, I went to a sauna one block from the house. We had agreed that on my return from the sauna I would push the door open and enter; that is what I did.

The door opened to a plot of land that was about 20 by 20 meters, on which a brick house was being built. There was a little room under construction to store materials. It measured four by four meters, and inside was only a bed. There was no light or water. In the surrounding area there was a vacant lot. We stayed there until almost 19:00 and during that time I handed her the package of mail I had brought for her hidden in my shoes. She was very happy and while she read, I saw how content she was; on occasions she cried with emotion and said, "I thought they had forgotten me." When she finished reading, on my request she burned everything that would not be of use to her at a later point. All she kept was the material related to the instructions she had been sent and she stuffed them into a key ring.

We took advantage of the afternoon to train her in the new surveillance and countersurveillance techniques. At the same time, we agreed to meet two days later, that is to say, on Thursday. On that day, I arrived and took a bath at the sauna; then I sat and drank a soft drink in order to observe Tania's arrival. I waited for almost half an hour and, as nothing unusual was happening, I went to the house, pushed open the door and went in. She was lying down. We worked together until almost 20:00. We used candles to light the house. I gave her classes in surveillance and countersurveillance, as well as in some security measures and counterintelligence, although just verbally, as the house was not adequate for more. Then we said good-bye.

For security reasons we agreed not to return to this house again. Besides, she still had to give classes to her pupils and had very little free time. So she asked me to wait a few days while she sorted out the matter. We agreed to see each other again at night in a little park close to the Seis de Agosto cinema, but at the first contact meeting she told me of her fears about a man who was head of immigration at the airport. Every time that he saw her, he told her to get her census papers in order. She could not sort them out because the fingerprints on her passport did not coincide with those in her identity card and on carrying out this procedure she would be put on record.

I suggested that we travel to the interior of the country and she said that would be better because in this way we could rent an apartment and carry out training there. We agreed to do it this way and used the remaining contacts to put the finishing touches to our trip to Cochabamba and talk about the latest international developments and Cuba's policy toward them.

Tania left in a bus for Cochabamba in order to wait for me in the city, where we would look for an apartment to carry out the training. Initially we had agreed to stay in the Bolívar hotel and to try to make progress in training while we were there. We couldn't do this because when I arrived in Cochabamba, Tania was waiting for me at the last stop. She told me that it was impossible to use this hotel as there were many people from the United States and some priests there for a conference being held in the city, and that it was dangerous for me to stay at the hotel. Given this situation, I sought accommodation in the Colón hotel.

On the following day we met in the park and began looking for an apartment, but we weren't successful. The day after the contact, Tania told me that Cochabamba was being subjected to a lot of control by the authorities and that she had been ordered to go to the security department in the locality so that some of her details could be noted in addition to her reason for visiting the city.

For this reason I invited her to go and visit some of the villages with me, such as Trinidad and Santa Cruz, with the goal of finding out whether we could rent an apartment in which we could work. She said to me that I should go and see if it would be easier in these places, during which time she could calmly search for one in Cochabamba. I agreed to her suggestion since I was interested in going to Riberalta to see don Ñico. We decided that if I found a house or apartment I would send a note to the hotel where she was staying.

On my return to Cochabamba, I telephoned Tania and we arranged to meet at a nearby cafeteria. She passed by and waited for me to get close to the park. We then we took a taxi and went to visit the monument to the Mujeres Próceres [Heroic Women] on the outskirts of Cochabamba. We spent some time there talking and taking photos of the city. She said that it had been entirely impossible to get a house, that the police had again gone to the hotel, and that it was dangerous to work in Cochabamba. There and then we decided to travel to La Paz as, in spite of everything, she thought that we would be safer there than in Cochabamba. We went to the train station and reserved tickets for the following day (this was my idea since she thought there wouldn't be any tickets until two days later).

During the time that she was on her own she had become friendly with three journalists from different countries who argued over her; due to them and other acquaintances she had made, it wasn't a good idea for us to be seen together. When I told her to avoid making acquaintances while she was working with me, she said, "I thought that I had to work on my cover, as a tourist and ceramicist." In this situation, I had to remind her on a number of occasions that, although it was important to keep up the cover story, she had to give priority to the work with me. I also warned her that when we were outside Bolivia she should abstain from making friends that would occupy her time, of which we were short. She agreed.

On the following day, February 2, 1966, we both went separately to the train station, although we traveled together and talked until we reached La Paz. On our arrival we took a taxi to Prado Street, where it broke down. We separated there and took different taxis to our houses, but not without agreeing to meet on the following day in a restaurant at lunchtime. We spent a number of days looking for a house but couldn't find anything.

On Sunday, February 6, I had lunch with Tania in a restaurant on Seis de Agosto Street. She found an apartment in the newspaper; afterwards we went to see it. It was very suitable and we arranged to meet the owner to sign the contract that afternoon in spite of the fact that she wanted three months rent in advance. But, talking to one of her daughters, we found out that her mother worked in the Bolivian Ministry of the Interior, so I did not show up at the appointment to sign the contract. Tania made excuses for me by saying that I thought that $120 a month was very expensive, since the maximum time we would spend there would be a month.

Given that we could not find a house that was suitable for our work, we decided to leave for Brazil in mid-February and we devoted the period between February 3 and 13 to searching for dead drops and making sketches, which is why we searched separately. We met at lunchtime at restaurants or in the park to decide on the times and days to test the dead drops. We had to reject some dead drops because the boxes of matches that we hid had disappeared when we checked. (So that Tania could have some practice at these operations, I had her fill the dead drops and arrange them, and I filled mine and she emptied them. We exchanged information in order to do this.)

Out of the dead drops chosen by Tania I rejected two; one because it was in the fence of a house which, although otherwise very suitable, belonged to Point 4, which is an organization used by the Yankees for infiltration, operating with Latin American personnel. I learned this one night when I went to empty the dead drop and on my return to the house, saw two Point 4 vehicles (a jeep and an Impala) at the entrance. The other dead drop was rejected because the box of matches that Tania used to fill it was missing.

On Saturday, February 12, we returned to the little room at Calacoto, to put the finishing touches on the group of dead drops we had selected. Tania took those that she had drawn in miniature on onionskin paper; we rejected those that we thought were of no use. I handed her my list so that she could make sketches to hide inside a secret compartment. We agreed that I would leave first and she, accompanied by her husband, would follow three days later. However, in order to keep her under surveillance, I stayed behind until she left for Santa Cruz. She did not have the census papers that were required for leaving Bolivia (which could not be obtained because the fingerprints on her passport were false—something which would be discovered by the authorities if they were to register her with the census).

To avoid problems with her departure, I would travel to São Paulo and send her a cable saying that we urgently needed her services as an interpreter and that she should travel to Brazil. In addition, I was also to send her the ticket for the trip, which would make the offer look more authentic. I also gave her some advice about leaving via Cobija for Brasilia and for Guajará-Mirum. This was so that she could use it in case there were problems leaving Bolivia even with my offer of work. Fortunately, she did not have to use these options, since on her arrival in Santa Cruz, her husband went to the airline companies Lloyd Aéreo Boliviano and Cruceiro Do Sul and asked for her ticket.

When I finally sent her the ticket through the República tourist agency, I had to show my passport because in order to pay for the trip I had to follow procedures of the Bank of Brazil. These were taken care of by Señorita María, who had become my friend at the time of the trip to the interior of Bolivia; I had sent her a New Year's greeting card. Things were easily sorted out since Tania, although she never received my cable, went to the Immigration office and showed them the ticket, and they authorized her departure without problems or asking any questions.

Tania arrived at the Handais hotel, where I was staying in São Paulo at the end of February. On the following morning, while I was waiting in the hotel talking to an Argentine couple and some Peruvians, she approached me, embraced me warmly, and joined us. We talked about football and politics and she defended me when it became apparent, according to her, that I did not speak like an Argentine, saying, "You have lost it, with all the time that you have been abroad. You don't talk like you used to," and she added, addressing herself to the others, "Isn't it true that he has lost his Argentine accent?" They laughed and agreed.

We went to a Japanese restaurant and then to a German restaurant, and then we returned to the hotel having made friends with the Argentines and Peruvians (one of the Argentines belonged to the armed forces in his country). He said that he had been involved in the war against the guerrillas and told us about his adventures. We praised him and congratulated him for his bravery. "Like all reactionary soldiers he was full of himself, presumptuous, and an imbecile." (Tania's words.)

It is important to indicate that *compañera* Tania is perhaps too frugal and I almost had to force her to buy clothes for going out, as she had almost nothing. When she went shopping, she always sought my advice, but even then she bought what was cheapest. I drew her attention to this, saying, "You are not thrifty, but stingy. Spend your money on better clothing and you will look more presentable. Besides lasting longer, the clothes will look better on you. Think about what you have said to people about your life. They think I am a man with money. Also, to be in a hotel you have to be presentable and you can't travel with such poor quality old clothes. Remember that you are young and all young people like to dress very well." In that way I convinced her but not without her first giving me a political speech about how hard it was for Cuba to get dollars.

I liked her all the more for this because she always tried to spend less money. She liked the least expensive places and in order to go anywhere by taxi, I had to convince her that it was easier for us to travel like this since we didn't know the places and we would get there quicker going by taxi. We spent a few days looking for an apartment or a house in São Paulo, but we were unsuccessful because they were too expensive. We talked about our work and the honor that we felt for being assigned special revolutionary work. She said, "You are right. That's why I would like to have a business that made money and be able to send dollars to Cuba." Her eyes filled with tears when she spoke like that and, of course, I too was moved because she expressed herself with passion that genuinely touched me. But at other times, I would ask her a question, she might suddenly, without any reason, answer "Don't be a fool" or "What a fool you are!"

One day we finally saw an advertisement in the newspaper for a furnished, two-bedroom apartment on the Itarare beach in San Vicente. On February 25 or 26, we went to the office that was handling the rental. When I was getting out of the taxi, I said, "You pay since I only have dollars on me." She paid and afterwards exploded saying, "This isn't right; you didn't change money so that I would have to pay. From this point onwards, we are going to share the expenses, half each. I will make a note of what you spend and then we will sort it out at the end."

We were angry at each other; we went into the office and she paid the equivalent of 80 pesos a month for the apartment. The man, who saw that we were angry at each other, thought that we were husband and wife and he made a note of it, as apartments were only rented to married couples. He gave us a document that stated we would have to hand over the keys to Mr. So-and-So and his wife when we left. By then her mood had changed and she was very pleased, but I pretended that I was still angry. She asked me, "Are you still angry? Look." And she started making faces, saying, "Little fish mouth." In the end she managed to make me laugh.

As we couldn't move into the apartment until the first of the month, she suggested that we look for a cheaper hotel for the next three days. Then she said, "This is the first time that I have stayed in such an expensive hotel; I have almost always stayed in very cheap hotels." I told her that it wasn't always a good idea to stay in very cheap hotels because your money could be stolen there, and besides, prostitutes tended to use these hotels. Then she told me that somewhere in Europe, she had been mistaken for a prostitute and had to show her identification. "Imagine what it is like to be a single woman in a capitalist country. After that incident they took me to the hotel in a police car and suggested that I be careful as it was dangerous to wander around alone."

On March 1, Tania moved into our apartment on the beach at Itarare; I stayed in São Paulo, since I had to go to the police to extend my stay in the country. Although it is said that Argentines have the right to spend three months in Brazil without a visa, on entering Bolivia I became subject to a law that gave me only 30 days. I went to buy the ticket for Europe while Tania was moving our things and organizing the new house, and I also went to the police to sort out this matter; the paperwork took an hour.

On the following day, March 2, I left the hotel and went to Itarare. Tania had bought some provisions and we had something to eat. Without wasting time we drew up a schedule of classes. These we organized in the following way: in the morning from 08:00 to 10:00, surveillance and countersurveillance; 10:00 to 12:00, charcoal and invisible writing; at noon, time on the beach until 13:30; after lunch, methods for obtaining and analyzing information up to 17:00; 17:00 to 20:00, counterintelligence and operation methods. After this we had dinner and immediately afterwards we reviewed what we had done during the day. Then we generally went out to listen to Radio Havana, when we could receive the broadcast, and we almost always finished after midnight. That was our first week.

During the second week, training was organized in the following way: from 08:00 to 10:00, observation; 10:00 to 12:00, cartographic studies; 15:00 to 17:00, microfilm (handling and locating only, because microfilm deteriorates with time); 17:00 to 20:00, security measures; 22:00 to 24:00, radio reception and a review.

During the third week of classes the schedule was from 08:00 to 10:00, karate; 10:00 to 12:00, locks; 15:00 to 17:00, correspondence; 17:00 to 20:00, a general review; 22:00 to 24:00, radio reception.

During the final week we drew up a plan linking Tania with Havana, as well as a plan for dead drops (the latter, Tania sketched and I put into invisible writing). For the final few days we carried out a general revision of all we had done during the month, but I made the mistake of wanting to ask Tania general questions and she exploded saying, "Listen, this way of asking questions was what annoyed me about my trainers in Havana, because it made me look stupid." When I told her it was to check that she had assimilated everything, she exploded again. Then I regretted it, "Listen, it is better that you tell me what things you want me to talk about and I will do it." I chose to do it her way, and that is what we did.

In spite of her tantrum, I was pleased with how much she had learned because it is worth pointing out that she has a prodigious memory and learns everything as if she had recorded it. At the end she said, "Now you see I'm not stupid." I said that I had never regarded her as stupid, that I admired her for her remarkable mind and tried to praise her, which she liked. In reality, it is right to recognize her merits, as she learned in less than a month what I had learned over more than a year.

In relation to ciphering with intercalations, we practiced this at different times of the day, mainly during our breaks because she told me that she knew it. That is why I only revised it with her and she quickly learned this way of writing in code, as she did devising secret compartments that we made in our spare time. In relation to her skills in code and radio, there was no need to review the material as she knew it perfectly. I only advised her not to do what she had done in the message of 3,000 groups, that is, cipher with the secret code and then insert part with the previous code, which she called an "emergency" code—in other words, without being doubly ciphered. She said that on that occasion, she had no other choice.

When on February 24 she was leaving for Montevideo,[2] I went to her and said, "*Compañera*, I want you to know that although we have had a lot of arguments, I am very happy to have given you training, and if I am ordered to come here again, I will do it with pleasure." I added, "As we don't know what might happen, I want to remind you above all that our slogan is 'Homeland or death,' and I know there is no need to remind you of this, but I have nothing other than 'Homeland or death' to say to you." She cried then and leaned on my shoulder saying, "That's why I didn't want you to say good-bye to me—I knew that you would make me cry." Then she said, crying, "Homeland or death."

When she returned from Montevideo, she was very pleased and said to me, "Look, I have brought some books for you so that you don't get bored with me, and I also brought you some *alfojadores* [a treat from the Río de la Plata region] so that you will have something to eat. There is also *maté* and a *bombilla*. [*Maté* is an herbal tea popular in Argentina and *bombilla* is the small piped container used to drink it.] Then she said, "I came back as soon as I could to spend a day with you and annoy you." When she was leaving on the following day she asked me to accompany her to São Paulo and to go to the

Sandaia hotel, and see if there was a letter there from Mariucho (that is what she called her husband). On arrival, she booked herself into the Inca hotel.

When I returned and said there was no letter for her, she took some paper and started writing. When I tried to talk to her she said, "Don't bother me. Can't you see that I'm writing?" I then went to the door of the hotel to let her write, but she got very angry and said, "Okay, I am not going to write anything since you are so sensitive and get mad for no reason." I said, "Don't be silly. Keep on writing and I'll wait for you." But instead of writing she became furious with me and then said, "Let's go. I am going to take you to the bus." I replied, "I'll go alone. You don't have to accompany me." But she insisted and after we had walked for a little while she said, "I can't walk with a person who doesn't talk to me. If you don't feel like talking I'll walk on because you're walking slowly on purpose." There and then she walked away from me saying in a very angry voice, "Do what you want to. I'll wait for you in the terminal."

I continued walking slowly. I went into a cafeteria and had a soft drink and then I took a taxi and arrived before her at the terminal. I sat down in a place where I could see her arrive. When she walked in I watched her. From time to time she looked to see whether I was coming and after 15 minutes she saw me and went to buy some of the candy she knew I liked. Then she came over to me and said, "Look what I have bought for you: the candy that you like."

I went to buy my ticket for the bus to Santos that was leaving in five minutes. She got angry again and said to me, "I want to see the ticket," and when she saw that I had bought it for two hours later she said, "You love to annoy me!" Then she said, "We have time to go for another walk," and went on to say, "One day we will meet again, when our cause has been victorious." With sorrow she said, "Maybe we won't be able to greet each other and we will have to pretend we are strangers, but with our gazes we will acknowledge each other, like good *compañeros*." And with tear-filled eyes she whispered in my ear in front of everyone, "I am very grateful for what you have taught me and for having put up with my moods. I've learned a lot with you." The bus driver called me and she shouted, "Wait just a minute," and without letting go of my hand she pulled me over to a corner and said into my ear, "Homeland or death" and "We will overcome!" I boarded the bus and she waved good-bye.

Conclusions:

On account of what I have written here, I have reached the conclusion that, in spite of the short period of time that was available for Tania's training, thanks to her excellent learning abilities, she fully understood everything I taught her. When she was not happy, I told her to take the matter up with whoever her next contact was. In this way she was satisfied and accepted my suggestion in good faith.

TANIA'S ORAL REPORT ON HER FIRST YEAR
OF WORK IN BOLIVIA

*Transcript of Tania's oral report on her first year of work in Bolivia,
given to Ariel during their meeting in Mexico on April 16, 1966.*

I landed in Peru on November 5 or 6, just when Víctor Paz Estenssoro
had arrived in Lima. I thought it would be a good idea to spend a
few more days in Peru to avoid entering Bolivia immediately because
its border with Peru was under tighter control at that time. In any
case, given my cover as an expert in archaeological, anthropological
studies, etc., it was better for me to go to Cuzco.

I traveled by plane from Lima to Cuzco. I stayed at the Rosedal
hotel in Cuzco, and as I have previously mentioned, I discovered
that the owner was Blanca Chacón. She was there with her niece,
who has a disabled leg.[1] I'm not sure whether they recognized me
or not. I spent a few days there, two or three. In the hotel I met a
young man who ate his meals there. While he was eating at a table,
he told me that he had been in Cuba from 1958 to 1959, fighting in
the mountains, and that he had left shortly after the revolution took
place. He had an olive green uniform or olive green shirt he said
he had brought from Cuba.[2] He was working in Cuzco, directing
a theater group that could have been a students' theater group
from Lima, or from Cuzco itself. I spent time with him in a cafeteria where, as in several others I have seen in Cuzco, politics was
debated from a Marxist point of view, and people defended Cuba,
discussed Fidel, etc.

I bought some local handicrafts for myself at a shop. While I
was there a middle-aged man came in and, when he heard my
accent, said, "You don't speak like an Argentine—you use Cuban
expressions." I answered that I had some Central American friends
and that was why I used some of those words. Apart from this, I did

not notice that anyone was checking up on me in Cuzco, although the political situation seemed to be a little tense.

Through the local authorities, I made contact with the person responsible for managing the folklore studies group in Cuzco, the lawyer Lino Fernando Casafranca. His home telephone number is 32-41; his office number is 39-96. He told me that there was a group of archaeology students who were devoted to researching folklore. The group included Argentines, Peruvians, and other foreigners, and he said that I could work with them if I stayed in Cuzco. He even introduced me to another student. I didn't see him again because I didn't have time.

I took a train from Cuzco to Puno. While I was still in Cuzco visiting the ruins, I met a Spanish woman whose name I don't have with me right now. (*Tania stops talking momentarily while car horns are sounding.*) She seemed strange to me. She was also traveling to Bolivia and she was on the same train as me. In Puno there wasn't much accommodation available and I shared a room with her. I continued to travel with her in a small truck until we reached Bolivia. I saw her later in La Paz. She spent a day in La Paz and then continued her travels. I wanted to visit some places in La Paz with her, but she said that she had to go alone, that she had some things to sort out. She's from Spain but has studied in the United States. Sometimes she expressed progressive opinions, but she seemed a bit odd in several ways. She was traveling throughout the entire continent and said that she was going to Spain, where her parents lived. I don't remember her name but I will try to see her again, to find out more about who she is and if she could be useful to us... Let me see if I can remember now.

Oh! From Puno I went to Yunguyo on the Bolivian border. Yunguyo is still part of Peru. At first they didn't want to authorize my exit because the border was closed when I reached it. Finally they let me through the border. From there I had to travel onward by donkey since there was no public transportation. There were no Bolivian police of any kind around. The customs building was a couple of meters after the border, and I declared my belongings there and continued my journey to Copacabana. This was the nearest town to the border and I spent the night in the Copacabana hotel, where they asked for my passport and other information but did not remind me to register with the police.

On the following day, I went to the police and explained that on the previous day there was no one on duty at the border. This was no problem with them. It seems that, normally, from a certain time onward no one patrols the border and the paperwork is sorted out later in the town. They gave me an entrance visa to the country. That was on November 18, 1965. Then I traveled to La Paz. First I went to the La Paz hotel and it was full. I spent a few days in the Sucre hotel and then I moved to the La Paz hotel for three weeks. In this hotel they asked for my passport and other information without telling me that I should register with the police. There was no problem. Quite a number of Argentines were in the hotel, as well as other foreigners and members of the Peace Corps.[3] Even the owner of the hotel's restaurant is Argentine.

I noticed that a lot of foreigners registered with the police, and after about 10 days I went to the National Tourism Office. I made some inquiries of a touristy, general nature and I asked if I should go to the police. I showed them my passport and they told me that the Bolivian embassy in France should have given me a tourist card, which is free of charge, and not the visa that they had provided me with, which cost $5. They must have done it to take advantage of me and to get $5 for themselves. However, they told me that to save myself a trip to the police I could use this visa and they would give me a free tourist card. They gave the card to me and ripped off the part that indicates the date of the border crossing, which they handed over to the police.

For the first few days I casually visited museums, the way a tourist would. In the Tiahuanaco archaeology museum I met the painter Moisés Chile Barrientos, who is a relative of President Barrientos.[4] He is married and has five children. He works as a sketch artist in the archaeology museum, which is part of the Ministry of Education. He took me to the Tiahuanaco ruins and flirted with me, etc. During the time I was with him, a man of about 28 to 30 years old, or perhaps less, approached. He studies economics, finance, and accounting in the university and introduced himself as the painter's cousin. He expressed left-wing ideas. The painter was also left wing in his politics although at times it seemed to be because he was snobbish, which is common among painters and artists in La Paz. I saw the cousin two or three times after that and then I never saw him again. In the beginning, he asked me some questions and seemed... the way he approached me, made me suspicious. I saw him last around New Year's Day or during the first few days of January.

Sometime before December, he took me to the Ministry of Education, where I talked to Dr. Julia Elena Fortín. She told me that there is a research committee registered with the Department of Folklore that currently has 30 or 40 members. All of them work voluntarily, given that the government does not finance them, and they do it as—what's the word?—an avocation. As enthusiasts, they are artists, intellectuals, teachers, etc. She told me there was no problem, that I could join this research committee, but that the Argentine embassy would have to provide me with a letter of recommendation.

Then and there she telephoned Ricardo Arce, who is secretary at the embassy... Where is the card Arce gave me? I thought I'd put it with another one. She talked to him. She told him about me, certainly giving him the impression that she, for her part, recommended me. On the phone she said, "There is an Argentine girl with me here who is interested in doing some archaeological research and we would like her to work with us." I think she was interested because I told her that I had a portable cassette recorder, which they don't have. In general, they have very few technical or economic resources in the Ministry of Education.

On the following day, at 11 a.m., I went to the Argentine embassy. I spoke to Ricardo Arce. He didn't ask for my passport. We talked for a while, and then he told me that I would have the letter that very afternoon. He introduced me to the Argentine who is the consul in

Santa Cruz, and also to some others, one or two who work in the embassy. Ricardo Arce is about 50 years old, maybe more. He is a bachelor who loves women. He invited me to lunch, but I refused the invitation. He said that he would like to see me again along with Dr. Fortín. That afternoon I returned and was given the letter of recommendation with my name, my age... I don't remember if it included my age. "The embassy recommends so-and-so to carry out folklore studies in the Bolivian Ministry of Education."

I saw him two or three other times, in the street. Once I greeted him. He asked if I wanted to go one Sunday to his house in... where are the golf courses? (*Tania talks to Ariel, trying to identify the place.*) No, farther away. After Aranjuez, La Florida... Where are the golf courses? (*Ariel answers, "Way out there, after La Florida, in Mayacilla."*) Yes, in Mayacilla, where almost all the diplomats live. I said that I would go. He told me to call him and gave me his telephone numbers: the number of the embassy and his home number. I ran into him at the La Paz club, where I had gone with a group of friends, on the last night of *carnaval*.[5] I had been to a party and at 4 a.m. we decided to go to the La Paz club. In the club, he [Ricardo Arce] was sitting at a table right beside us. He invited me to dance. He was quite drunk. He took me around the room and introduced me to everyone as someone who worked in the Argentine embassy, which some of the people that I later became friends with believed.

I saw him again later, once or twice. Once I saw him on the high plateau, at a folk festival held on the shores of a lake [Lake Titicaca]. General Barrientos was also there. Official invitations had been given to diplomats for a special lunch with the president. A barbecue was held there. The people from the ministry and I did not have invitations. He [Ricardo Arce] took me to the lunch as if I were his wife... I kept telling him that I had to do research, that I didn't want to spend time with diplomats, but I went with him anyway, and also with the Mexican Juan Manuel Ramírez, whom I will talk about later. We spoke to [President] Barrientos and also to several members of the Protocol Division of the Ministry of Foreign

Affairs, people with whom I still have contact given that they have been useful… After that I don't think I saw him again.

From the La Paz hotel I tried, using the newspapers, to get a room… Have I already said that? For the first few days I went to Coroico and I explored the city of La Paz itself. Then I went to the National Tourism Office. Then I found a room. I moved to the room that is on Juan Street, number… This is the first room that I lived in. I stayed there for a month, until January. The address is 232 Juan José Pérez Street. The owner of the house is Alcira Dupley de Zamora, and she lives with her third husband. She was widowed twice. He works in some kind of factory. He is an administrator in a factory in Bincha. I think it's a cement factory. I'm not sure. She often travels to Argentina because a brother of hers is in Buenos Aires, at the address I previously mentioned. She travels every two months or so and brings back things to resell. It is a kind of elementary smuggling that is carried out in La Paz, Bolivia, done mostly by women.

Her daughter, Sonia Azurduy Dupley—Azurduy because she was born during the first or second marriage—is a bilingual secretary. She studied hairdressing in Argentina and then was in a boarding school there. She also studied and worked in the United States for two years. During the Paz Estenssoro era she was secretary to the British Mission in the Ministry of the Economy. After Paz Estenssoro's fall from power, they got rid of almost all the secretaries and many other employees too. However, she got a job a few months ago as secretary to the minister of planning and development. It's not a ministry; it's more a Bureau of Planning and Development. In general, she is a very strong Catholic and is quite reactionary or, in part, apolitical. But recently she has changed a lot because she married a Nationalist Revolutionary Movement (MNR) university leader,[6] Marcelo Hurtado, a law student who is about to finish his studies in a few weeks' time. Together with the current leader of the university federation, he has recently run into a lot of problems. The government and its party, the Christian Popular Movement

(MPC),[7] have accused them of being communists or of supporting the Leftist Party.[8] There are a range of parties that have organized themselves in the university and have adopted a position of total opposition to the government. I think that they also lead—what's it called?—the Human Rights Organization. I see them often, and her every month or two. I am a friend of theirs. I often have contact with the mother, the owner of the house. She treats me like a daughter and gives me advice.

In the same building, Ana Henrick and her mother rent a room across from mine. She is originally from Beni but has lived for a long time in Cochabamba, where her husband is. They are separated. Her husband is Yugoslav and, according to her, belongs to a group of Yugoslavs who get together, organize activities, and are in contact with the Yugoslav embassy and the Yugoslav government. I had to be careful with her as she is quite alert and very knowledgable about things, and maybe the MNR or other groups are using her. After the fall of Paz Estenssoro, she lost her job as secretary to the Senate. She had a lot of friends and close relationships with Senate leaders and employees.

Currently, according to Sonia Azurduy Dupley, Ana Henrick is working as secretary to the president of, the head of, the Revolutionary Authentic Party, Guevara Arce. For a few months, she [Ana] has been closely involved with, as his girlfriend, an official from the United States who lives behind my house, but they have sent him… She said they were going to get married but her Yugoslav husband hasn't given her a divorce yet. The husband—I don't know his name—is in Cochabamba and is the owner of the Boston hotel. The official was sent to Panama two or three months ago and from Panama to Vietnam.

At the beginning of January she took me to a party held in Mario Quiroga Santa Cruz's house; he is Marcelo Quiroga Santa Cruz's brother, who has been a well-known journalist and writer for some years now. He is currently working for the newspaper *Presencia*. They produced the newspaper *El Sol*, which was published for a few months and then disappeared. It seems that this was due to economic and also political problems. Among the editorial staff there were as many right-wing people as there were communists. Mario Quiroga Santa Cruz offered me a job working on the editorial staff as a proofreader. I couldn't accept because the shift was from 3 to 5 a.m. and this didn't suit me. He promised that at a later stage I would be offered another job with him, but he gave me the employment certificate that I needed for my residency.

At the same party where I met Mario Quiroga Santa Cruz, who is of a political tendency that is close to certain falangist[9] and Christian Democrat ideas, but who, in part, expresses himself as an intellectual with some left-wing ideas… In his house I met two falangists who had left Peru in 1952, at the same time as the falangist lawyer Vascope Méndez—whom I will talk about later. They live in Lima and have managed to get ahead; they are financially well-off. They had come to Bolivia because they are close friends of René Barrientos and other members of the government. Above all, they are friends of the current Bolivian ambassador in the United States, Sanjinés Goitía, who was the minister of the economy at that time. They spoke to him to see if they could get positions that suited them, similar to those in Peru. But it seemed that they weren't successful and for this reason they remained living in Peru.

One of them, Oscar de la Fuente, is the sales manager for FEREICO, located at 3080 Panamericana Avenue, in Lima. He wanted to go out with Ana Henrick. The other was René Segadan, who is at 757 De Pierola, Office 610, Lima, and works in a company where he appears to be his brother's partner. It is a construction company: highway and road laying and other things related to civil engineering. He has studied engineering, specializing in economic affairs, in Brazil and the United States. He is married and has two children. I flirted with him and went out with him two or three days later, thinking that it would be convenient for me to have a friendship of this kind in Lima in case it was necessary to travel there or to have a connection in the city. I saw him only once after that, in March or April of last year, two or three months after I met him. He had spent a few days in Lima and said that he had been in Argentina. His company works with US capital. He had been in the southern part of Argentina, in the pampas or farther south, because they were going to do some construction work in these places and were doing some things that he mentioned in passing to me. It seems that they were looking at some constructions of a military type in Bolivia. He said that he was going to move to Argentina with his family and live there for two years on account of work. I have not seen him again.

All of these people are also friendly with Vascope Méndez, whom I met a few days later, also through Ana Henrick, who was romantically involved with him too. Vascope Méndez is a lawyer who has been out of the country for 10 or 12 years, spending most of this time in Peru. When I met him, he was the leader of the FSB Information Commission, but it seemed that he was also involved in the security corps belonging to the falange. She [Ana] introduced him to me explaining that I was interested in obtaining residency. It looked like he too... well, he liked women. His wife was in Cochabamba, and he chased after any woman that crossed his path. He thought that by getting me the passport he could have his way with me, although he knew that I, according to his group of falangist friends, was involved with René Segadan, who lives in Lima. And they thought that I wanted my residency in order to travel to Lima to see René Segadan and that having residency meant that I wouldn't face any problems entering and leaving the country.

Believing that this was the case, he [Vascope] hastened the procedures and completed the application, explaining that I wanted to stay in Bolivia to research folklore and that I was a member of the Folklore Research Committee in the Ministry of Education. The employment certificate that Mario Quiroga Santa Cruz gave me had to be attached to the application along with a certificate of good conduct. I went to the police to request the certificate and was told to return the following day to collect it. I asked whether they could give it to me sooner, and they wanted 5,000 pesos—which equals about half a dollar. I gave them more than 5,000 pesos and

I was given the certificate in half an hour. With the certificate of good conduct on me, I went to see the doctor that the lawyer had referred me to and got the medical certificate. In addition, I had to get the signature of a guarantor, which the lawyer himself took care of. We handed this in and on the following day I went back to... This had to be given to Immigration on Arce Avenue, in the Government Ministry. On the following day I went back and it still wasn't ready. So I went to see the lawyer to ask whether he could get it for me through his friends, but it was clear that at that time everyone was acting cautiously on account of the political situation and because the FSB was attempting, successfully, to place people in the ministries and they didn't want to have any trouble.

However, two days later when I went... no, it was the following day, no the same day, when I was sent to go buy some document stamps, and I think it was the second day when I was told, "Wait a moment, I am going to talk to the boss, the main Immigration official." And I waited half an hour and I didn't say anything at all. Then he simply, ceremoniously, handed me the passport and told me, "Congratulations. You now have residency in Bolivia." He instructed me to go to the police and ask for an identity card. That was at 5 p.m. and I thought, in view of the problem of the fingerprints and my passport... Like the time when I went to ask for the certificate of good conduct and saw that all the people getting their identity cards had to give their fingerprints and other things...

So at 5:50 or 5:55 p.m. I went to speak with the head of Foreign Affairs. I showed him my passport and told him that I wanted an identity card. He said, "Go and buy a blank identity card." He said that because it was already very late, I would have to return the following day to resolve everything else. I went to buy the card and saw that, without asking for documents, they sell blank identity cards for 40,000 pesos, currently 40 pesos.[10] On the following day, I went to the police... Now it is not Immigration; it is the police station on Junín Street, opposite Foreign Relations. I went to the Department of Personal Identification and Foreign Affairs. I went in and straightaway went to the office where I had been the previous day and said, "Could you see if my passport is here?" They searched everywhere and couldn't find it. So I said, "I must have mislaid it and I need to travel to the interior of the country and I don't have any other documentation." I showed them the letter that those in the ministry had written for me when I had informed them that I was going to travel to the interior of the country.[11] They had given me a letter stating that I belonged to the research committee and that I was to be given all the help I needed to carry out my research.

I showed them this letter and said that I needed to travel to the interior of the country and asked them if I could travel with just an identity card. They said... It was the same person I had seen on the previous day with my passport and residency permit. He told me it should be fine, but that he would have to talk to the head of Personal Identification to make sure it could be done. However, I would have to go back to Immigration and ask for a certificate, a letter, explaining that I had been given residency and what the number was, etc. I returned to Immigration and explained... No, I didn't go straight back to Immigration. I went to talk to my lawyer. My lawyer told me to put an announcement in the newspaper *El Diario* stating that I had lost my passport. Before going to Immigration I placed the notice in *El Diario*. The notice offered a reward for recovering the passport. And when, on the following day... (*Ariel asks a question.*) What? Yes, everything with Vascope. He told me to put the notice in the newspaper. He wrote on a little piece of paper how I should word the notice and I placed it with the newspaper. So then, on the following day, with the notice in *El Diario*... Besides, when I told Vascope what had happened he said, "Don't worry, I can sort this out for you, because the falange has many ways of getting passports and I can get you a new passport from Argentina." The FSB has no problem in this respect; it is very well organized and has a lot of documents.

With the Foreign Affairs paper I was sent to Immigration, as I have already mentioned. In Immigration I showed them this paper, explaining that I had lost my passport, and they immediately gave me a letter stating that I had been given residency on the previous day, what the number was, etc. I returned to Foreign Affairs and showed the letter to them, and they started procedures to get my identity card. They took all my fingerprints. I think they took them twice for two different forms in the same office and they also took my thumbprint for the identity card. Then and there they took photos of me. Then, after finalizing all these technical things, I had to speak to an official, not from Foreign Affairs but from Identification. He asked me a series of questions, some of which were trick questions. For example, he wanted to find out what languages I knew, why I didn't speak Russian if it was the most important language in those days, what countries I had traveled to, etc.

The card records not only my name, but also my parents' names, ages, and dates of birth. I gave those that were agreed upon for my cover. In addition to my parents' names, the card records my father's address, and I gave them the place where my father lives in Frankfurt. Furthermore, I was asked for the names of people abroad and within the country who know me. For people in the country, I gave the address of the house where Alcira Dupley lives, and for abroad, the address in Lima of René Segadan, as well as another one in France of a French woman I met in Paris. She is an 80-year-old woman who (*inaudible*) to Paris from Austria and whom I was writing to... I continued writing to her even though she had not replied to me in a while. It might have been my fault since I didn't write to her for several months in the beginning. Perhaps she has died... Alicia... I can't find it... Her name is Alice Multner and she lives at 121 Simón Bolívar Avenue, Paris 19. She has written to me before but for the past month or two I haven't heard from her. This is the other address I used as a reference for the police documents. Besides them, I met a Turkish teacher who worked in France at the Organization for Economic Cooperation and Development. I met him in Lima when he was organizing an economic development conference. His name is Nejat Erner. His address is 2 Rue André Pascal, Paris 16. This is the address of the organization I mentioned.

I think that the official who asked the questions... What else can I say? In relation to the official who took down the details, I think he recorded them, that he had a recorder. The desks are in the center of the room and close by there is a hallway with a handrail, and when I walked down the hallway and looked behind me, I thought I saw a microphone in the left desk drawer. A day later they gave me the identity card and at the same time, in the same Foreign Affairs building, they issued a document that registers the domicile, and this always has to be carried with the identity card; the address is registered in this and also in the census. That was the only thing that I had left to do: change my address again and register in the census, which I hadn't done because it involved going back to Immigration and presenting both documents to them and asking for a card. Lately, they have been insisting on this. And in Cochabamba there are very tight controls; at least in January and February of this year they were very tight. Hotels were constantly checked and foreigners were told to go to Foreign Affairs.

I went before they told me to go. At the hotel where I was staying, a 15- or 16-year-old boy stopped by, and he told me that the identity card is useless and that it is only used to acquire a passport. But this didn't make sense. It seems this boy didn't know much about the matter. I went to the Foreign Affairs office and asked what was happening, and the boy was there. I told them what he had told me about my papers not being in order, and they said that this was not the case. They said my papers were in order, and that I also had to carry my passport on me along with the census card. I said that all I had was the identity card because they had told me this would be enough, and that the other documents were in La Paz. I said this was because I was researching folklore and had to travel into the countryside, and I didn't want all my documents together in case I lost them. They didn't ask me any more questions. Then there was another police check in the hotel where I was staying, which was a smaller hotel, the Bolívar hotel. And in the other hotel, the owners said that I was from the Ministry of Education and there were no problems. But that is how I realized that they are currently asking for the census registration together with the identity card.

Lately, I have been seeing a friend whom I became acquainted with at a little party, although he lost interest when he saw that I wasn't paying attention to him. He appeared to be flirting with me. I didn't pay him any attention. Then he lost interest. Later I bumped into him in the office of Immigration Control in the El Alto airport, and he took me by jeep to the city center. He asked if all my papers were in order and if I had my census registration card, and I said yes, I did. Later, I phoned him. I wanted to take advantage of the situation to get to know him and to see if the registration could be done with just the identity card, and quickly, but when I went they asked for both documents and they asked me for photos. So I said, this is just before Christmas… Now, lately I have been avoiding the issue and I haven't gone. He phoned me for New Year's and invited me to a party and I said that I couldn't go because I was with my boyfriend. Since then I have seen him a few times in the city but he didn't ask about the matter. He'll probably ask me, when I return, whether it has been resolved. Finally, in order to obtain a census card, all foreigners are asked for their identity card and passport and also photos and some stamps. I think that the right thing to do is personally go and request a census card by presenting my passport, in order, with the correct fingerprints on it…

I have just jumped forward, so now I have to go back again. All right? In January I moved. Where I was living was not suitable, the conditions were not good and I moved… I am not going to go into details about why because it would take too long to explain, but I moved. I tried to get another room and while I was doing so I bumped into that same young man in the street who worked in the Government Ministry.[12] At that time I wasn't aware of this and, while talking to him, I asked if he knew anyone who rented rooms and he told me about a young man who had a business that helped people who were looking to rent. Through him I got a room where I stayed until a short while ago, before leaving Bolivia.[13] It is an apartment in a building that belongs to a trade union, a guild.

The apartment is rented to Alfredo Sanjinés and his wife. He is 80 years old. I think she is 70. He is a diabetic. For 40 years, up

until 1948, he was a diplomat, first in Europe, in Spain, in France...
then in Mexico, during the Cárdenas era.[14] He spent some years in
Cuba, until 1948, when he retired. His politics are very reactionary,
although in his time he held a relatively progressive position. He
published a book, the first of its kind to be written in Bolivia on
agrarian reform.

Alfredo Sanjinés was also president of the Indigenous Congress
held in Mexico. He visited Trotsky. He spoke to Trotsky, and he has
some books with some inscriptions written in them or Trotsky's signature. Broadly speaking, Sanjinés currently holds a very reactionary
position. This was apparent when the mining problems arose,[15] and
the problems in the Dominican Republic.[16] Almost everybody in
Bolivia, even the most reactionary people, had a positive position
toward those issues. He had a very reactionary position then, and
in other situations as well.

His son is a manager at Royal Dutch Airlines (KLM) in La Paz.
He is married and has four daughters, aged from 10 to 15 years old.
Alfredo Sanjinés's other daughter is married—I don't know if she
still is—to the lawyer Arrieta who was in the research commission
of the regime back then, which I don't think exists any longer. She
is a teacher, she teaches French, but she is financially quite well-
off. Alfredo Sanjinés and his wife don't have much money. His son
gives them money. What they do have is the government pension,
which is currently very little. I think it is about 280 pesos.[17] I have
seen the receipts. What was a lot of money when he retired is now
worth nothing. That is why they rent rooms out.

They rented one room to me. There were two students occupying
the other room when I arrived. One of them, Ávila, has falangist
politics, and he left shortly afterward because he took a room in
Anticrético. The other, who has left-wing politics, Fuack Nasar Casat
Vargas, of Arab origin, was around 22 or 23 years old and was in
the second year of a geology degree. He must have moved into the
third year by now. He is one of those young men who like to talk
and to be interesting, and that is why he says that he belongs to the
National Leftist Revolutionary Party (PRIN), which is with Lechín.

He always had leaflets—I don't remember what the newspaper was called—printed by communist students in the university, and journals from Cuba. He has portraits of Fidel and Cuban flags in his room as well as slogans posted such as "Homeland or Death." He studies with Edmundo Arriem, who is from Cochabamba and studies in La Paz. His father or uncle has been to Cuba. He [Arriem] also has left-wing politics, although he is very cautious when discussing them. Just recently, they have been more open with me and, for example, I saw him with the Cuban edition of *History Will Absolve Me*.[18] When I asked where he had gotten the book, he said that they were given out only within communist party groups in the university.

Around May or June—I had moved in January 1965—two other students arrived. One of them is the man I am currently married to, the eldest, who is 21 years old, Mario Antonio Martínez Álvarez, and the other is his younger brother, Gonzalo. During their first few days there, I asked him—the student I talked about before—Nasar, who is from Padilla in the Chuquisaca region... When I asked him if those two shared his politics... By the way, he believed and believes me to be quite reactionary, but at the same time quite objective, that I see things neutrally or objectively—I have tried to convey this image of myself so they don't clam up too much on me... He said that he is from the Peking Line and that the others are from the Moscow Line.[19] The other two, according to what they have always said and to what my current husband says, are not politically active, but they do have left-wing ideas. Mario often says he is not a good student, that he doesn't like to study here because it doesn't make sense. He says that only when communism prevails will it make sense to study and to become something. But he would like to study in another country and, if possible, in a socialist country.

They often read Marxist journals or leaflets and Edmundo Arriem brings a lot of them. Those two, the Martínez brothers, study engineering. The younger brother studies industrial engineering and Mario studies electrical engineering. Both of them are poor students. First they were at a technical school, but to enter the university, it seems that they will lose another year because a number of their classes will not be accepted. In their free time they drink a lot, like the majority of students. They get together sometimes at night and although they don't have any money, they get drunk on *pisco*,[20] the cheapest they can find... (*Ariel asks a question.*) I met those two during the first weeks of June. I didn't talk to them much. Later, they started coming to my room to listen to music; they like my recordings and in Sucre they sing the Argentine zamba a lot. So very often we ended up talking.

At that time, I was trying to see if I could find someone to marry in order to get [Bolivian] citizenship. Compared with other persons I had met, I would prefer a person... I realized that if I married a professional, who was financially well-off, I would have to stay at home and I wouldn't be able to go out. I would be completely dependent on him, and I would have an active social life that I wouldn't want. Instead, this way I could be freer, since he doesn't have any money other than what is sent to each of them by their father—which is 350 pesos—I would have more options, so it would be better to be with him. Besides, he isn't a known politician or activist. Although he does get involved in some political activities, it looks like he doesn't go to meetings or become too involved. When there are demonstrations or something in the university he participates, but only in a marginal way. This is what I've been able to see, but it remains to be checked out whether he is an activist in the [communist] party or any other organization. His father is a mining engineer in Oruro, Huanuni.[21] According to him [Mario] his father also has left-wing politics, but his parents don't want to commit themselves or create problems. His mother is in Sucre with the other two brothers who are attending secondary school at a German college, and there is a little sister who is 13 or 14 years old. They live at 110 Loa Street, in Sucre. Details concerning his parents are in the documents I turned in.[22]

A few months after I met him, I asked him what he thought about getting married to me. This way we could be together anywhere, without restrictions, and travel together without running into problems with people who always gossip. He said he would do it, that it would be fun, and that as long as nobody found out about it we could do it; that way everything would be so much simpler. I think that was how he put it then, but right now it seems to be about being in love. Several times I spoke to him about us getting married, and he was impatient to go ahead with it. He always asked whether I had changed my mind. Recently, before leaving, I quickly checked with a lawyer, Galindo—I will tell you later how I met him—what the procedure would be. I explained the situation and told him that Mario didn't want anyone to know about it, that it was to be a secret. To a certain extent this suited him.

The lawyer, Galindo, put me in touch with an official from the Civil Registry Office. I explained the case, and I told him that I wanted to get married right away because I had to travel and did not want to risk having problems with the police on account of my papers. The official said that there would be no problem, that I could get married right away if I wanted to, or on the following day, if I brought witnesses with me. The only difficulty, as far as he was concerned, was that Mario was 21 years old, about to turn 22. That makes him a minor under Bolivian law and therefore he needs parental authority to go ahead. I took Mario there, and the official spoke with him and asked him if he thought that his father would object. Mario said that his father would get angry with him but he didn't think that he would create any problems, and he wouldn't go directly to the courts. We got the witnesses and the documents, and three days later we got married. The procedure cost 200 pesos, which is less than $20—it is $16. The notice was not published anywhere, although it really is an obligation to publish it within eight days.

We were still living in the same house, where we didn't want anyone to know about the wedding, so we had a small party at Yolanda Rivas's house—I will explain who she is later—and a few days later we traveled together by bus from La Paz to Santa Cruz. I had to pay for the trip as he didn't have enough money, and then we spent two or three days in Santa Cruz until I got the ticket. I had agreed beforehand with *compañero* Juan to send me the ticket as a signal from Brazil.[23] In this way my husband was convinced that I had been sent a ticket to work as a German translator with some Germans, which is what I had told him and some friends in La Paz. He [Mario] returned to Sucre from Santa Cruz. According to what we had agreed, no one was to find out about it—our wedding—not even his parents or his brother. He will continue to live with his brother, but two or three times a week he'll come to the house where I will be living. At this point I have my belongings in Yolanda Rivas's house, but as soon as I return I will look for an apartment or a room for a married couple.

What else can I say in relation to him? Well, when I return, I have to check to see if he really is waiting for me... What I want to do when I get back—since I have been traveling for such a long time and up to now he has never been abroad—is to suggest to him that we travel somewhere nearby as soon as I have a vacation. I think that in July or August I have a week or a few days free, and perhaps we could go to Peru or Chile. I will tell him to request passports for the two of us so that we can travel together because my passport identifies me as a single woman and he would like everything to be in order, and our marriage registered on the documents. That is what I have to sort out when I go back, to find out whether I can still count on him or whether, in the meantime, he has decided to annul the marriage because of my long absence while traveling... (*Ariel asks her a question.*) It is not certain; it might be that everything goes well... Well, we agreed, we talked before I left, that even if he met someone else while I was away, when I got back we would try to be together, and that if we still liked it we would continue together, and if not, we would separate. But let's wait and see what he says when I get there. He might say, "Go to hell, you've been away for a long time, and I don't like that." He might not be interested anymore and then again he just might. Now, if we continue together, I am going to suggest... At least he doesn't have a complex about whether I am going to pay; I have more or less dealt with that... (*Ariel asks a question about how long the trip will last.*) No, he cannot be away for long. It's just a few days, in order to get the passport. If not, I have no motive for requesting a passport. It is to go, for example, to Arica. Everyone goes for just five days. Isn't that true? So then, he goes and gets the passports for the two of us and we travel to Arica together, but I will have to see about that when I return. What I need now is to check…

Well, until recently, he had always been able to prevent his parents from finding out that he is with me, although his brother knows. However, when I last went to Cochabamba he was on vacation. He had time between exams and had traveled to Huanuni and there, sure enough, as he told me later on… There his father said, "Listen, I have been told that you are with a girl and that's why you are not studying." Then he told him that it was just the opposite, that I made sure he studied and that it was not my fault… By the way, this problem was raised by his brother and his other friends. All of them said that I didn't let him study because they wanted to separate us. He told me about this a short time ago… In January he talked to his father and told him. He talked about me, who I was, my age, and everything else. His father advised him to think about it, saying that it was a decision he had to make for himself and that even though he was his father, he could only tell him that he was very young and that he should finish his studies, but he had to decide for himself what he wanted to do. So, his father knows about us being together, but we have tried up until now to prevent his father from finding out about us getting married. At least I, for my part, told him not to let his father know… Most importantly, I advised him not to say anything until a few months had gone by, when he could prove with his grades that he was studying harder than before; if he didn't, then his parents would be opposed to our marriage.

I don't know what he will have been doing in the meantime. His parents don't know that we are married. They know he is with me, but they don't know we are married. If they find out, I think they will be angry with him. They will give him advice. But, given what I have seen up to now of how his father treats his children, he is an intelligent man, and I'm sure that he will say, "If I go against him, it will be worse." In the beginning, he [Mario] used to always say that he would prefer to marry so that we didn't have to behave like that with people, but that his father would cut off the money he sends him and so on… Until now there have been no problems, and I don't think his father will make a big thing of it, but there is no reason for him to find out, because it hasn't been publicized and not even his brother knows. It is possible that he could become emotional, get drunk, and let off steam about it. What is important for me, to really find out about, is his political position. Right? I need to know whether he really is an activist or not. He could be very politically active and not say anything about it. Right? He could be keeping it a secret. Perhaps not; I don't think so. I don't know. It could be a cover, but I don't think that is the case. But I have to see about it, because anything could be true…

Another thing is that I cannot work according to the plan drawn up[24] while I am living with him. Not even living apart, as agreed, with him coming two or three times a week to my house, would work. What I want is to return, to sort out my passport as soon as possible, and to get rid of him. I need help for all of this, and his situation is that he could be sent abroad to study. (*Ariel asks a question.*) What? That is why, to send him away to study and since he is really interested… It is a problem because of his attitude, if he wants to know and see what I am doing, that is a problem. What I really have to do is work hard almost every day on the thing about hideaways and all of that. So what I have to do is be free of him. I can do very little with him around. It is a problem. Besides, they are very jealous types. The fact that everyone knows each other and gossip spreads quickly is a problem there… (*Ariel asks a question about Mario's willingness to study abroad.*) He would, without any problem, without blackmail or anything. The best way to do it would be this way, the ideal…

I don't know whether this can be done quickly or not, because I have to get the identity card and passport. Maybe it could be done quickly because it is likely that, if I go to the Bolivian embassy and say, "I have lost my Argentine passport, but I am married to a Bolivian citizen," they would have to give me a Bolivian passport and even pay the return for me. But I have to find out about this when I get back. (*Ariel asks another question.*) Yes, I am Bolivian, but I have to do the paperwork for this. No? Of course, I have to present my papers and ensure that they are all in order. But they could ask, "Why haven't you registered with the census yet?" Of course, perhaps now that I am married, I can go to the Identification people and say, "Listen, I got married and want to be issued a Bolivian identity card." Maybe there won't be any problems this way. But there might be. I don't know. The ideal thing would be, first the census and then afterward...

(*Ariel speaks.*) Of course, that would be one more option now, but that is up in the air because I don't know if he has broken off relations in the meantime. The best thing to do would be to go back and even if he has broken up with me, as I still have these papers, I can still be issued a Bolivian identity card and do something. The ideal thing would be this: find him, live the first few weeks with him, get him out... There is even a reason to get a passport issued. He might say to me, "What do you want a passport for if you have yours?" The first thing is to be married according to the passport. But before that there is another reason. I could say to him, "Let's travel to the north of Argentina," and what happens then is that if I... That's why I mentioned it before. If I travel to Argentina, even though it is revalidated I will have to do all the paperwork again. If you enter the country with the passport, then it is annulled. It is not annulled; rather, another passport has to be issued in order to leave. If I don't have the identity card... He knows that I don't have an Argentine identity card, and if not, I'll tell him, "I lost the identity card..." He has never asked me, I think. But all I have is the passport.

Now, if I want to travel to Argentina and have no problems on my return, I shouldn't travel with an Argentine passport because I might have to go and do a whole lot of paperwork that costs a lot of money. I have been told that Argentine passports now cost 50,000 pesos.[25] That's a reason then. Even if I don't travel a lot inside Argentina, perhaps I could just go to Salta or Jujuy. Right? That is the least of my worries, but the problem is finding a pretext to get a passport using a totally legal and normal procedure, without running into any problems. This is what I want to do… (*Ariel asks a question.*) No, this is the one I talked about. Not another one. What I am saying is this. Get it with him. (*Ariel talks.*) Oh yes! (*Ariel talks.*) No, because in any case he wants me to have the passport of the country, even though that has been arranged. (*Ariel talks.*) If I have the census papers then I won't have any problems at all.

But the ideal thing would be for me to have a passport that has been issued entirely legally, one that doesn't cause me any problems so that the day won't come when I have to go to the Argentine embassy. I should get a passport with him. I will be Bolivian because I am married to him. Why do I want to be Bolivian? I am already Bolivian, but the problem is that I don't know if you can simply go and get the identity card and the passport or if you can just get the passport. Or perhaps you have to go to Foreign Affairs and ask for citizenship. I don't know whether it is easy or not. In reality, that is something else that I have to see about, and that is why it is best for me to have the passport just about sorted out. Maybe when I go there, they'll say, "You will have to renounce Argentina, Argentine citizenship." And then I will have to go to the embassy. Maybe not, because I spoke to several people and they told me that, according to the law, someone who marries a Bolivian—an Argentine who marries a Bolivian—becomes Bolivian but continues to be Argentine because in Argentina's view they are still Argentine and for Bolivia… If that is the case, then there won't be any problems. But the best thing is for the passport to be right.

Let's say that I go back and talk to him. I arrive and say, "Let's go traveling." Then he [Mario] goes with his identity card and says that I want to be issued a passport. Maybe they'll give it to him right away. Maybe they'll say, "Your wife is a foreigner. Let's see if all her papers are in order, let's see if her papers as a foreigner are in order." Of course, what I am going to try to do, even if they give me this…

No, in any case, because if they don't give this to me, even though I try to get a passport I am running a risk. Because they could... he could go with the two identity cards or with me and they could say, "Okay, let's see if her papers are okay." Then they see that the census registration is missing. She is Bolivian now, but before she was a foreigner. Where are the census papers? Maybe they won't ask and maybe they will. I don't know. Perhaps I will have to go to the embassy. So I really need to have all this in order. Now, in any case, I want to get a Bolivian passport, even though this one is in order. It is much better to have the Bolivian one in order, even though it has a drawback: the Bolivian one has to be requested again even if I don't leave the country. But I am now a Bolivian citizen. I can get my Bolivian identity card, but I need to have this in order in any case. So then, with regard to him, it is clear what I need after I sort out these things, the documents.

Now, regarding the code decided upon with the *compañero*,[26] there is also a code in the music for me, in the music that is broadcast on Radio Havana.[27] There is a code for things that I send by telegram and, at the point where numbers are included in the text, it will mean that I sorted out the problem or that I need them to get my husband abroad. It will be in the code that they are going to receive... (*Ariel talks.*) It will be in there. I have memorized what to do, and I know how to put the numbers there. So then, when they receive this they have to...

(*There seems to be part of the meeting that was not recorded.*)

Well... What? Another thing that remains to be seen, that he also wants, is for him to study in Argentina or Brazil, and that might be in our interest. So, he would go away to study and I would have my excuse to travel to these countries, which is something else that has to be checked up on. That is to say, first, I need him. When I don't need him anymore, he can be taken away somehow or the other. The good part is that we have the fact that he wants to study abroad. So there is no problem in suggesting that he go away to study.

(*Ariel speaks.*) This refers to the relations in the house where I was living. Before I moved to the other house, Anis or Ana Henrick knew that I was looking for some work. I was looking for the kind of job that would give me some freedom, a translator or something like that. She knew Gonzalo López Muñoz, the editor of the *IPE*. This is a weekly publication called *Información Periodística*, a cultural, political, and economic journal sent by mail to those who pay for an annual or six-month subscription. He was also beginning at that time to edit the journal *Esto es*, which comes out every fortnight— now it is not as regular as it used to be. Right now, the journal is considered to be the best in terms of the quality of the material, photographs, etc.

First she introduced me to the painter Ortega Leyton. This painter was working with Gonzalo López Muñoz. Ortega Leyton lives in a house in Miraflores, where left-wing and moderate intellectuals often meet and have orgies, political debates, and a little of everything. He is a very good friend of the writer Tristán Marof, who shares the same house with him when he is in La Paz. His real name is Gustavo Navarro and he lives in Santa Cruz. Tristán Marof recently published some books; one is called *El Jefe* and ironically describes Paz Estenssoro. This man, Ortega Leyton, joined the editorial staff of *Esto es*, which was then in the same office used by *Visión*.[28] Gonzalo López Muñoz is a correspondent there. Besides him, Sergio Cobarrubias, the *Visión* representative in charge of subscriptions, is also in this office; Gonzalo López Muñoz was away traveling at that time. First I met Sergio Cobarrubias, who currently has an office in the Oversides building, on Mariscal Santa Cruz Street. His politics are falangist, although he says he cannot join the party because it is not permitted by his job as representative of *Visión*. Gonzalo López Muñoz always criticized him and said that he wanted him out of the office because he is very reactionary.

Left-wing intellectuals met in López Muñoz's office. For example, the journalist Luis Raúl Durán, who is the media director at the National Treasure Oil Reserves,[29] was there, and some others. They debated political matters. He also talked about his trip to Europe, about his time in Europe, and how he got into an argument with some Germans because they were fascist. He always adopted a left-wing position, although sometimes this seemed to be a little artificial. I have been to Gonzalo López Muñoz's home, where he has an extensive Marxist library. He showed me photos of himself with several representatives of the Cuban embassy during the time when the embassy was still in Bolivia, and he also had journals from Cuba. He always said that, politically speaking, he didn't know where he stood at that stage. He didn't know what was best. It was best to be neutral. One day, when I went to see him I found him with an application to join the PCB. He filled it out in front of the other person who was in the office and when it was completed he took it to the PCB. He says that he saw the PCB person who belongs to what they call the Moscow Line under Monje's leadership.[30] As I was saying, I always adopted quite a reactionary position; because of this they often made fun of me in the office and asked me what I was doing there with my ideas and with my falangist friends, because they knew I was friendly with Vascope, the falangist lawyer.

On one occasion, Gonzalo López Muñoz made some comments to me while telling me about when he was in West Berlin, at a conference as the *Visión* correspondent... He showed me the place they were staying. It is not a very well-known place and he asked me about it. I didn't know where they were and he replied, "When you study maps, you don't get to know the place very well. Who knows whether you've been to Berlin or not. I know about these things and you could very well be a bit of a spy or something and that is why you are traveling a lot." There were other people in the office at that time. That was, in truth, the only time he made a remark of this nature. Once they also made comments among themselves about the spy thing, etc., and he said, "Well, in reality the United States thinks you spy for Russia and Russia thinks you spy for the United States, and that is why no one recruits you."

There was also a young Argentine working in his office for a while, a 19-year-old journalist, René Capriles Farfán, who talked about activities he had participated in with the Argentine Communist Youth and mentioned that he had been in prison. He expressed very left-wing ideas, saying that instead of belonging to any party, it was better to just be left wing and make the revolution happen. In Gonzalo López Muñoz's office there was a party flag and there was a hat he often wore, one of those given out by the Cuban embassy: olive green, with some black and red.[31] He would wear it even when people came to the office.

A few weeks later I met Alberto, Gonzalo López Muñoz's brother, who never talked about anything and was recently put in charge of the journal because Gonzalo Muñoz was appointed the national director of Information Services for the Bolivian presidency. Then, on January 2, he began to work as editor of the newspaper *La República*. Recently, on February 11 or 12, he resigned. I haven't had anything to do with him for months. I broke off contact on purpose, but I still ran into him every once in a while. According to his brother-in-law, who is married to his sister, he has a plastics business on Evaristo Valle Street, called Plásticos Lor. I went by there the day after—or the same day—he resigned. He remarked that he had resigned because the MPC was trying to take over the newspaper, and he didn't want to be ruled by any party so he resigned. He might still be working for the journal; he always had worked for the journal and he always had worked as a *Visión* correspondent.

Around February of last year Gonzalo López Muñoz's brother, Eduardo Olmedo López, appeared in the office in a very secretive and mysterious way. The name he used as a poet is Olmedo López. He began to use it when he started publishing his first books. First he introduced himself under another name, which I can't recall, but recently, when he felt more relaxed with me, he told me his name. Besides, it seemed like he was interested in me. He also began to tell me who he really was. He used to restrict himself to coming to the office, working and then taking a taxi home, and he didn't let anyone see him outside. In the end, he told me he was half in hiding because he was accused of killing Teresa Siles, who was Siles Zuazo's niece.[32] After this he had left the country and, recently, a few months before the government of Paz Estenssoro was overthrown, he returned. He had been secretary to Paz Estenssoro and also a diplomat in Argentina and Uruguay for some time. Ruth Arrieta,

Eduardo Olmedo López's first wife, is in Cuba with two children by him. He showed me a photo of the children that was taken on 5th Avenue. And the second wife, a Uruguayan, also has a child by him. She is in Uruguay. He is currently married to a woman who is infamous for having had a lot of affairs with heads of government until the time he married her. His family hates her because they say that she is a loose woman. Besides, she has a very bad temper. He has a child with her, who is now two years old. He spent over a year and a half abroad after the problem with Siles Zuazo's niece. According to him, the niece committed suicide. After he returned to the country, he turned himself in to the authorities. He thought he was going to get help and that they were going to let him go free and be in the country under normal conditions because Ciro Humboldt, a government minister, was a close friend of his.[33] On November 4, his brother Alberto López Muñoz helped him escape.[34]

He [Olmedo López] hid in the house of some friends while the court at Oruro decreed that it wasn't homicide but suicide and that he could be out on bail until the Supreme Court in Sucre delivered a verdict. But he had escaped from prison and he could be charged with that. He remained in hiding until he finally began to go out and work for the journal *Esto es*. The dead girl's father began to put pressure on him, asking him for money. He went to the office—he or his son, that is, the brother of the dead girl—and asked him for money and said that if he didn't hand it over they would inform the authorities. He doesn't have any money anymore; it seems that he spent it all during the time he was in exile and on his family because he didn't work throughout that whole period. And then he was detained in April of last year. They took him to the DIC. First he was taken to the DIC cells on Ayacucho Street and from there he was taken to the Panóptico [prison]. It was a very public affair. He had on a vest that he still had from the time he was secretary to Paz Estenssoro, and they took it away from him.

Since then, he [Olmedo López] has been in prison. He was incarcerated for the rest of the time that I dealt with them. He continued to work for the journal *Esto es* from jail. He defends Cuba and has adopted, in some respects, a clearer position than Gonzalo López Muñoz. López Muñoz tried to get me involved with Olmedo López because he wanted him to divorce his wife. That is why he sent me to the Panóptico. I went there quite a few times until, precisely because of this matter related to his wife, I found a reason to break off contact with all of them. Can you understand this? I used exactly that as a pretext. When I stopped going to Gonzalo López Muñoz's office, I said to my friends that he had sent me to see Eduardo Olmedo López and there was trouble with his wife, and that was the reason I stopped going to see him. Of course, on the day that Gonzalo López Muñoz said he was joining the communist party, he went to the Panóptico. He was there when I said to Eduardo, "Look, your brother has joined the PCB. He is crazy." Then Gonzalo López Muñoz told him that he had joined the PCB, but that the people in the party had said that this was a secret. If he was going to stay, then he shouldn't advertise it; instead, he could cooperate with them through the press, publishing articles that they would bring to his attention. Eduardo said that this was stupid, that you can be more useful to the revolution outside rather than inside the party. I managed to break contact with them on May 2.

I went to the office and spoke, first of all, to the *Visión* representative. He recruited me as subscriptions agent, but this was quite difficult work and, above all, I didn't know whether it suited me because it was very public. It involved going to a lot of places, which could be both positive and negative. When Gonzalo López Muñoz arrived, he also made me a subscriptions agent for the *IPE*, which, to a certain degree, was easier because people had already subscribed; it was a question of renewing their subscriptions. For the first subscriptions, of so many—I don't know the amount—they paid me 10 percent, and after a certain point, 20 percent. As, at that time, I did not have a job, I couldn't avoid it and so I did this work for a few weeks and was able to move around. I got access to a lot of places through this subscriptions job. They… Oh! That painter had introduced me to Gonzalo López Muñoz because he wanted to learn German; I gave him a few lessons. But then we couldn't agree on times. In the meantime, I had begun to teach German in private lessons.

Through the newspapers and friends in Gonzalo López Muñoz's office, I also got to know Víctor Sanier, who is the editor in chief of the newspaper *El Mundo* in Cochabamba. He is very closely linked to René Barrientos and was working in the presidency when I met him. But they say that he hasn't been given a post there. He wanted a post as diplomat and they said he didn't get it because the US embassy is opposed to him; he has been labeled a communist or left-winger. He says he spent some time in the PRIN, but he never belonged to the communist party. He traveled for a while through Europe. He was in Czechoslovakia and the GDR. His views are relatively favorable, with ideas both for and against communism. I met Víctor Sanier's brother in Cochabamba. He had studied enginee-ring in Prague for eight years. No, machinery installation. I don't know what he studied. Something like machinery installation. He is currently the head of the telephone company in Cochabamba. Another of Víctor Sanier's brothers was in Cuba during the early years, 1959 or 1960. He had been sent there to study, but he says that he didn't like it and he returned. He is currently studying agriculture in Cochabamba. Víctor Sanier has just gone back to the position of editor at the newspaper *El Mundo*, which came out a month ago in Cochabamba. Through Víctor Sanier I got to know his sister-in-law, who is married to an elder brother, the eldest brother. He is a mining engineer. They are not political. This sister-in-law found me many students from very good families, students of German.

What else? Wait. I want to see whether there was something else regarding Gonzalo López Muñoz. Nothing. So then, in May, I managed to break off contact with them. He often insisted that I stop by. I met his sister, whose name is Colombia. (*Ariel discusses the remark López Muñoz made about Tania being a bit of a spy.*) No, he said that once, but jokingly while he was laughing. They make a lot of jokes of this kind… I think he said it to see whether it was true. Per-haps he imagined it could be possible, but he probably didn't mean it directly, thinking that it was the case, but just wanted to see. It might be possible and that is why he tested me. Who knows? The fact is that he never made any other similar comments after that. What he was after was to get me involved with Eduardo Olmedo López. After that I didn't go there again and I stopped seeing them. Afterward, I saw the sister Colombia a few times. She is married to a Chilean. Oh! This Chilean, in addition to the business of… he also had left-wing politics that he would talk about, but always in a relative way, never adopting a concrete position.

This Carlos Casi Goli, who is married to Colombia López Muñoz, has, in addition to the plastics business, Plásticos Lor, a publishing house—the name of which escapes me right now. He publishes a lot of books covering official government matters for the Ministry of Education, but left-wing people publish some things with his company as well… I can't remember the name of the publishing house. They live at 31 Pasos Canqui Street in… Gonzalo López Muñoz lived on Estados Unidos Street in Miraflores, but I don't recall the number. I went one time to his house and met his wife—who is the niece of the poet Jesús Lara. I have been there once. I saw them a few other times, but he insisted that I go to the office. I had a good excuse when I broke off contact, and it didn't seem artificial. So at any time I could go and see them and talk to them without a problem. They weren't angry; they saw it instead as having something to do with this mess that I was involved in with Eduardo Olmedo López. I went to the Panóptico a few times and his wife got jealous. I did it on purpose so that there would be trouble, although I had to be careful because she is a little dangerous and it could have turned out badly. I got to know the Panóptico well. I met some political prisoners there, such as… Who is the man with the German name, whose brother was a well-known MNR leader? The guy in jail is the one who managed the police academy. Walter Kauner? Wasn't he the boss? The brother, then, the other one, one of the two. One was outside. The other was in prison. One was in exile, right? The other one was in jail. That's the one I met.

I also met the gang that carried out a huge robbery in Calamarca and all of them were prisoners there. The leader was Argentine and there were others there, one from Borcocaina. I don't remember the others' names very well. But I do know the Panóptico from one end to the other. The entrance is completely open. On Thursdays and Sundays there are no problems entering. We just had to say whom we were visiting and we could spend the whole day there. They barely check who takes in a bottle of liquor, and that is just about it. Okay? I have also been inside the DIC. The day that they caught him [Olmedo López], they took all his things from the office. I tried to stay away from it all, but when I could no longer find a way to get out of it, I helped to bring him a mattress. They had taken him to the DIC and had put him in a DIC cell. It was an isolated cell and, in truth, security was so poor that we went right in. With Gonzalo López Muñoz, we went in through the backyard, where there was an iron gate. He opened the chain himself, opened the iron gate, and in there was a group of young men playing volleyball. And Olmedo's cell was behind them, in a corner. We went straight through to the back, without anyone stopping us for security reasons. He was isolated, he was kept alone in there, because they thought he was inside for political motives and they wanted to charge him—although later they couldn't produce any evidence. They thought he was involved with Paz Estenssoro, because he appeared there out of the blue...

(*Ariel asks her about the Bolivian security corps.*) Oh! The DIC matter. Over the past few months the security forces have changed a few times; they have been reorganized. As far as I understand, there is an organization called the National Guard for Public Security, which, I believe, has its main office—in La Paz at least—on Junín Street, opposite Foreign Affairs, where Identification is. The Identification Department, which I haven't been to for a few months, and I don't know if it is still there... Yes, it is, because the *compañero* [Mercy] went there. This National Guard for Public Security is divided into three units: traffic, security, and the DIC, which is the Criminal Investigations Headquarters. According to journalists and press reports in general, prisoners who are very political go directly to the Government Ministry on Arce Street. Some are taken first to the DIC and some also go to a garrison, which is on... Loaiza Street, I think, or Colón Street. One of the streets opposite the hotel called the Noima, Niuma… (*Ariel speaks.*) That's it.

(*Ariel asks about other relations she has.*) Not like those, no. I know them but I am not that familiar with them. The ceramicist visits now and so does Rosario, the lady who has the post office box. On another occasion, when I was in Gonzalo López Muñoz's office, I met some other people, from other parties that went there. Afterward, another time, I was introduced to Lechín outside in the street,[35] just three days before they got him out of the country, but we barely spoke… He, Gonzalo López Muñoz, wanted me to go with him when he was going to do some interviews in Lechín's house, but I always tried to get out of it. Right? It was always a problem. He also wanted to take me to several places like this. (*Ariel talks about the political position she had adopted.*) Always the same. Now, of course, for example, I pretended to be more reactionary there, while with the young people I was anticommunist, but more objective. For example, I said that I had been to Berlin, but that there were good and bad things in Berlin, and it is true; they were right that some things are bad, but that in cultural terms, communists do good things and that the literacy campaign in Cuba is good… I talked about random things like that. But, in general, my position was one of opposition. I laughed at them when they started going on about pro-communist things, but never in an extremely reactionary way.

(*Ariel talks about the students who rent rooms in the same house as Tania.*) Of the three who live in the house, I think so. We have to check it out. (*Ariel talks about Mario.*) No, I think, I think so, but it is very difficult for me to verify it, isn't it? It is difficult, although he lives with them. That's true; in general he doesn't go to the meetings. No, he was sometimes there the whole day when we were seeing each other. He went to classes and then came back. He was at home, but it is difficult to tell. It could be a good cover, but it would be too good, he would have to be congratulated. What else? Not anything particularly strange. (*Ariel asks about other people that she might have known.*) Wait a minute. Now, others like that? Well, I met the director of education… but this one, the man from Lima I met, the Bolivian who lives in Lima, knew I wanted residency. He told me to telephone someone from the Ministry of the Economy, René Pacheco, who was, at that time, the private secretary of the minister of the economy. He gave me the telephone number and everything, but between one thing and another I don't think that he still works there.

Others like that? Well, after this I tried to keep away so I wouldn't create problems for myself, until I could sort things out. I was always writing down who all these people were and everything, and whether they could be useful or not. But I wanted to avoid problems. It was mainly on account of the work matter... They even put a free announcement in the journal for me for translation work and German lessons without adding my name to it. They simply put the office telephone number in the advertisement, but after that I tried to distance myself a little... Afterward, for example, I noticed that the falangists could be helpful. Later, the falangists were very involved in the opposition, so then they weren't worth my time. In the beginning they were. Everyone praised them. So I became involved with them through the lawyer [Vascope Méndez]. I met other falangists. Afterward, he himself said to me one day when I bumped into him, "Listen, do you know what we are up to now? We are armed." He showed me the weapon he had and said, "If ever I have any problems I will go to your house and hide there." I told him, "The problem is that it is not my house. It belongs to someone else." The problem is, he knows very well that the people in my house are very pro-falangist, because they are good friends of Gonzalo Romero, who is the leader of the FSB. And then he wanted to know, perhaps, in this respect... So then I tried to avoid the falangists somewhat. There was a period when they were raiding the houses for falangists and everything.

Well, through the first painter I met, Moisés Chile Barrientos, I met Rosario Sarabia Iturri. She never told me her age because she is an old spinster who doesn't want anyone to know how old she is. She still thinks that someday she will get married. She is from a family that, seemingly, used to have a lot of money, but that isn't the case any longer. That type of family. The family is very bitter and the parents haven't spoken to each other for 15 years. There are serious problems between them. She is very Catholic. She always goes to church, but her ideas are not very clear; she is very prejudiced. For example, when they suggested doing an exhibition (*inaudible*), that is, a traditional fair with the indigenous people, she didn't want to. They would have given her a building to put it in, but she is put out by the indigenous... On the other hand, she is Luis Raúl Duran's very good friend—perhaps lover, I don't know as she is very reserved about this; she never tells me private things, making it seem as if she has nothing and no one. Through him, I got to know a number of people who say that they have been in socialist countries and so she is influenced by some left-wing ideas. Although she has never spoken directly in support of Cuba, she has some left-wing politics.

Her [Rosario Sarabia's] sister is quite reactionary but she was the girlfriend of a man who was once at a meeting with some friends that... if he is not a communist party activist, his ideas and his politics are very left wing... (*Ariel asks for his name.*) I don't know. I have only seen him once and I wasn't able to ask. He is the sister's boyfriend. And her other sister, the one who has a child, is divorced and lives with her child in the same house. She works for the army. I think she is an office worker or has a job in a workshop because once she said that they have a lot of leather goods there and that she could get leather boots. So it might also be that she has a job in the storehouse or something like that, but it is something with the army. Well, this Rosario Sarabia does some little paintings with cloth and straw and silver and things like that, and she sells them at exhibitions. Although she didn't go herself, her paintings were exhibited in Czechoslovakia and the United States.

I became friends with her and often went to her house. I told her that I had a friend who had to write to me at her house because he was married. But I don't trust her completely and I want to try to get another address for mail because hers is not safe. Until now I haven't been able to test it. Besides, she is a very mixed-up kind of person: she has left-wing politics, but also right-wing as well. She is like that—she doesn't know what she wants. It turns out, according to what I was told recently, that she tried to get a scholarship or something like that, a trip to an exhibition here in Mexico. I think it was in Mexico. But they didn't want to award it to her. Yolanda Rivas told me—I will talk about her later—that the United Nations Educational, Scientific, and Cultural Organization (UNESCO) told Rosario Sarabia that they didn't want to give her the scholarship because she was too involved with communists and had very left-wing ideas.

In the middle of last year I went to a conference at the university and I was introduced to Yolanda Rivas there. She is one of the best ceramicists in Bolivia and I had heard about her but no one had introduced me to her. When she found out I was teaching German, she asked me to give German lessons to her nephews. I said that in exchange for the lessons I would like to work in her workshop and be taught ceramics by her. I became friends with her and shortly afterward I found out that her husband was Czech, that he had left Czechoslovakia about five years earlier. He is a geology professor; he finished his studies and graduated in Czechoslovakia. She won a scholarship from a contest in Bolivia that paid for her to study ceramics in Czechoslovakia for three years. She only spent a year and a half there and during this time she completed her studies and left. She says that she didn't like it much, but she has objective opinions on certain things such as culture: she says it is not true that there is no freedom. She says there is quite a lot of freedom, although in general she is anticommunist in her views.

Yolanda Rivas's brother is also a geology professor at the university. His name is Rivas. I don't remember his full name. He is married to a Bolivian woman. He spent a number of years studying in Nuremberg or Munich. Also, while she was in Europe, she was married to a Bolivian artist who turned out to be homosexual; she separated from him and stopped living with him. She was still married when she was in Czechoslovakia. That is where she met Plosconca, the Czech professor—he is an engineer—but she wasn't in a serious relationship with him yet. When she left and returned to Bolivia, he, according to what she told me, managed to leave the country after a whole lot of paperwork, because he has a Uruguayan passport, as he was born in Uruguay. His parents were in Uruguay and then they returned to Czechoslovakia after the war. His family still lives in Czechoslovakia. He gets letters and packages from them. They say that he wants to bring his mother to Bolivia, but he needs $3,000 to do this and if this amount isn't paid then they won't let her leave Czechoslovakia. He left Czechoslovakia without any money and went to West Germany, where he met up with her sister, and later he went to Uruguay. In Uruguay he couldn't find any work as a geology professor, and he traveled to Bolivia—where he started off working in the mines—and then he married Yolanda Rivas. She also spent some time with him in the mines. He is currently a geology professor in the university.

I have become quite friendly with Yolanda Rivas because she is more open. I can talk to her more openly, not like Rosario Sarabia, who is more complicated. Also, I saw an opportunity in the ceramics work and I began to go to her house often, and I could go to the workshop at any time of the day to work on ceramics. We have recently set up the Bolivian Association of Ceramicists, of which I am a founding member. I am also a representative of the association. In different countries I make contacts in order to have exchanges between the Bolivian Association of Ceramicists and, say, the one here [Mexico]. It didn't exist in Bolivia until now, and everyone used to work alone on his or her own projects, and there were problems. For example, once the US embassy contacted the wife of a very good painter from there. She is Inés de Córdoba, also a very good ceramicist. But when they contacted her and said that she could exhibit in the United States, she said that she had no items to display, and that she was the only ceramicist. Since then, there have been fights and they said that in order to avoid this kind of problem in the future we should create an association of ceramicists. The truth is that this association was set up just recently, only a few weeks ago. I brought some papers that describe our purpose, etc.

They have the association's letterhead, and I personally sent them to the printer.

They—Yolanda Rivas and her husband—live at 795 Antonio Díaz Villamil Street, in San Pedro. The house belongs to her mother, or really, to all of them. It is a three-story house and has a lot of rooms. Her sister, who is divorced and has three children, also lives in the house. She works in the Ministry of Employment. Her mother travels a lot. Before, they had a lot of mines but, according to what she told me, the father often got drunk and spent the money. Now they don't have much money and they even have debts. They have a plot of land in Calacoto. This land has a modest house. I asked for the keys thinking that perhaps one day we might need to use the house in one way or another. And as I had a boyfriend—who is my husband right now—I always asked for the keys. I have used the house for the *compañero* [Mercy] and myself on a couple of occasions. The conditions aren't the best because there are a lot of diplomats in the area, and it is on a piece of land with nothing else. It is at the end of Calacoto, and just opposite is a house where the gardener lives; he has the keys to the little house so that he can look after it. So he always knows whom I am going into the house with. But in any case, it was useful for us on a couple of occasions to be able to speak at ease. I have the keys with me now because I brought them along without realizing it (*Tania laughs*) and I wrote to her to say that the gardener has the other keys. It is a simple, makeshift house, just to use for the time being.

In reality, she is my closest friend. I have less contact with her husband. I go to her house. I can go there whenever I feel like it. I eat there. I work there in the workshop. I teach German to their nephews. She was a witness at my wedding. We got married in her house and I confided in her all that stuff about my boyfriend and other things. My belongings are currently in her house. But I really need to have more information, above all, about him [Yolanda's husband] to see whether I should keep a distance or whether everything is okay. She has a post office box that could be used in his plans.[36] This [the post office box] could be used to send me

mail, open mailings like magazines with something. To this post
office box... Now, what cannot be sent to this post office box... It
could be things that have to do with folklore, archaeology, culture
in general, but not ceramics, because if ceramics material is sent,
well, the Bolivian Association of Ceramicists could be using this
post office box too. Then they will want to keep the magazine for
themselves, and getting it back, or tearing out some pages from it,
will be a mess. So they have to be different things. I also explain
that in there.

Regarding the people from the house that I used to live in,
Rosario Sarabia is very complicated. I am sure that they are a little
angry with me right now because I left without saying good-bye.
She is one of those bourgeois women, very old-fashioned. You have
to excuse yourself and arrive on time and when you arrive late
she gets angry. These very complicated people have to be spoken
to very carefully so that they don't get angry. On the other hand
there is Yolanda, who is quite the opposite, and who also shares
my opinion of Rosario. The one who knows about my problems,
for example, in my relationships, my private problems, is Yolanda
Rivas... Also Rosario, but Rosario doesn't know that I got married.
Yolanda Rivas, and nobody else, knows this.

(*Ariel asks a question.*) Wait a minute. Let me think about it. Well,
through the lawyer Vascope Méndez, the falangist lawyer, I first
met a cousin by marriage, or, in other words, the woman married
to his cousin, Armando Vascope, who was an MNR leader and
the head of a telephone company. When Paz Estenssoro fell from
power he, Vascope himself, the falangist, put his cousin in a car and
took him to the Mexican embassy for asylum. He told him to seek
asylum there (*she laughs*); he himself exiled him. Vascope was in Cochabamba and, with a group of falangists, he caused a commotion
in Cochabamba. The first thing he did when he got back to La Paz
was to put his cousin in a car and take him to the Mexican embassy
because, well, he is a relative; that's why he took him.

The other one, Rita de Vascope, was still in La Paz. When I met
her, she wanted to be friends with me; she was looking for support.

She is a 26-year-old woman. She has four children from her first marriage and three to him: seven children. She is very attractive and she began to ask for my advice because she has a crush on the Mexican Juan Manuel Ramírez.[37] Then she told me that for three years her husband Vascope didn't sleep at home. He had a mistress with whom he had another child, and everything was a big problem like this. This girl, this woman, was there with her seven children until she finally asked for a passport to leave and she ran up against problems. I get the impression that at one point Vascope tried to steal my passport for her to use; all the signs were there. There was a trip abroad that they wanted me to go on and I think he said something to her. And, besides, once he studied my passport in detail. It seems to be true that the FSB has a strong network for all of these things, for falsifying everything. It is well known that the falangist network has documents and it can get anything at all. It looked like he wanted to take it from me. It seemed that way because of several signs that were there. Well, I never saw her again. Ever. I tried to avoid her because it was logical to suppose that they were keeping an eye on her and I think they have checked me out, but only in relation to my contacts with her. It makes sense that they watch her because she has traveled; she traveled abroad once and returned…

(*Ariel asks her if she has ever discovered that she was under surveillance at any point.*) When I was with Olmedo López and when I was with her, I noticed something, but together with them, not alone, at that time. Besides, it had to do with them and that is why I attempted to break off contact, but I immediately tried to develop links with the falangists to see… Besides, I was Vascope's friend, not hers. They knew Juan Manuel Ramírez from the Mexican embassy very well because he had granted asylum to the cousin. They went out a lot together, although he often criticized him to his face, saying, "You are Franco's falangists; you are reactionary." Then when he drank a little, and the other one too, he answered, "No, I am against Franco and I do not agree with Spain; it is a dictatorship and we are democratic revolutionary falangists." (*She laughs.*) At some meetings the falangist spoke up... For example, he said, when they were talking about exactly that, he said, and it's true that we acknowledge things... For example, he said to the other person, the Mexican, "You, you who support the Russians so much—it is true that they have some good things. I have seen some Soviet magazines and what I most admire are their morals and their treatment of women. I think that in the socialist countries"—this is what the falangist said—"education and many other things are better than in capitalist countries..." He had opinions like this!

The Mexican wanted to have a relationship with me. He wanted me to go... He invited me to his home, which is next to the consulate offices, in the Guerrero building, on Mercado Street. The building they live in at the moment is the main residence because the ambassador is not there. He is the chargé d'affaires and was in... This is the place where the former ambassador lived, beside the Ministry of Defense in Baroa Square. I went there a few times and taped his records of the *Misa Criolla* (Creole Mass).[38] We talked a lot. He made advances toward me but realized that I wasn't interested in him, that there was someone else. I made up a story and he left me alone; he talked to me and that was all. The last time I saw him... No, afterward I saw him; he moved when the ambassador arrived. He moved into a house on Estados Unidos Street, in Miraflores. I went to his house for a small party and after that I went to the embassy just to say good-bye to him. That was where he introduced me to the new ambassador. The new ambassador took me home in his car and... who knows what his name is. He is a journalist or a writer, I don't know, and I said good-bye to him and I asked him what he was going to do...

I went to the consulate quite a few times. Once I left there with a bottle of whiskey; I would be given some books and things like that. But, generally speaking, I didn't go there on purpose. I tried to avoid the Mexican embassy and the last thing he said as he was leaving was, "I am going because the altitude is bad for me and I am happy because I have been told to go to Cuba." He had told me that he had been to Cuba a number of times and he spoke to me about Cuban women. (*Ariel talks.*) What? He should go there and be happy there. I asked him if he was afraid of traveling behind the Iron Curtain, about being behind it, and what they might do to him, and so on. But he was happy and very positive about it. Generally, when we weren't in an official setting, he was very supportive of Cuba and showed me music records and journals from Cuba, saying that these were from the time when democracy still existed in Bolivia, when there were relations, etc. He was friends with a very reactionary man, the ambassador for Paraguay, Do Santos or Santos, something like that, whom I also know in La Paz. An old man. He is older than this one and a drunkard too. This one is also a drunkard but the Paraguayan is more of a drunkard than the Mexican. Well, in the Mexican embassy, I didn't know the ambassador very well because he had just arrived. However, I know a young man who is around 20 years old, whom they call a chancellor but he works on consulate affairs. I can't recall his name, but I know him quite well.

What was I talking about? (*Ariel speaks.*) I was just about to say something, *che.* Oh! What I wanted to say is that in the Ministry of Education, besides Julia Elena Fortín, I also met those who work in anthropology and just a short time ago, before traveling to the interior of the country, I asked some of them if they had any friends there I could approach. When I talked to one of the secretaries, I don't remember his name, but he was tall and slim. I think he is one of her secretaries, works directly with her, a young man who is from Beni… When I asked for some details… I don't know what date. I wanted to see if the person that he knew is in Beni, just in case I go to Beni… He took out a card. A UJC card with Che on it.[39] This secretary then approached me. I looked at it like this. What a card! It wasn't a card. It was one of these calendar things, a desk calendar, and on the other side it said, "Viva Cuba! Communist Youth Federation of Bolivia."

So then someone who had come with me asked the question, "Are you one of those?" And he replied, "Yes, we are the best." He said something like that, I don't know exactly, and then he put it away. The other one wanted to keep the calendar. He spoke to me about a professor in Beni. I didn't make note of it. (*Ariel asks if this had been done on purpose.*) No, judging by the way it happened, I don't think so. There is someone that I have worked with the most at the ministry, whom you have to be careful with: Hugo Ruiz. When I arrived he was in one of the departments there, doing a very simple job recording folk music. Afterward, he was sent on a trip, and he was in charge of the Cevallos Museum... He came here, to Mexico, on work-related matters. So this Hugo Ruiz was left in charge of the museum. He is a strange type and it just might be the case that they have placed him in the ministry for security reasons; that is possible. That is how he comes across to me. He also attended a course from Program 208, on rural development, etc. Sometimes he said he was a falangist but he had a strange look. He asked me some weird things. I have done a lot of recordings in the city with him and in the high plains, recording and compiling information. I also know the general director of education, who is the former head of the University of Santa Cruz; his name is Sanabria. After him I also got to know some others, for example, López Sánchez from the National Tourism Office. Generally speaking, it is the people from the National Tourism Office that I know well.

I have pupils from Calacoto among my German-language students. I got them partly through *El Diario,* and also through Víctor Sanier's sister-in-law. One of them... Well, I don't think I have them anymore. I have left them. Maybe they have found another teacher by now. I gave lessons twice a week, three times a week to one boy, sometimes to three of them. One was from the González family; I am not really friends with them. The boy's father is an engineering professor. I think that he is the head of the engineering college in La Paz. The Encina family is another one. He is living in Songo because he is an electrical engineer at the Power.[40] And other students are part of the Granado family. He is the boss of an international funding company with headquarters in Switzerland. Then the other students I had: one was a Bolivian, named Palsa, an architect. I taught two sons of a woman from the United States who has some businesses where Seis de Agosto Street begins. She is quite closely linked with the US embassy. I developed a friendship with her. We are close enough, but I have never asked her any questions. Just recently she has opened a cake shop in the same building, because in their building there are some shops on the ground floor, and he works with the Four Point Program.[41] They have six children, all of them young, three boys and three girls. I have given German lessons to two of the boys. Other students… I don't think they are very important.

On one of my trips to Calacoto, while talking to someone on the bus, on the *góndolas*,[42] about German lessons, someone from the United States turned around who spoke Spanish with a US accent. At that point he was wearing a uniform and he asked me about the German lessons, as if it was something he was really interested in. And, of course, he also began to flirt with me a little. He talked during the whole trip and asked for my telephone number so that he could call me at home. I gave him the number and he didn't call. I didn't see him again and then, a few weeks later, he bumped into me in the Prado. He invited me to have a drink with him. On that day he was dressed partly as a civilian, but with a suit, I think, that was military. That was precisely when there was all that trouble in May, or a little after the problems in May.[43] So we had something to drink. He had a very nice folder with him, a plastic one. I asked if he could get me one like it. I told him that I thought it was very nice and that in Bolivia there were none like it. He showed it to me and it had an FBI inscription on it; inside it were a series of paper sheets with Spanish typewriting on them and I asked him if he belonged to the Peace Corps. He said no, that he was from the "war corps" and that he had previously been in different countries, first in Japan or Vietnam, but as a soldier. He had trouble because he wanted to marry a woman from the place and that was why they took him out of there and suspended him. After that he said he was in his country's embassy in France and in the embassy in Moscow and some other country. He said he could speak a little Russian. He had learned Spanish when he was a child in New Mexico.

His name is Álvaro Cristian, and he is between 28 and 30 years old. He is tall, slim, wears glasses, and is ugly. He has a horrible face. He really tried to... I don't know. He continued to say that he was still interested in German lessons, but he also made it clear that what he wanted was to take me out, to be romantic with me, but he didn't call. I only ran into him on a few occasions, on public transportation, on the same route, and it was always sometime before 3 p.m., and at 3 p.m. on the dot he had to be in the Calacoto Officers Military Academy. It is the only school of its kind in Calacoto. No, the police academy that's in Següencoma is before you get to Calacoto; it is the one that belongs to the army. He told me that he teaches classes there. After that I bumped into him on a few occasions. I told him that I was traveling to the interior of the country to do research in Beni and some other places. Once I bumped into him in the street and he invited me to have a drink with him and he said, "Oh! I have to rush off now because our boss just passed by and if he sees me here I'll be in trouble because at such and such an hour we always have to be on our way back to Calacoto, where we are living. If I have to, I could sleep here in La Paz, but it isn't right and then they won't let me leave Calacoto for two or three days."

Through Rosario Sarabia Iturri, I met the lawyer Erdulfo Val de Escobar, who is a Spanish teacher in the school of administration and commerce on the corner of Aspaciu and 20 de Octubre streets, and he has an office on Ayacucho Street. He has been in the United States several times, for a few months each time, attending courses— which he didn't elaborate on—and he has also been in Mexico. He was there just recently and he went back again a short time ago for matters related to the OAS. On the day I met him, he showed me slides from the trip he had been on, and just recently when he returned, he also wanted to show us slides from his trip. He is an irritating man who is always after women but in a way that is very low-key. He called me a couple of times at the beginning of last year, when I met him, and after that I saw him only occasionally.

Alfonso Vascope Méndez, the falangist lawyer, was first working in the Ministry of Public Works as a legal advisor and now he is a consultant in the National Road Service at 1829 20 de Octubre Street.

I see him, but I try to avoid it… I haven't seen him much over the past few months, only by coincidence in the street. He always asks how my research is progressing, how I am, and whether I have any problems. He is always very polite; he's the one who sorted out my residency in Bolivia.

In Cochabamba I also met Carlos Bekar, the editor of the newspaper *Prensa Libre*. *Prensa Libre* belonged to the MNR in Cochabamba. He is also acquainted with the same falangists in Cochabamba that I know, but his politics are left wing. He says that Gonzalo López Muñoz is shameless, that he is a revolutionary only because he is a snob and that in reality he does nothing, and that you have to be careful where he is concerned. He was astonished by the fact that although I know people like him, my politics were even more right wing and that I was opposed to Cuba. He generally supports Cuba and, at least for the time being, it seems he does not belong to any of the MNR groups, or at least to the new MNR group led by Andrade, which had its last meeting precisely during those days when I was in Cochabamba at the end of January or the beginning of February.[44] He did not go to the MNR conference held at the end of January under the Andrade faction's leadership. He had been invited, but he did not attend this conference or many of the meetings and neither did he publish anything in his newspaper for them. This guy from *Prensa Libre* is thinking about going to work in Miami, as he may have a contract to work there at a newspaper; he says he has no hope of going further in Bolivia because he is already the editor of *Prensa Libre* and it is difficult to go higher than this unless you get a post like the one Gonzalo López Muñoz has, but he sold out to the army, etc.

The former staff of the newspaper *El Mundo*, edited by Víctor Sanier in Cochabamba, now publishes the newspaper *Extra*, managed, among others, by Canela; one of his brothers works at Prensa Latina in Bolivia.[45] At this point he is in Cuba, or someone from the staff is. At least the editor of *Extra* was not in Cochabamba at that time; he was in Cuba. I am not sure if Canela was, or someone else. They told me about this because I went there to sort out some things on behalf of Yolanda Rivas. She needed some information that had been published in Cochabamba about her exhibition. That is why I went to the editorial department, first in *Extra*… In *Extra*, oh, they told me that the editor wasn't there and I spoke to someone else who may have been Canela, or maybe not. I don't know his name. He told me to come back the following day because he didn't have the information at hand.

Then I went to the *Prensa Libre* office. Once there I discovered that the editor was Carlos Bekar. I knew him because he was a very good friend of Vascope's, although he is against the falangists, but they had gone to school together. When I told him I had been in the office of *Extra*, Bekar said, "Oh, maybe the situation is not that good, because the editor of *Extra* is in Cuba and the editor's brother is working at Prensa Latina." I asked him, "What is Prensa Latina?" He asked me how it is that I don't know about Prensa Latina if I worked with Gonzalo López Muñoz, that Prensa Latina is in the La Paz hotel, so on and so forth, etc. Right? The *Extra* staff once worked for *El Mundo*, but when they had problems with Víctor Sanier, they left *El Mundo*. And the newspaper stopped being published. They formed a cooperative that published *Extra* in Cochabamba. And so I was told that the editor was… In January he went to the Tricontinental Conference, etc.[46] Well, that was Carlos Bekar. I have already explained about Víctor Sanier, about Cochabamba, and about Víctor Sanier's family.

I know someone from the university, Julio Mendoza López, who is secretary in the rectory, and who also works at *Extra*. He was getting me in touch with… He had prepared a program of folklore studies for me in Cochabamba, in connection with those on the research committee who study folklore. He is part of the Cochabamba Folklore Committee, which is not doing anything at all; it was established a short time ago. I also met other ceramicists like Jorge Medina y Medina, who recently taught a ceramics course organized by the municipality.

In terms of work, expenses incurred, and what my life was like there: in the afternoons I gave German lessons almost every day, from 2 to 8 p.m. I went to my students' homes and earned between 800 and 900 pesos a month.[47] I could quite easily and very naturally drop the lessons or change the times, etc. This kind of work left me with a lot of freedom. In general, I would go to the ministry in the mornings, and I have been out a lot with Hugo Ruiz to research folklore. It was impossible to do much research during the state of emergency; it was very difficult and very risky to make recordings, especially because the markets are in the highest part of the city, which is exactly where the strikers are entrenched, etc. There was gunfire; for a period of several weeks it wasn't a good idea to go to these places.

Oh! Wait a minute. My trip out of the country. I decided to leave via Santa Cruz because if I had left as I was told to, via Chile, I would have had to ask for the exit permit in La Paz to leave directly from there. Then it would have been more difficult to sort out the trouble if I had to present my passport and identity card. I traveled with my husband to Santa Cruz, and in Santa Cruz I didn't have to show my identity card, just my passport. If they had asked for my card I could have said, "As I am traveling abroad I kept my card at home." In Santa Cruz, they gave my ticket to me with no problem as it had been paid for in Brazil by the *compañero* who had sent me a telegram saying, "We want you to come here quickly as a translator." They did not give me the telegram, even though I went to the post office. I think they lost it, and that's why they didn't give it to me. (*Ariel talks.*) To get the ticket that was at the agency, I went with my husband. I went to the São Paulo post office and they said they had sent the telegram, and I myself went to the Santa Cruz post office where they keep all the telegrams and I searched them together with my husband and we didn't find it. Let's see if they send it. It's better if they did take it; it said right there that they wanted me as a translator and everything…

Well, then, a day before I left, around noon or in the afternoon, I went to the Foreign Affairs Department. There, the police and Immigration are in the same place. You have to go to two places in La Paz, first to Immigration and then to the police, where you tell them you are leaving so they stamp your papers. In Santa Cruz, you have to go to one office. I went and my husband explained that I had to work abroad as a translator and that I had to go because they had already sent me the ticket and I needed a visa because I was to leave on the following day. The guy said, "So fast? First we need to send a telegram to La Paz." Then he wrote the telegram himself and sent me to the post office across the street to pay for the telegram. So, there, you can send the telegram yourself. I could have chosen not to send it, but I did. But then I said to him, "I need this straightaway because I am leaving tomorrow and I can't wait. Please, imagine my situation." He said, "If there is a problem, I'll sort it out for you." Five minutes away, opposite the post office, is the police station. I went back and right then and there he sorted everything out. He stamped it and the only thing he said to me at the end was, "That will be 20 pesos." The truth is that they shouldn't charge anything; no doubt those 20 pesos were for him. But I needed it, so I asked, "How much is it?" and he replied, "It's 20 pesos."

(*Ariel speaks, inaudible.*) The cable says, "Laura Gutiérrez is on a tourist trip to Brazil." I said that I was going to work, but he said that it was better this way because, really, it was like a tourist trip. "Laura Gutiérrez is traveling as a tourist to Brazil," is what it said. But there and then he gave it to me and I didn't go back to the police after that. Do you know? That day I was waiting to see whether anyone turned up, and the following day I flew out. My husband went at noon. He really did give it to me in 10 minutes, without asking for the identity card. They asked for my passport, they stamped it and gave me an exit permit, and that was it. I left without any problems. At first this trip was only to Corumbá, because they said there was no room. Then there was space and so I flew to São Paulo without any problems. That is where I met up with the *compañero*.

On the trip... And why have you mixed everything up? I had some things separately arranged there. Oh! During the flight...

Well, when I was in Brazil, we tried first of all to find a house, first in São Paulo, and then we realized that it was more economical and convenient to be in Santos; we could be in a comfortable house on the beach at Santos without drawing attention to ourselves. I was in the same hotel as him in Yantana. He was my uncle there, in that hotel. What a niece! In the house at Santos they thought we were married, but they never asked any questions. We got the place through the newspaper; we paid for it in São Paulo and from there we went to Santos. In São Paulo, they gave us the key of a beach apartment and we spent a month there. I decided to travel to Montevideo so that I could justify a trip to Buenos Aires, from the point of view of both the authorities and my friends. Right? I could write and tell them that I went to Buenos Aires, and they wouldn't know that I had been in Montevideo. That way it is very easy to go to Buenos Aires.[48]

Right now, the flight... Well, I asked about this because the *compañero* said that I would have to take a lot of lessons and so on. When I told him that I had to make a trip to Montevideo, I explained why, and he said that it was nonsense on my part. I thought that this was best: I could enter Montevideo with my identity card, and then I could say whenever I liked that I had been to Argentina. That was what the money was for. You can see that, because the trip to Montevideo cost another $200. Do you know what a trip there costs—$80. Okay? So then I flew to Montevideo and during the flight I met a German who was sitting by me. His name was Hans Arthur Von... something... I didn't understand the other last name. The Von part means he is from the nobility. First he spoke to me in Spanish and then we spoke in German. He left in 1950, something like that, 1950 or 1952. During those years he left the GDR, and he is in Brazil now. He has a coffee plantation in Londrina; he can be reached at PO Box 166... Well, he is totally reactionary in his politics. He probably is in contact with one of the many Nazi groups in Brazil. He was on his way to Uruguay, so that in Uruguay he could head for a place in the interior of Montevideo that is on the border with Argentina. He belongs to a family from the nobility from the northern part of the GDR. They had land there that was taken from them when the cooperatives were set up. He managed to leave the GDR and he is with his family in Brazil... (*Ariel talks.*)

No, he talked about the problems in Germany and his departure from the GDR, what he went through there, how they took his land, that he belonged to the nobility and the problems he had because of this, and other things. No, it is very likely that he is in touch with Nazi groups. No, I told him about myself, that I am in Bolivia. He was also interested in the state of the German schools in Bolivia. He has friends who want to send their children there because it is less expensive. I told him that I would find out if boarding schools exist and that I would let him know. That could be of interest to others. Well, at least to the Germans. It is very likely that he is linked to the Nazi groups there.

I stayed in the California hotel in Montevideo. I checked out things to do with ceramics as well. I got in touch with a cultural center in the city. Two days after my arrival at the hotel, I got to talking to a young man who works at the reception desk. He showed an interest in me, and we chatted and went out. We went to the television lounge in the hotel. He said he was very tired, that he had a lot of work. I asked what he did, whether he was only employed in the office... I am looking for his address... Well, I asked him. He said that in addition to working at the reception desk—and that this job was a break for him—he did something else of a very special nature. I continued to talk to him. I told him about my work as a ceramicist and how interested I was to make contact with a ceramicist in Uruguay on behalf of the Bolivan Association of Ceramicists. He told me, after we had built up some degree of trust between us, that he worked for the Special Police. I asked him what the Special Police did. He told me that some worked on the political situation and that his work was in relation to contraband. Although he didn't give me any more details in reference to this, he said that this was the reason he had problems with his family. They didn't like him working for the police.

I went out with him a few times and he told me that his job was dangerous and exhausting. He had a lot of female *compañeras* and they were the most agile, particularly in their judo and karate classes... He showed me some exercises that they make them do with their hands in karate, etc. Apart from that, he also told me about the problems within the Uruguayan government. He said that there were a lot of government members who were involved in smuggling and that it was all linked to political problems and that it was very difficult for them to act against those involved in contraband… His name is Julio César Olivera, and he lives at 225 Guaná Street, Apartment 5. He works from 2 p.m. until 10 p.m. in the California hotel… Switch off the recorder for a moment while I think about something… The hotel salary is between 400 and 500 pesos, but he says that in the police he earns some 800 or 1,000 Uruguayan pesos, and he works there four times a week in the mornings. He is 20 years old. When he was 18, first he traveled to Brazil and then he traveled onward to see whether he could find a better situation; after that he returned to Uruguay. He says that they wanted to recruit him as an "anti-Castro guerrilla." Something strange about him is that he uses a swear word that is not normally used in the southern countries; he says *coño*,[49] which caught my attention. People, particularly Uruguayans from Montevideo… He speaks like everybody else, but specifically uses this word.

What else? I have seen Zamora,[50] but I don't know whether he recognized me. I don't think so. I saw him once in the Pedaiquir restaurant during the first few days after I arrived in Bolivia, shortly before Christmas. He sat down at the table next to mine with some other student leaders, but I don't think he saw me or recognized me. After that I saw him once more in the street. Recently, over the Christmas and New Year's period, I saw him again in the street, close to the *El Diario* office. He was talking to other people, and I passed right by him. I saw him at the very last moment but I don't think he noticed me. He didn't show any sign of having seen me.

(*Ariel asks a question.*) I can give you very little information in relation to the parties because lately I have tried to keep away, to be as uninvolved as possible in these matters, waiting for contact to be made so that I can show an interest in these things and these problems. Last year, around April or May, Gonzalo López Muñoz wrote an article for his weekly publication that[51]—according to what he was given to believe—was an instruction to him by communists from the line with which he was affiliated, the Moscow Line. He included information in it. The old communist party, the original, is still led by Monje,[52] while the other faction is led by Zamora and others. The office is on… No, there it is, where Gonzalo López Muñoz's office is, on Juan de la Riva Street. In this weekly publication, they included the exact address and so on; they wrote, "We know that Zamora has been in Prague, working in the International Student Union, and that he is very closely linked to Czechoslovakia." It was written in a style that was a little insidious, on purpose, but this group belongs to the Peking Line and they have some arguments to make, but we will have to see.

(*Ariel asks a question.*) Well, I don't remember very well, but I think that he said that he did it because the other party told him to oppose it. The matter of the secretary of the party on Ayacucho Street… I don't know when that was. They raided it and I think they closed it down, but it continued to operate afterward. I don't know if it is still there opposite the Escala. There was a government communiqué saying they had raided it and closed it down, because they had found detailed notes recording the times that the president passed by the front of the building in his car… on Ayacucho Street, right in front of them. They accused them of planning an attack on the president. We didn't hear much about the party in the last few weeks of January. There were a number of notices, statements in the newspapers, in *El Diario*, in… (*inaudible*). Different remarks were made about different parties. When they wrote about the falangists and the communists, they called them the best organized but said that the communist party, on account of the split, appeared to be more focused on fighting among themselves than on carrying out any activities. That is what was said in *El Diario*, in the official press, but then, in January and February, something else was said…

Apart from the usual university matters, some meetings were held to celebrate the anniversary… I don't know what they celebrated. I was in Cochabamba. I think they celebrated the anniversary of the communist party, using the cinema…[53] The cinema that is at the

end of Comercio Street, the Roíz, I think it is at the end... There is
the Princesa and then, at the end, the Roxi, at the end of Comercio
Street. That's where a party meeting was held. I think that it was
Monje's people. During that period a lot of big and small posters
came out with the slogan, "Viva such and such anniversary of the
party."

During the period that I was in contact with the falangists, they
were in a very strong position. They were obtaining a lot of posts
in the ministries, in public administration, etc. But after that they
grew closer to the opposition, and they had more difficulties and
more internal problems. Now they don't operate the way they did
in the first few months...[54]

(*End of report.*)

DOCUMENT DENYING TANIA'S LINKS
TO THE STASI

Official communication sent to Nadia Bunke's lawyer by the federal commissioner for state security documents of the former GDR denying Tania's link with the Stasi.

Federal commissioner for state security documents of the former GDR

BstU. Postfach
218 . 10106 Berlin
Attorney's Office
Ulrich Dost
18 Edison Street
12459 Berlin

Reference Code   Berlin
AUI.5.03-026510/97 Z
October 17, 1997

Use of personal documents from the state security services of the former GDR.
    Request dated 28/07/1997
    Sender: Nadziega [Nadia] Bunke

Dear Sir,

The inquiries in the files of the central documents office and foreign documents office in Berlin have revealed that there is no indication of documents belonging to the daughter of the sender. Nevertheless, in documents belonging to third parties, the name of Tamara Bunke is mentioned.

In these cases the documents are: Mfs Gh 99/78.

According to Article 3, Section 3, related to Articles 12 of the state security documents, you may have access only to that part of the documents which contains information on the sender's daughter. These documents include a total of 10 pages. If you wish, they can be sent to you.

In the copies, according to Article 3 of the law on state security documents, the names that relate to personal information to people referred to and to third parties, are blacked out in order to respect the anonymity of these persons, preserving their right to protection. All the information relevant to Tamara Bunke and related to her will remain visible on the documents.

I would like to point out that this information refers to the state security documents researched to date. Nonetheless, we cannot exclude the possibility that future research may uncover documents about your daughter.

On account of the vast amount of requests still pending, I am sorry I am not able to provide information in each case on new documents found. You can contact me again within two years to extend the research, which will continue uninterrupted until then. Please communicate with us using reference code at the head of this letter.

I ask you to refrain from making further requests until then.

Yours sincerely,
Manager, Swick
Documents
Mfs Gh 99/78 (10 pp)

DOCUMENT DENYING TANIA'S LINKS
TO THE KGB

Report by the chief of the press office of the Russian Federation Foreign Intelligence Service denying links between Tania and the KGB.

Foreign Intelligence Service
Russian Federation
Press Office
Moscow 119034   Tel. 247-19-38
Osteshenka, 51/10   Fax. 247-05-29

Dear Mrs. Bunke:

In accordance with current international practice, we do not comment on matters relating to whether a person or persons belongs to the Soviet/Russian intelligence service.

However, taking into account that this case relates to your beloved daughter, who unfortunately cannot defend herself, we assure you that the Foreign Intelligence Service holds no materials or documents that confirm the report that Tamara Bunke collaborated with the KGB Foreign Intelligence Service.

Very respectfully,

(Signed)
I.G. Kobaladse
Head of the Press Office
Russian Federation Foreign Intelligence Service
December 5, 1997

DOCUMENT DENYING TANIA'S LINKS
TO SOVIET INTELLIGENCE

Handwritten note given to Nadia Bunke by the former lieutenant general and head of KGB operations in the Americas, N.S. Leonov, stating that Tania had no links with Soviet intelligence.

I, Nikolai Sergueievich Leonov, resident of Moscow, 15 Chéjov Street, Apartment 24, lieutenant general in Soviet intelligence, standing in for the PGU[1] director, in charge of work on the continent of the Americas, certify that our intelligence service had no relationship with Tamara Bunke (Tania) linked to Che Guevara. All presumptions in this respect are defamatory and aim to disgrace the memory of Tamara Bunke and discredit Soviet and West German intelligence services.

N.S. Leonov
December 12, 1997
Moscow

MY BATTLE FOR TRUTH:
AN INTERVIEW WITH NADIA BUNKE

Interview by Christoph Wiesner, published in Junge Welt,
March 7-8, 1998.

Junge Welt: In September 1997, [German publisher] Aufbau Verlag published a new book on Tania. What are your objections to the book by the Uruguayan writer José A. Friedl Zapata?

Nadia Bunke: A series of errors stand out in the book, denigrations of the worst kind and obvious falsehoods. The author's main thesis is that Tania must have been an unscrupulous triple agent, that Tania must have been in the service of Cuban espionage and GDR security services, as well as those of the Soviet Union.

The GDR security services do not hold any document under the name of Tamara Bunke. Nevertheless, her name is mentioned on at least two occasions by Günter Männel, a former officer in the GDR security services. Männel escaped to the West on June 29, 1961 (just a few weeks after Tamara departed for Cuba); afterwards two disciplinary files were opened on him for drunkenness and sexual harassment. Tamara left on May 9, 1961, from the airport at Schonefeld for Argentina, via Cuba, and my son and I went to say farewell to her. She had been born in Argentina and was automatically granted citizenship of the country. She wanted to join the struggle of the Argentine Communist Party, banned and forced to operate clandestinely.

According to Männel, Tania, on the contrary, had dropped her plans to return to Argentina and wanted to settle in Cuba and request citizenship of that country. The final sentence is indicative: "After Männel's betrayal she stopped pursuing this goal." Contact with the GDR security services was broken reciprocally from the moment of her departure for Cuba.

The accusation of her working for the KGB is also groundless. I personally went to Moscow, where I met with the head of the press office for foreign services of the Russian Federation and with the Soviet security service officer who was in charge of the Americas for a long time. He assured me in writing that Tamara Bunke had never collaborated with the Soviet security services.

This officer, who has 33 years of active service behind him, said that he was willing to declare this in court, if necessary.

JW: What support have the Cuban authorities given you in your research?

NB: Fortunately, my Cuban friends have helped me enormously. If they hadn't helped I would have been afraid of going to Moscow. I used to feel at home in Moscow, and in fact I worked there for five years as head of the Translations Department in the Ministry of Foreign Trade. But nowadays, given the new political situation, Moscow has become a very dangerous city. That is why I am grateful to the Cubans for having given me somewhere to stay, for having welcomed me at the airport, and accompanied me wherever I wanted to go. The Cubans have put into practice an example of what internationalism should be.

JW: Nevertheless, the accusation of being a triple agent does not constitute the only critical element in the book in question. Are there other statements in the book that do not reflect the truth?

NB: Of course. The book contains so many falsehoods and slanderous claims that I can't count all of them. For example, Zapata claims that the Stasi had spoken to us, Tamara's parents, and that we had no objections whatsoever to her working in these services. And not only this, he states that our house had been used to hold "conspiracy meetings." If we had in reality been informed of Tamara's supposed collaboration with the Stasi, we would have thought carefully about giving our consent, simply because we knew that our daughter wanted to work for the Argentine Communist Party. We were very worried, as we feared that sooner or later she would be arrested pursuing this desire]. If her collaboration with the Stasi had been publicly known, what would have happened to her?

The second issue that I have with Zapata's book, which has hurt me deeply, is his reference to the education that her parents (particularly her mother, according to the author) had given to her from a very young age. He states that terms such as "subversion" and "world revolution" must have been forced into the girl's mind. It is also claimed that Tamara was forced to go to meetings held by the Argentine Communist Party and to attend impassioned debates. This is quite simply unbelievable. First of all, the meetings that are mentioned were held at night, after 9 p.m., when the children had been asleep for some hours. Besides, for obvious reasons to do with revolutionary security, we had to ensure that our children were unaware of anything said during these meetings to prevent them from slipping up at school and saying something dangerous without realizing it.

Furthermore, Zapata writes that Tamara hated her parents because they forced her to leave Argentina and to go with them to the GDR. Of course, Tamara was happy in Argentina and she would have continued living there, but she was also interested in the plans to build socialism in the GDR. From the time of her first meeting with FGY, Tamara was filled with enthusiasm and she moved on in leaps and bounds in order to become a member of the FGY. She accomplished this in September 1952, immediately after registering at the Clara Zetkin High School, not in 1955 as Zapata would have us believe. Tamara also joined the German-Soviet Friendship Committee and the Society for Training and Sports, where equestrian skills and shooting are practiced, and the team from the Stahl Company [steel]. In short, she was involved in numerous social activities.

In 1956, after graduation, she moved to Berlin to work in the Ministry of Foreign Affairs. During this period, and afterwards, when she enrolled in Humboldt University, she often served as an interpreter and attendant for many Latin American delegations. Here, it is worth telling you a revealing story. A Latin American who lived in Paris had to travel to Berlin. They asked him, "How will you manage if you don't know anyone?" He replied, "No problem. I just have to say the word 'Tamara' and someone will look after me." And it really was like that. On more than one occasion Tamara was called to help young Latin Americans who didn't know a word of German and all they had to do was to say her name.

When she was 18, she was accepted as a candidate for the GUWSP, in the city of Eisenhüttenstadt. Tamara managed to convince the party leadership of her political maturity to the extent that they made an exception for her by reducing the admission period from two years to one. This was the first time that this had happened. It meant that a student could take part in cell meetings set up for professors, on an equal footing.

Zapata also writes that I got married in Germany while the Nazis were in power, that my husband had been forced to leave his school on account of my Jewish origins, and that we were forced to live clandestinely. This is not true! To put it simply, in order for all of this not to happen, we held back from getting married in Nazi Germany. We arrived in Argentina on December 19, 1935, and we quickly completed the necessary paperwork and got married in Buenos Aires, on December 28 of that same year.

JW: The cover of Zapata's book has the title: *Tania, the Woman Che Guevara Loved.* For decades there have been rumors circulating about Tania being Che's lover. Does Zapata have evidence to back up this argument?

NB: Not at all! In the entire book the only reference that appears is in part of a sentence about this matter, when he refers to Che's trip to the GDR, a visit that lasted two days. As president of the National Bank of Cuba, Che first visited Leuna and then Lipsia. In Lipsia he attended a meeting with Cuban and Latin American students. The FGY Central Committee sent to that meeting its own representative, accompanied by Tamara Bunke acting as interpreter. From Lipsia, Che traveled to where he signed some trade agreements, and from there he left by train for Poland. The book claims, without any proof, that on that occasion Tamara became intimately involved with Che. It is just a single, ambiguous sentence. The rest of the book does not deal with the matter again, except for the title. Needless to say, this libel has no evidence whatsoever to back it up.

At the same time, there is supposedly no one at all who did not have intimate relations with Tamara: a Cuban in the consulate in Prague; a painter who was a relative of the Bolivian president; the head of Information Services at the Presidential Palace; the first secretary of the Argentine embassy; and apparently she was even often seen in the company of President Barrientos... In short, Tamara is portrayed by the author as a cold-blooded and calculating secret agent, unscrupulous and with no emotions, who changed lovers more often than she changed her shirt, as she pleased. He could not imagine that Tamara Bunke, or rather Laura Gutiérrez Bauer, the name Tamara used in Bolivia, had qualities and abilities that were different from those he describes. Tamara was popular with those who knew her because of her personality, for the joie de vivre that is typical of a young and attractive woman, because of her linguistic abilities, her interest in folklore, archaeology, and ethnography. She knew how to make a lot of friends who appreciated her qualities and tried to help her. But Zapata was obviously not interested in these people's testimonies.

JW: But is this slander and defamation new?

NB: No, for 30 years such rumors have constantly been around, and they continue to be endlessly repeated in new variations. The reactionary press quickly started its own libelous campaign, that is to say, from the beginning of March 1968, when the first articles appeared in the Cuban press about the sacrifice of the revolutionary hero Tania, Che's *compañera* in the struggle. The first to write something slanderous was the already mentioned Männel, an officer who deserted from the Stasi and who, in the reactionary paper *Welt am Sonntag*, wrote that Che not only valued Tania for her military abilities, but also for her feminine abilities. He added that the Soviet security services had taken advantage of this to keep her on his trail and that this must have happened in 1961 (because it was only from this date onward that Tania went to Cuba)! In 1961, Che was minister of industry. Why would the Soviets want someone to spy on him in order to keep tabs on him?

Whatever the case, from 1968 onward the reactionary press began to spread slanderous rumors about her. Antonio Arguedas, former government minister in Bolivia, denounced the CIA during a press conference in La Paz (around 1969–70) for having forced him to spread articles of this nature in the official Bolivian press. In these articles, Tania is described as a triple agent and Che's lover. It was only from this date onward that similar articles began to appear in the *The Observer* (Britain), the *New York Times*, and also in newspapers in Brazil, Finland, and other countries.

JW: On December 23, 1997, you managed, through a lawsuit lodged at a Berlin court, to prevent the book from being distributed. How was this verdict reached and on what grounds was it based?

NB: On August 15, 1997, after the imminent publication of the book was announced, I sent a detailed analysis to the publisher Aufbau Verlag about the lack of evidence put forward in Zapata's book. In my letter I warned the editor that if the book to be published included the systematic compilation and embellishment of the libel that had been published in the reactionary press over the past 30 years tarnishing the memory of my daughter, I would be forced to take legal action. Evidently, the editor did not take my letter into account. In September 1997 the book was published and distributed. My lawyer, Dr. Christian Scherz, requested in vain that the book be withdrawn from the market. But later, when the facts and evidence were presented during the hearing, it was easy to obtain a verdict in our favor.

The verdict was given on December 23 and it was a wonderful Christmas present for me. The publication of 14 claims of different types is now prohibited on the penalty of a fine of 500,000 marks or a six-month prison sentence. The prohibition includes any references to Tania as a triple agent, my marriage, teaching my children to hate, etc.

JW: What do you plan to do now?

NB: Before the verdict was announced, the publishers had practically sold out of the edition (with the exception of 75 copies). So much poison circulated against the memory of my daughter and me. But the publishers have accepted the verdict.

As long as I live I will continue defending the honor and dignity of my daughter with all my strength. This is my battle to have the truth respected.

JW: In the GDR, there were over 200 youth brigades, women's groups, children's nurseries, and schools that were named after Tamara Bunke. How many of them have survived the annexation by West Germany?

NB: According to the information I have, only one; it is a children's nursery in Berlin-Friedrichshain. The rest were renamed or no longer exist. But this doesn't mean that the memory of Tamara Bunke has disappeared. Many people still ask me if I am a relative of Tamara Bunke—taxi drivers, bartenders, hospital doctors… it is good for my heart to know that my daughter has not been forgotten.

There are many groups and institutions that are named after Tamara Bunke, or Tania, in Cuba. Also in Bolivia, a lot of children have been named Tania or Ernesto. I know at least three families where the girls are called either Tania or Tamara. In Nicaragua and Chile, and perhaps in other places, there are institutions that carry her name.

JW: In 1997, the remains of Che Guevara were recovered together with those of six of his *compañeros* in the struggle. What will happen to Tania's remains when they are found?

NB: The excavations in Bolivia were carried out during a period of approximately 600 days until the remains of Che and his *compañeros* were found. They were taken to Cuba and interred there. I have entrusted the task of finding and identifying Tamara's remains to the Cubans. My deepest wish is that she be interred in Cuba. In the mausoleum in Santa Clara, where Che's remains rest, a total of 38 alcoves have been prepared, the same number as the guerrillas who were killed in Bolivia, including Tania.

NADIA BUNKE'S LETTER TO FIDEL CASTRO, REQUESTING THAT TANIA'S REMAINS BE BURIED IN CUBA

Nadia Bunke, BSc. Econ.
23 Paris Commune Street, Dep. 1801
10243 Berlin-Friedriehshain

December 25, 1995

Dearest *compañero* Fidel Castro,

As the mother of Tamara—Tania—I would like to ask for your support, help, and permission in matters related to the mortal remains of my beloved daughter, who fought and fell alongside Che's guerrilla combatants on August 3, 1967, in Río Grande, Bolivia.

According to news that has reached me via various sources from Bolivia, it would appear there are certain possibilities to claim the remains of my beloved and remarkable daughter, Tamara-Tania. In Berlin I have already signed a general power of attorney over to the Cuban Jorge González Pérez, so that he can represent us to the Bolivian authorities in their exhumation procedures and the subsequent departure of her remains.

I should like to nourish the hope that it is possible to find and positively identify them. Her full name: Haydée Tamara Bunke Bíder, known in Bolivia as Laura Gutiérrez Bauer. My most cherished desire is that you, dearest *compañero* Fidel Castro, would give permission for my beloved daughter to have her final and permanent resting place on Cuban soil, in a socialist country, alongside the Cuban guerrillas, united in struggle and in death with Che's guerrilla movement.

Tamara admired the Cuban Revolution and loved and felt closely united to the heroic Cuban people.

The three years Tamara lived in Cuba, and participated with so much enthusiasm and selflessness in the construction of the new society, were the happiest years of her life. Of her almost 30 years (all but 2 months) Tamara lived two-thirds of her life in Latin America.

In her soul and mind she was a Latin American.

Haydée Tamara Bunke Bíder was born on November 19, 1937, in Buenos Aires, Argentina. She was a native Argentine all her life (also according to Argentine law). During the nine years of her stay in the GDR she had dual citizenship. At the initiation of our party she made an application to return her GDR citizenship. Tamara arrived in Cuba on May 12, 1961, with Argentine citizenship.

She had a great desire to receive Cuban citizenship.

Tamara has fought and fallen for the liberation of the Bolivian people from poverty, hunger, and brutal exploitation, and has spilt her blood for a Latin American nation.

I feel and believe that Tamara would have been happy to know that one day she would permanently rest on her beloved Cuban soil.

With profound honor, respect, and affection,

Yours,
Nadia Bunke
Mother of Tamara—Tania the Guerrilla

FIDEL CASTRO'S REPLY TO NADIA BUNKE

Havana, April 1, 1996
Nadia Bunke

Dear *compañera* Nadia,

I have read with profound emotion your recent letter in which you ask for our support in the tasks of the discovery, exhumation, and identification of the remains of your beloved daughter Tamara, immortalized forever as our Tania the Guerrilla.

You can count on our unlimited help and support for such a sensitive request.

With my sincerest admiration and respect,

Fidel Castro

APPENDIX 16

FIDEL CASTRO'S SPEECH AT THE BURIAL OF THE REMAINS OF CHE GUEVARA AND HIS *COMPAÑEROS*

Che Guevara Memorial
Santa Clara, Cuba
October 17, 1997

Relatives of the *compañeros* killed in combat;
Guests;
People of Villa Clara;
Compatriots:

With profound emotion we experience one of those moments that will never again be repeated.

We are not here to say farewell to Che and his heroic *compañeros*. We are here to welcome them.

I see Che and his men as reinforcements, as a movement of invincible combatants, which on this occasion not only includes Cubans, but also Latin Americans who came to fight with us and write new pages of history and glory.

I also see Che as a moral giant who grows with each passing day, whose image, strength, and influence have multiplied throughout the earth.

How can he fit beneath a memorial stone?

How can he fit into this square?

How can he fit into our beloved, but small, island?

Only in the world that he dreamed of, which he lived and fought for, is there enough space for him.

The greater the injustice, the greater the exploitation, the greater the inequality, the greater the unemployment, the greater the poverty, hunger, and misery that prevail in human society, the greater his figure will be.

The values he defended will appear more elevated in the face of growing imperialist power, hegemony, domination, and interventionism that deny the most sacred rights of humanity, particularly the rights of the weak, underdeveloped, and poor peoples in what were for centuries colonies of the West and sources of slave labor.

His profound humanism will always stand in stark contrast to growing abuse, egotism, alienation, discrimination against indigenous peoples, ethnic minorities, women, and immigrants. It will stand against child labor and the sexual commodification of hundreds of thousands of children. It will stand against ignorance, disease, unemployment, and insecurity.

His example as an upright, revolutionary, and principled man will be ever more outstanding, as long as corrupt politicians, demagogues, and hypocrites exist everywhere.

Admiration for his personal bravery and revolutionary integrity will grow as long as the numbers of cowards, opportunists, and traitors on earth increase. While others flinch from their duty, the greater will be the respect for his iron will. The more people lacking integrity, the greater his sense of honor and dignity; the more skeptics there are, the greater his faith in humanity; the more pessimists there are, the greater his optimism; the more fear there is, the greater his daring; the more idlers there are who waste the products of the labor of others in luxury and leisure, the greater his austerity and his spirit of work and study.

Che was a true communist and is today an example and a paradigm of the revolutionary and the communist.

Che was a teacher who forged men and women like himself. Consistent with his actions, he never failed to do what he preached, or demand of himself what he demanded of others.

Whenever a volunteer was required for a difficult mission, he was the first in line, both in war and in peace. His great dreams depended on his willingness to give his life generously. Nothing was impossible for him, and he was capable of making the impossible possible.

The invasion from the Sierra Maestra through vast and unprotected plains and the capture of the city of Santa Clara with just a few men are among those feats that show his amazing capabilities.

His ideas on revolution in his own country and in the rest of Latin America, in spite of enormous difficulties, were possible. Had he made them a reality, perhaps today the world might be different. Vietnam proved it could fight against the interventionist forces of imperialism and defeat them. The Sandinistas triumphed against one of the most powerful puppet governments of the United States. The Salvadoran revolutionaries were just about to win victory. In Southern Africa, apartheid was defeated in spite of the state possessing nuclear weapons. China, thanks to the heroic struggle of its workers and peasant farmers, is today one of the most promising countries in the world. Hong Kong was returned after 150 years of an occupation established through the Opium Wars.

Not all historical eras or circumstances require the same methods and the same tactics. But nothing can stop the march of history; its objective laws are immutable. Che based himself on these social laws and had an absolute faith in humanity. Very often revolutionaries and those seeking profound social change do not have the privilege of seeing their dreams realized as quickly as they had hoped or desired, but sooner or later they are victorious.

A combatant may die, but not their ideas. What was a man from the US government doing up there where Che was wounded and taken prisoner? How could they believe that by killing Che he would cease to exist as a combatant? Now, he is not in La Higuera; instead he is everywhere, wherever there is a just cause to defend. Those who wanted to kill him, to make him disappear, were not able to understand that he would leave an indelible footprint in history and that his luminous prophet's gaze would transform him into a symbol for all the earth's poor in their millions upon millions.

Young people, children, the elderly, men and women who have learned about him, honest people throughout the world, regardless of their social background, admire him.

Che is taking up and winning more battles than ever.

Thank you, Che, for your history, your life, and your example!

Thank you for coming to fortify us in this difficult battle we are engaged in today to save the ideas you fought so hard for, to save the revolution, our country, and the achievements of socialism, where some of the great dreams you cherished have come true!

To carry forward this heroic achievement, to defeat the imperialists' plans against Cuba, to resist the blockade, to achieve victory, we count on you.

As you can see, this land is your land, these people are your people, and this revolution is your revolution. We continue to fly the socialist banner with honor and pride.

Welcome, heroic *compañeros* of the reinforcement! The trenches of ideas and justice that you defend together with our people will never be conquered by the enemy! And together we will continue to fight for a better world!

Ever onward to victory!

APPENDIX 17

RAMIRO VALDÉS'S SPEECH AT THE BURIAL OF THE REMAINS OF TANIA AND OTHER INTERNATIONALIST COMBATANTS

Che Guevara Memorial
Santa Clara, Cuba
December 30, 1998

Relatives of the deceased combatants;
Compañeros;
People of Villa Clara:

Four decades ago, when Cuba was approaching the end of its struggle for freedom, a young communist activist born in Argentina, Tamara Bunke, was following the progress of those events from far away in the GDR. She lived there with her parents who, in spite of the distance, were beside us in their sympathy and solidarity.

The triumphant Cuban Revolution, which represented the most radical historic change in the hemisphere, bound the destiny of that brave, intelligent, and thoughtful young woman to the cause of our country. As a clandestine combatant, she provided invaluable service to the Latin American revolutionary movement and then, as Tania, she filled a glorious page in the history of Che's actions in Bolivia, giving her life in a hostile environment, side by side with other Bolivian, Peruvian, and Cuban *compañeros*.

When, at the outset of the search for her remains in Vallegrande, we asked her mother, Nadia Bunke, who is with us today, where she wanted her daughter's remains buried, Nadia did not hesitate to say that Tania should rest here, together with the remains of Che and her *compañeros*.

More recently, asking Nadia which flag we should place over the coffin when taking it to the memorial, she immediately responded, the Cuban flag, the flag of her other homeland for which she had fought and which had honored her by accepting her into the Cuban Communist Party.

We are also here to welcome a brave soldier in our Rebel Army who came from the Sierra Maestra in the vanguard of our Ciro Redondo invasion column.[1] Here, in the former Las Villas Province, Captain Manuel Hernández Osorio (alias Miguel) distinguished himself in all the battles waged during the final offensive against the dictatorship. He proved himself again in Bolivia as a strong, steady, and disciplined revolutionary.

We welcome to Cuba the doctor Octavio de la Concepción y de la Pedraja (alias Moro), a combatant in the Frank País Second Eastern Front,[2] and an internationalist fighter in the Congo. He was one of the Cuban *compañeros* whose commitment had been proven and who were selected personally by Che to be by his side in the initial nucleus of a revolutionary project conceived to expand the struggle for liberation throughout the heart of this continent.

Furthermore, it is an extraordinary honor that we will have in our land, from this day forth, a man we held in high esteem and admiration, combatant Roberto Peredo Liegue (alias Coco). Che considered him, together with his brother, Inti, to be bastions in the struggle, with enormous potential for development. Coco Peredo was one of those revolutionary activists who took part in the organization of the guerrilla during the early days. These men never doubted Che's leadership and never gave up or lost their faith in victory.

The relatives of a group of distinguished and heroic Bolivians, who are with us here today, also wanted the remains of their loved ones to rest in Cuba. They were young revolutionaries who knew how to respond to the demands of their time and their country: Mario Gutiérrez Ardaya (alias Julio), Aniceto Reinaga Gordillo, Jaime Arana Campero (alias Chapaco), Francisco Huanca Flores (alias Pablito) and Julio Luis Méndez Korne (alias Ñato).

Also with us are the relatives of the Peruvian Lucio Edilberto Galván Hidalgo (alias Eustaquio), who also asked that the remains of this brave fighter be interred in Cuba together with his *compañeros* in glorious deeds.

Each of them symbolizes the spirit of Latin American solidarity on which that struggle was based. Their presence in Cuba represents the unity of ideals, history, and the common destiny of the peoples of Our America, as José Martí described it; they were called on then, as we are today, to struggle to achieve full and definitive independence, integration, social justice, and a truly humane development in this region.

Last year, when in this same place on the 30th anniversary of the death of the heroic guerrilla, we paid tribute to Che and his *compañeros*, Fidel said that he saw Che and the other *compañeros*, whose remains have been interred here, as a movement of invincible combatants come to support us in the difficult battle our people are engaged in. This is a battle against the Yankee enemy that is trying to destroy us and in the defense of the ideas of the revolution, solidarity, and socialism.

In this way, today, receiving the remains of Tania and the other nine internationalist combatants, we can say we are better prepared and even more invincible because of the power of their example, their morale, and their revolutionary message for present and future generations.

Currently in Bolivia, the scene of Che's campaign, a group of *compañeros* is still searching in the hope we can find the remains of those still missing. We are confident that we will be able to bring the rest of the members of the guerrilla movement to Cuba.

Times change, as do conditions and methods, but 31 years after the death of Che and his *compañeros* in Bolivia, we can say that the goals for which they fought continue to be an essential part of, and an aspiration for, the future of Latin America.

Today, US imperialism aspires, more than ever, to perpetuate the subordination, underdevelopment, and division of Latin America. Neoliberalism aims to ensure that the market, with its blind laws, dictates the economy and life of every country. Powerful countries support self-centered and elitist globalization that, with each passing day, makes the rich richer and the poor poorer.

The US government is trying to place itself in the position of a world government that can impose its political and military laws on other countries, using different methods, including the use of force. They want to establish a single way of thinking and a single social system and to punish those who refuse to accept it. They argue for interventionism in Latin America and the Caribbean, for armaments and conflicts between countries. Transnational companies are taking over media and cultural concerns throughout the world in order to erase the identity of peoples and impose on them their uniformity, manipulated facts, and banality.

Imperialists are capable of presenting their reactionary policies as modern or ultramodern, but those who seriously analyze Che's and Fidel's ideas must acknowledge that within them is a true vision of progress to which humanity should aspire, especially on the threshold of a millennium which overflows with aggression, threats, and danger.

That is why now, as in the past, we are striving to transform reality, to combat the main enemy of our people and of all exploited peoples on this continent and throughout the world. Because we have different conditions, because the way can no longer be the same, we strive to open up paths to new ideas of freedom and justice. Given that the situations we face now are more complex and unfavorable, we will continue fighting for our just cause, our just ideas, without the slightest concession to anyone, and placing above everything else the principles of independence, revolution, and socialism.

Compañeros: Forty years ago, on a day like today, a hard battle was fought in this city of Santa Clara. At the same time, on the afternoon of December 30, one of the most daring, memorable captains of our Rebel Army died in combat, Roberto Rodríguez (Vaquerito). His death, just a few hours away from victory, is today a symbol of all those who sacrificed their lives so that we could be free and have the right to control our own lives.

The joy of triumph was born then, compensation for all the commitment and the pain of remembering all those *compañeros* who died along the way, from Moncada until the last day of the war.

We knew then that we were facing new challenges, new dangers, and new events. Nevertheless, we could not have imagined what these decades, now a part of history, would be like, or how many new figures would distinguish themselves in missions for the revolution. We could not have imagined how difficult and complicated the path our country has followed would be, that we would be virtually on our own, as we were at the beginning, with no support other than the solidarity of other peoples, facing a powerful, unscrupulous enemy, determined to wipe us off the face of the earth at any price.

So when you, brothers and sisters of Villa Clara, begin on January 1 to celebrate the 40th anniversary of the liberation of the city, and rejoice in that battle where people stood beside the combined invading forces of Columns 8 and 2,[3] the Revolutionary Directorate, the combatants of the July 26 Movement, and the Popular Socialist Party, who rebelled under Che and Camilo's leadership, once again genuine happiness is reunited with the solemnity of this moment. We are placing the remains of Tania and her Bolivian, Peruvian, and Cuban *compañeros* in their final resting place, in their battle trenches.

We should not welcome them with sadness. We should welcome them with pride. We should accept them in our midst as a new reason to be inspired and committed to the cause of the revolution.

We value, as if it were yesterday, the example set by Vaquerito, who was killed in the prime of his life, an example which inspired our people in the final battle against dictatorship. Today we are in the presence of Tania and her *compañeros* who, together with Che and the other combatants, are now in the heart of this island. They should be held up as examples for our young people, an inspiration for all workers and everyone to fulfill their duty. They should aid in the development of our consciousness in the face of internal difficulties and the realities of the world we live in. They should inspire decisive support for the general strategy of the revolution, led by Fidel and Raúl at the forefront of our party and our government.

The progressive and solid recovery of our economy, the constant reaffirmation of our moral and political values, and an indefatigable nation is the monument we have to build every day in homage to Che and those who are interred in this monument; in homage to those who have been buried in our country from the time of La Demajagua until today;[4] and in homage to our magnificent fighting people who truly deserve it.

Welcome, *compañeros* of the new reinforcements, who have arrived to join us on the eve of this glorious 40th anniversary!

Welcome, Tania, immortal example of a woman and a communist!

Welcome, heroic combatants for the cause of the Cuban Revolution, for fraternity and solidarity among peoples!

We say today with Che, Ever onward to victory!

And we repeat with Fidel, Socialism or death!
Homeland or death!
We shall overcome!

NOTES

PREFACE

1. Marta Rojas and Mirta Rodríguez Calderón, *Tania the Unforgettable Guerrilla* (New York: Random House, 1971). Published first in Spanish in 1970 by the Cuban Book Institute, Havana, as *Tania la guerrillera inolvidable*.

2. On April 11, 1964, Haydée Tamara had sent a letter to her parents telling them of her relationship with Ulises. Sections of this are reproduced in *Tania the Unforgettable Guerrilla*.

3. Currently named the People's Democratic Republic of Congo, this country was founded by Patrice Lumumba and others, on June 30, 1960, after winning its independence from Belgium. Following the CIA's assassination of Lumumba and his main followers on January 17, 1961, the country became known as Congo Leopoldville or Congo Kinshasa. In 1970, the dictator Joseph Desideré Mobuto (also known as Mobuto Sese Seko) renamed it Zaire. After Mobuto was overthrown on May 17, 1997, by a prolonged people's uprising led by President Laurent Kabila, it recovered the name given it by its founders. During the period described, the National Council of the Revolution of Congo Kinshasa was presided over by Gastión Soumaliot and included, among others, Laurent Kabila, with whom Che had several disagreements. Those interested in further details of these events can consult Che's *Congo Diary*.

4. Pierre Kalfon, *Ernesto Guevara, una leyenda de nuestro siglo* (Ernesto Guevara: Hero of our Century) (Plaza & Yanés Editores S.A., 1997).

5. Jorge G. Castañeda, *La vida en rojo: Una biografía del Che Guevara* (Life in Red: A Biography of Che Guevara)(Argentina: Espasa, 1997).

6. See *Los cuadernos de Praga* (The Prague Notebooks). Ulises Estrada has never spoken to Abel Pose, yet in addition to inventing a story about the supposed romance between Che and Tania in Prague, Pose

attributed comments to Estrada that the author never expressed, such as describing Che's time in the Congo as a "disaster."

7. References made to Tania by Che Guevara in *The Bolivian Diary*, forthcoming from Ocean Press in 2005.

8. Carlos Conrado de Jesús Alvarado Marín (alias Mercy) was a captain in the Guatemalan police force. He opposed the CIA-backed mercenaries who in 1954 overthrew the democratically elected government of Jacobo Arbenz. In these circumstances he met Che, who helped him go into exile in Argentina. In 1960 Carlos traveled to Cuba. A tireless defender of the Latin American peoples, he agreed to work with the newly established Cuban state security organizations. He died in Cuba on November 14, 1997. Until recently, it was not possible to reveal Mercy's real identity because his son, Percy Alvarado, worked as a Cuban agent who penetrated the ranks of counterrevolutionary and terrorist groups operating in Miami, specifically the Cuban American National Foundation.

CHAPTER 1

1. July 26, 1953, the day of the failed attack on the Moncada garrison, is seen as the beginning of the armed struggle against the dictatorship of General Fulgencio Batista. Batista's rule commenced on March 10, 1952, and concluded on December 31, 1958. During this period the Democrat Harry Truman (1945–53) and the Republican Dwight Eisenhower (1953–61) were presidents of the United States.

2. On December 2, 1956, the boat *Granma* landed on the Cuban coastline. The boat contained 82 men, the majority of whom were founders of the July 26 Movement and who subsequently went on to fight in the Rebel Army. They included Fidel and Raúl Castro, Juan Almeida, Camilo Cienfuegos, and Che Guevara.

3. For further information see Jane Franklin, *Cuba and the United States: A Chronological History* (New York: Ocean Press, 1997).

4. When the Cuban Revolution was victorious, the only "independent" countries in the Caribbean were Cuba, Haiti, and the Dominican

Republic. The remaining Caribbean nations were subject to British, French, Dutch, and US colonial domination.

5. For further information see Luis Suárez, *Century of Terror in Latin America* (New York: Ocean Press, forthcoming 2006).

6. For an analysis of the different tendencies within the New Left in Latin America and the Caribbean, see Donald C. Hodges, *The Latin American Revolution* (William Morrow Co. Inc., 1974).

7. Refers to the continuous attacks against Cuba by Colombian President Alberto Lleras Camargo (1958–62), in close coordination with the OAS and the White House. Lleras Camargo, in the wake of several incidents between the two countries in December 1961, broke off diplomatic relations with Cuba that same month.

8. As candidate of the Intransigent Radical Civic Union, Frondizi was successful in the presidential elections of February 1958 under a reformist program that had won him the electoral support of the followers of the banned Justicialista Party (also known as the Peronist Party) and other progressive Argentine sectors. Pressure by the armed forces and the United States gradually undermined the promises made by the president until he was finally overthrown by a coup d'état that made José María Guido the president. Guido immediately banned all candidates belonging to the Justicialista Party who had been elected in the legislative elections held at the beginning of March 1962.

9. After several years of struggle, on July 5, 1962, Algeria obtained its independence from France. However, well before that date there were reciprocal relations of solidarity between the Algerian National Liberation Front and the Cuban revolutionary government. In that relationship, Masetti played a crucial role.

10. The Ministry of the Interior (MININT) in the republic of Cuba was founded on June 14, 1961, under the leadership of Ramiro Valdés Menéndez.

11. For further information see Gabriel Rot, *Los orígenes perdidos de la guerrilla argentina* (The Lost Origins of the Argentine Guerrilla)

(Buenos Aires: Cielo por Asalto, 2000).

12. See Manuel Piñeiro, *Che Guevara and the Latin American Revolutionary Movements* (New York: Ocean Press, 2001).

13. For further information see David Deutshmann (editor), *Che Guevara Reader* (New York: Ocean Press, 2004).

CHAPTER 2

1. Juan Almeida Bosque was a participant in the Moncada garrison attack and in the *Granma* boat expedition and was a founder of the Rebel Army. In the final stages of the insurrection against Batista, Almeida Bosque led the Mario Muñoz Eastern Third Front. He is currently a member of the Political Bureau of the PCC's Central Committee and is vice president of the Council of State. Celia Sánchez was one of the principal organizers of the July 26 Movement in Manzanillo and one of the first women to join the Rebel Army, in which she held a leadership position. Celia fulfilled key missions during the insurrection and after the revolution, and served as one of Fidel Castro's closest confidents. At the time of her death in 1980, she was a member of the PCC's Central Committee, in addition to occupying the post of secretary in the Council of State.

2. Orlando Pantoja Tamayo (alias Olo) was a member of the July 26 Movement and, from 1957 on, of the Rebel Army, in which Che promoted him to the rank of captain. After the revolution, he contributed to the foundation of MININT, fulfilled an international mission in Bolivia preparing for Masetti's mission to Argentina, and was subsequently the head of the border patrol. He was selected by Che and, after intensive military training in Cuba, arrived in Bolivia on December 19, 1966. He died in combat in the Quebrada del Yuro pass on October 8, 1967.

3. José María Martínez Tamayo (alias Papi) belonged to the clandestine network of the July 26 Movement in the city of Holguín. In April 1958 he joined the Rebel Army and after the revolution he worked closely with Che. When MININT was established he joined Department M,

from where he fulfilled several international missions, including preparing conditions for the arrival of Jorge Ricardo Masetti's guerrilla column in Argentina. Papi also accompanied Che to the Congo, and then traveled to Bolivia in May 1966 to prepare conditions for Che's arrival. When Che arrived, Papi joined the newly formed guerrilla movement. As a member of the ELN, he died in combat on July 30, 1967.

4. The Second Declaration of Havana proclaimed by the Cuban people in February 1962 was the response to the decision of the Organization of American States (OAS) to expel the Cuban government.

5. Refers to a statement made by José Martí when, during the 1890s, he was involved in preparing the recommencement of armed struggle waged by Cuban patriots against Spanish colonialism.

6. The address is 3308 18th Street, between 33rd Street and Lázaro Cárdenas Avenue, in Miramar, Havana.

7. At this time the first steps had already been taken to prepare for the guerrilla struggle in Argentina. Support for the MOEC survivors in Colombia continued, in addition to the backing of those Colombian *compañeros* who would subsequently form the Colombian National Liberation Army. In the case of Peru, the Cuban Revolution supported the founders of the Peruvian National Liberation Army (ELN), as well as the Movement of the Revolutionary Left. In Uruguay and Venezuela, Cuban solidarity focused mainly on preparing the military wing of the communist parties in both countries. In the case of Venezuela, support intensified after 1962. In response to the banning of the Venezuelan Communist Party and the Revolutionary Left Movement, a decision was taken to found a national liberation army there.

8. The address is 772 47th Street, between Conill and Tulipán streets, in Nuevo Vedado, Havana. The Che Guevara Studies Center currently operates from there and is open to all those interested in his life and work.

9. José Manuel Manresa was a soldier and typist in Batista's army. When, during the first few days of January 1959, Che occupied the Cabaña fortress, Manresa performed different military functions,

but soon afterwards, requested permission to be discharged from duty. Discovering he was incapable of farm work, he changed his mind and asked Che to be reinstated. Che accepted him back, and Manresa was so efficient and discreet that within a few weeks he became Che's personal secretary, a position he held until 1965 when Che left for the Congo. For further information see Orlando Borrego, *Che, recuerdos en ráfaga* (Che, a Gust of Memories) (Havana: Editorial de Ciencias Sociales, 2004).

10. The name of Operation Sombra is taken from the book *Don Segundo Sombra* by the Argentine Ricardo Güiraldes, published in 1926.

11. Coco and Inti were the aliases of the brothers Roberto and Guido Peredo Liegue, members of Che's guerrilla movement and the Bolivian Communist Party (PCB). Coco helped to prepare for Che's clandestine arrival and was a founder of the ELN. He was killed in action on September 26, 1967. Inti, a member of the PCB's Central Committee, joined the guerrilla movement on November 27, 1967. He was one of the few survivors. After Che's assassination, he undertook—together with Rodolfo Saldaña and other *compañeros*—the challenge of re-founding the ELN. He was assassinated in La Paz on September 9, 1969.

12. Javier Heraud was a young, prize-winning Peruvian poet. Following his military training in Cuba, he joined a guerrilla column that in May 1963 attempted to enter Peru via Bolivia at the border port of Puerto Maldonado. The column was taken by surprise by the Peruvian army and he was killed in action. The survivors of this column, under the leadership of Héctor Béjar, founded the Peruvian ELN.

13. De la Puente was considered one of the most prestigious former leaders of the Peruvian Aprista Party (APRA). In 1959 the party split, and de la Puente became the main leader of the APRA Rebelde division. De la Puente also founded the Movement of the Revolutionary Left in Peru, in which he was general secretary until he was killed in combat in January 1966.

CHAPTER **3**

1. The People's Defense Militia was among the organizations that were created in the first years of the Cuban Revolution for defense against the mulitiple terrorist attacks from the United States and internal counterrevolutionaries.
2. A dead drop is a prearranged hiding place used by agents to exchange messages without having to meet in person.
3. Tamara sent a letter to Captain Antonio Núñez Jiménez from the GDR on August 22, 1960. For further information see *Tania the Unforgettable Guerrilla*.

CHAPTER **4**

1. The address is 1080 Third Street, third floor, between 18th and 20th streets, Miramar, Havana, Cuba.
2. A target is the focus of an intelligence operation.
3. The real names of colleagues mentioned in this paragraph cannot be revealed. They are called by the aliases they used during the time they were training Tania.
4. An operations house is a base that agents use to carry out their missions.

CHAPTER **5**

1. Iván Montero (alias Renán) was a combatant in the clandestine struggle against the Batista dictatorship. In danger, he traveled to Mexico, where he joined up with a group of exiled Nicaraguans. When the Cuban Revolution took place he returned to Havana, maintaining contact with the Nicaraguans. In 1959 and 1960, with Che Guevara's support, he joined the first attempts to wage armed struggle against the Somoza dictatorship (1936–79) by joining the FSLN. When the Sandinista revolution was victorious in 1979, he was appointed head of the intelligence department in Nicaragua. Prior to this, Renán had been an active part of the clandestine

apparatus supporting Che in Bolivia. When problems arose with the documentation he used for a cover as a salesperson, Che advised him to return to Cuba to resolve the matter. Subsequent developments did not allow him to rejoin the network in La Paz.

2. Jorge Ricardo Masetti and his two columns entered the Salta region in northeast Argentina from Tarijas, Bolivia, on September 31, 1963. They began to set up a number of camps until their presence was detected in February 1964, and the repressive Argentine forces began to surround them. This siege ended in April, following the collapse of the guerrilla column and the capture, disappearance, or death of several *compañeros*, including Masetti, who died on April 21, 1964.

3. Papi arrived in Bolivia in mid-1963, just a few weeks after Masetti. Che assigned Papi the mission of establishing a support network for the guerrilla column on the Argentina-Bolivia border. Papi traveled to Bolivia, Peru, and Argentina on a number of occasions. After Masetti had entered Argentina, Papi returned to Havana.

CHAPTER 6

1. At this point Ulises was the alias used by the author of this book; his real name was Dámaso Lascaille.

CHAPTER 7

1. This is a particularly Cuban way of performing boleros which, at that time, were popular on account of performances by famous singers, including César Portillo de la Luz, José Antonio Méndez, Elena Burke, and Moraima Secade.

CHAPTER 8

1. A reference to the Czech communist and journalist Julius Fucík, who, after being imprisoned for nearly a year and a half, was assassinated by fascists on September 8, 1943. Before he died, he wrote his famous book *Report from the Hangman's Scaffold*.

2. Although the message is addressed to the MOE, the tone is informal, and it is evidently written for the author of this book (see appendix 5).

CHAPTER 9

1. The Revolutionary National Movement (MNR), under the leadership of Víctor Paz Estenssoro, headed a popular uprising on April 11, 1952, that in the course of several battles overthrew the professional army and began the Bolivian Revolution. In spite of the political inconsistencies of Paz Estenssoro and in the face of widespread pressure, the mining resources of the country were nationalized. The demands of the miners were taken into account and agrarian reform was approved. A substantial though insufficient quantity of land was handed over to the rural and indigenous population. The radical nature of this process was also evident in the temporary substitution of a professional army for a people's militia in which the militant mining workers had a decisive say. Nevertheless, little by little Paz Estenssoro betrayed the principles of the revolution by making several concessions to the United States, including the reestablishment of a professional army. As a consequence of these concessions, he named in May 1964 the pro-imperialist general and chief of the armed forces René Barrientos as his vice president. On November 4 of that same year, Barrientos led the coup d´état that signaled the death knell of the 1952 revolution.

2. A few kilometers to the west of La Paz, these ruins are the remains of a ceremonial center of the Aymara culture, the foundations of which probably date back to 300 AD. The Tiahuanaco culture was the main pre-Columbian civilization that was based in what is currently Bolivian territory. In the 15th century, the population was dominated by the Inca Empire that was centered in Cuzco, Peru.

3. General Alfredo Ovando (1919–82) was the commander in chief of the army when the coup d'état overthrew President Paz Estenssoro. Ovando belonged to the military junta which, headed by General Barrientos, governed the country until July 1966. In this year,

following fraudulent elections, Barrientos was appointed "constitutional" president of the republic, a position he held until he lost his life in an airplane crash in 1969. Immediately after the crash, Ovando became the de facto president of Bolivia until overthrown in 1970 by a civilian-military rising led by the nationalist general Juan José Torres.

4. Refers to the old Bolivian peso. In response to the devaluation of this currency, the Barrientos government created a new Bolivian peso that was equivalent to 1,000 old pesos. At the time of the monetary reform, approximately 12.5 new Bolivian pesos were worth US$1.

5. Mining is one of the main economic activities in the Oruro region, located in the Bolivian eastern Andes. Tin has traditionally been extracted, together with associated minerals such as bismuth, gold, silver, wolfram, and zinc.

6. At that time the company National Treasure Oil Reserves was a state-owned organization responsible for locating and exploiting hydrocarbon (oil and gas) reserves.

CHAPTER 10

1. Tania's departure from Havana for Prague is the date of reference used here.

2. The United Republic of Tanzania, the capital of which is Dar-es-Salaam, adopted this name after July 1965. Before then, it was known as the United Republic of Tanganyika and Zanzibar, in recognition of their unity in the struggle against imperialism, colonialism, and racism.

3. Tuma and Tumaini were the aliases used by the Cuban Carlos Coello throughout his involvement in the international guerrilla movement in Bolivia. Coello accompanied Che during his reconnaissance of different Bolivian cities and took him to the guerrilla camp on the Ñacaguazu ranch between November 5 and 6, 1966. He died in combat on June 26, 1967, as part of the Bolivian ELN main column.

4. Pombo was the alias used by Harry Villegas Tamayo, currently division general of the Cuban armed forces. Pombo took part in the invasion of western Cuba as part of Che's column during the struggle against Batista. He also fought under Che's command in the internationalist struggles in the Congo and Latin America.
5. This term comes from Ramiro Valdés, the head of MININT at that time.
6. The term *quemar*, to burn, is colloquial and used in clandestine work to make it clear that a person should not be given assignments that might lead to them being detected by the enemy.

CHAPTER 11

1. Alberto Fernández Montes de Oca (alias Pacho or Pachungo) was born in Santiago de Cuba on December, 28, 1935. After traveling through several European countries, he joined Che in La Paz on November 3 and left for the Ñacaguazu ranch two days later. He belonged to the guerrilla movement, together with Che, until he died in combat at the Quebrada del Yuro pass on October 8, 1967.
2. The Bolivian Julio Dagnino Pacheco (alias Sánchez) acted as the mediator for Pombo and Papi, with the Peruvian ELN leader, Juan Pablo Chang Navarro (alias Chino) and with the PCB's Peking Line.
3. Moisés Guevara Rodríguez led a dissident group known as the Peking Line that had broken away from the PCB. In March 1967, Moisés and some of his other *compañeros* in the struggle (along with some traitors) joined the guerrilla movement as combatants and in April he was assigned to Joaquín's column. He remained heroically loyal until his death in the ambush at Puerto Mauricio on August 31, 1967.
4. Until 1968, Antonio Arguedas Mendieta was Bolivian government minister. Prior to this, in 1964, the CIA had recruited him. After Che's assassination, Arguedas kept Che's hands (after they had been amputated from the corpse), a postmortem mask, and a copy

of the diary Che had kept in Bolivia. In a brave and honest gesture, Arguedas secretly sent those items to the Cuban government through journalists belonging to the Chilean journal *Punto Final*. Because of this, he was the target of an attack on May 8, 1969, that forced him into exile in Mexico City. Several years later in 2001, in circumstances that have yet to be clarified, he died a violent death in La Paz. For further information on Arguedas's account of Tania's life see *Tania the Unforgettable Guerrilla*.

5. The author's claim was corroborated by Loyola Guzmán's testimony to the Cuban historians Adys Cupull and Froilán González on June 29, 1983. According to Loyola, in mid-1966 Papi asked for help in obtaining a scholarship for the Bolivian student Mario Martínez (although at the time she did not know who the person in question was or what was behind this request). There were two scholarships available from the Bulgarian Communist Party, and she, in her position as a leader in the Communist Youth Federation of the PCB, asked Mario Monje for one of these scholarships.

6. Adys Cupull and Froilán González, *La CIA contra el Che* (The CIA against Che) (Havana: Editora Política, 1992), 101.

7. Interview by the Cuban researcher Adys Cupull with Ángela Soto Cobián, in Ángela Soto Cobián, *La muchacha de la guerrilla del Che, Tania: Leyendas y realidades* (The Girl from Che's Guerrilla, Tania: Myths and Realities) (Montevideo: Impresora Grafis Ltda., 1999), 83-84.

8. Adys Cupull and Froilán González, *Che: Un hombre bravo* (Che: A Brave Man) (Havana: Capitán San Luis, 1994), 312.

9. See the interview with Mario Gonzalo López Muñoz by the Cuban historian Froilán González, in *La muchacha de la guerrilla del Che, Tania: Leyendas y realidades*, 76-77.

10. see *The Bolivian Diary*.

11. Ibid.

12. Jorge Vázquez Viaña (alias Loro or Bigotes) was born in La Paz on January, 5, 1939. He joined the guerrilla movement at its inception and remained within its ranks until April 22, 1967, when he was

injured in combat in Taperrillas. He was captured and brutally tortured by the CIA and the Bolivian intelligence services, and assassinated in cold blood in the hospital in Camiri. His body was thrown from a helicopter somewhere in the Bolivian jungle. His corpse is one of the few that has not been found to date.

13. According to the Cuban historian Froilán González, this place is also referred to as Ñacahuasi, Ñacahuasu, Ñacahuazú, Ñancahuazu, and Ñancahuazú. In the deeds of the ranch signed by its seller, Remberto Villa, and by its purchaser, Roberto Peredo, this site is identified as Ñacaguazu. For further information on this matter see *The Bolivian Diary*.

14. Another ranch in the region was also purchased in Caranavi, in the area of Alto Beni, to the northeast of La Paz.

15. Antonio Jiménez Tardío (alias Pan Divino) was born in Tarara, Cochabamba, in 1941. He joined the ranks of the guerrilla unit on December 31, 1966. He died in combat in the foothills of Iñao, near Monteagudo, on August 9, 1967.

16. Monje's statement was taken from Che's account of the meeting held with the Bolivians. Those interested in reading about this may consult *The Bolivian Diary*.

17. A reference to the Cuban fighter Leonardo Tamayo Núñez (alias Urbano), who joined the recently formed guerrilla movement on November 27, 1966. He was one of the few survivors of the Bolivian struggle and is currently a colonel in the MININT in Cuba.

18. René Martínez Tamayo (alias Arturo) was born in Mayarí, Cuba, on February 2, 1941. He joined the guerrilla forces in December 1966 and died in combat at the Quebrada del Yuro pass on October 8, 1967.

19. Refers to the eighth anniversary of the Cuban Revolution of January 1, 1959.

20. Atahualpa Yupanki is one of the most famous singer-songwriters of folk music in the Argentine pampas. Because of his strong commitment to progressive causes he is considered as one of the most prominent figures in protest music and the "political song

movement" that extended throughout a number of Latin American countries from the 1960s.

21. see *Tania the Unforgettable Guerrilla*.

22. Pedro Domingo Murillo (1756–1810) was born in La Paz to a poor family. Influenced in his youth by the principles of the Enlightenment, from 1805 on he began to promote the cause of emancipation in opposition to Spanish colonial domination. He was a key figure in the uprising that took place in La Paz on July 9, 1809, and he was appointed some days later commander of the square and president of the junta for the rights of the king and the people. A few months later, in November 1809, during the battle of Irupana, Murillo was taken prisoner by the Spanish royal forces. He was subsequently tried and executed in La Paz in January 1810.

23. see *The Bolivian Diary*.

24. In March 1967, Ciro Roberto Bustos (alias Carlos or Pelao) attended a meeting with Che. While attempting to leave the guerrilla zone, together with the French intellectual, Regís Debray, he was taken prisoner on April 20. Bustos remains accused by history of having drawn sketches for the Bolivian army and US security services that allowed them to confirm Che's presence in Bolivia.

25. The author is referring to the account that Loyola Guzmán gave in July 1983 to the Cuban historians Adys Cupull and Froilán González. Other Latin American authors have indicated that Tania, presumably working as the head of the intelligence operation, belonged to the leadership of the recently established urban network. However, this claim does not appear to be confirmed either in Loyola Guzmán's account or in the one published in the United States by the Bolivian Rodolfo Saldaña, another member of the urban network who has since died.

26. Juan Pablo Chang Navarro (alias Chino) first made contact with Che on December 1, 1966. His plan, according to Che, was to send 20 men from his organization (the Peruvian ELN) to train in Bolivia. Che did not agree with this plan and decided to wait until he had talked to the general secretary of the PCB, Mario Monje. In any

case, fulfilling his agreement with Che, Chino returned to Bolivia in mid-March 1967, with a Peruvian doctor and a radio technician. While in Bolivia, the attacks started and Chino decided to remain in the guerrilla column under Che's command. He was taken prisoner at the Quebrada del Yuro pass on October 8, 1967, and murdered in cold blood one day later in the little school at La Higuera.

27. Dr. Restituto José Cabrera Flores (alias Negro) was born in the port of Callao, Peru, on June 27, 1931. He joined Che's guerrilla force in mid-March 1967. When the column was separated into two, he remained in Joaquín's column until the very end, following Che's order to look after Tania. He carried out this instruction to the end of his life. Following Tania's body downstream, he managed to escape from the ambush at Puerto Mauricio on August 31, 1967, but a few days later on September 4, he was captured and assassinated by the Bolivian army.

28. Lucio Edilberto Galván Hidalgo (alias Eustaquio) was born in Huancayo, Peru, on July 7, 1937. He joined the guerrilla movement in mid-March 1967 and died in combat in the Cajones region on October 12, 1967, three days after Che was assassinated along with his *compañero* in the struggle, Chino.

29. see *Tania the Unforgettable Guerrilla*.

30. Ibid.

31. Vicente Rocabado was an agent of the Bolivian Criminal Investigation Headquarters (DIC). Immediately after his desertion, he notified the Bolivian armed forces and the Government Ministry, and through them the CIA, of all details (including Tania's presence in the guerrilla camp) he had learned during his stay on the Ñacaguazu ranch.

32. The guerrilla base, a ranch on the Ñacaguazu River, had a house with a corrugated zinc roof that came to be known as the "zinc house."

33. Salustio Choque Choque was taken prisoner by the Bolivian army on March 20, 1967. For a long time, he was considered an informer for the Barrientos dictatorship; however, according to testimony

given years later to the Cuban historians Adys Cupull and Froilán
González, he never gave any compromising information about the
organization and composition of the guerrilla column.

CHAPTER 12

1. see *The Bolivian Diary.*
2. As there are different accounts about the outcome of this battle, the
   details of the dead and injured in the Bolivian army were taken
   from Communiqué No. 1 by the Bolivian ELN that appears in *El
   Che en Bolivia: Documentos y testimonios* (Che in Bolivia: Documents
   and Testimonies) (La Paz: Cedoin, 1996), 269-70.
3. see *The Bolivian Diary.*
4. Communiqué No. 1 of the Bolivian ELN, in *El Che en Bolivia:
   Documentos y testimonios,* 269.
5. After a number of failed attempts, Communiqué No. 1 of the
   Bolivian ELN was made public for the first time on May 1, 1967.
6. This claim was taken from the testimony of General Harry Villegas
   (alias Pombo). See *Tania the Unforgettable Guerrilla.*
7. see *The Bolivian Diary.*
8. see *Tania the Unforgettable Guerrilla.*
9. Serapio Aquino Tudela (alias Serafín) was born in La Paz, Bolivia,
   in October 1951. He was a farmhand on the Ñacaguazu ranch at the
   time hostilities began. To protect his life, Che integrated him into
   the guerrilla force as a "refugee." On April 17, he joined Joaquín's
   column as a combatant. He died in combat on July 9, 1967.
10. see *Tania the Unforgettable Guerrilla.*
11. Che's opinion on the deficiencies of these Bolivians was partially
    confirmed over the following months. In spite of having been
    formally reincorporated as combatants into Joaquín's column, Julio
    Velazco Montana (alias Pepe) deserted in May 1967. Nonetheless,
    he was brutally tortured and then assassinated by the Bolivian
    armed forces. Eusebio Tapia and Hugo Choque (alias Chingolo)
    left Joaquín's column at the beginning of August in the same year

and were both taken prisoner. Some accounts indicate that while the former bravely resisted the torture from the Bolivian army; the latter, after being tortured, gave the specific location of the caves where the guerrilla column had hidden several documents, as well as the places where reserves of weapons, munitions, food, and medicine had been set up near the Ñacaguazu ranch. For his part, José Castillo Chávez (alias Paco) remained in Joaquín's column until the group was attacked in the ambush at Puerto Mauricio on August 31, 1967.

12. Juan Vitalo Acuña Núñez (alias Joaquín) was born in Purial de Vicana, Cuba, on January 27, 1925. He joined the guerrilla movement under Che's command on November 27, 1966. Because of his distinguished revolutionary career in Cuba and his military experience, he was appointed second in command of the unit and commander of the rearguard of the Bolivian ELN guerrilla column. He was killed in combat on the banks of the Río Grande on August 31, 1967.

13. In the campaign diary published by the US firm Stein & Day, the second in command of the rearguard platoon of the Bolivian ELN column, the Cuban Israel Reyes Zayas (alias Braulio) states, "Tania was there, she stayed with us because she had a wounded leg." The diary of the Cuban Pacho indicates, "The center is making very slow progress. Tania's legs are swollen." For those interested in consulting both documents see *El Che en Bolivia: Documentos y testimonios,* 141 and 177.

14. see *Tania the Unforgettable Guerrilla.*

15. Ibid.

16. Ibid.

17. For further information see Adys Cupull and Froilán González, *De Ñacahuasú a La Higuera* (From Ñacahuasú to La Higuera) (Havana: Editora Política, 1969), 324-48.

18. see *The Bolivian Diary.*

19. Antonio Sánchez Díaz (alias Marcos) was born on the Cantera ranch in Pinar del Río, Cuba, on December 7, 1927. He joined the guerrilla

movement on November 20, 1966. He was head of the vanguard and subsequently transferred to the rearguard as a combatant. He died in an ambush near Bella Vista on June 2, 1967.

20. Casildo Condori Vargas (alias Víctor) was born on April 9, 1941, in Coro Coro, Bolivia. From the beginning, he was part of Joaquín's column. He died in combat in the vicinity of Bella Vista on June 2, 1967.

21. *De Ñacahuasú a La Higuera*, 327.

22. see *Che: Un hombre bravo*.

23. Interview with Froilán González, in *La muchacha de la guerrilla del Che, Tania: Leyendas y realidades*, 78-79.

24. Ibid.

25. A *chigoe* is a parasite found in the Americas and throughout Africa, similar to the flea, but much smaller and with a larger proboscis. The fertile females penetrate the skin of animals and human beings, mainly through the feet, and lay their eggs, producing a severe itching and serious ulcers that make it difficult to walk.

26. *De Ñacahuasú a La Higuera*, 339.

27. José A. Friedl Zapata, *Tania la guerrillera: La enigmática espia a la sombra del Che* (Tania the Guerrilla: The Mysterious Spy in the Shadow of Che) (Germany: Aufbau Verlag, 1997), 168-70.

28. *Tania the Unforgettable Guerrilla*.

29. Ibid.

30. Gustavo Machín Hoed de Beche (alias Alejandro) was born in Havana, Cuba, on February 1, 1937. He joined the guerrilla movement on December 11, 1966. In view of his revolutionary career in Cuba and his military experience, he was appointed head of Operations, a post that he held until April 17, 1967. Because of serious health problems, he was transferred to the rearguard. He was killed in combat at Puerto Mauricio on August 31, 1967.

31. *Tania the Unforgettable Guerrilla*.

32. Ibid.

33. Israel Reyes Zayas (alias Braulio) was born in the Sierra Maestra, Cuba, on October 9, 1933. He joined the guerrilla movement on

November 27, 1966, and died in combat in the ambush at Puerto Mauricio on August 31, 1967.

34. *De Ñacahuasú a La Higuera*, 341-42.

35. Freddy Maymura Hurtado (alias Ernesto) was born in Trinidad, Bolivia, on October 18, 1941. He joined the guerrilla movement on November 27, 1966. He was tortured and assassinated by the Bolivian army near at Puerto Mauricio on August 31, 1967.

36. *De Ñacahuasú a La Higuera*, 342.

37. see *The Bolivian Diary*.

38. Ibid.

39. Ibid.

40. Manuel Hernández Osorio (alias Miguel) was born in Santa Rita, Cuba, on March 17, 1931. On November 27, 1966, he joined the guerrilla movement where in March 1967 he was assigned to lead the vanguard. He was killed in the ambush by the Bolivian army at the pass in Batán on September 26, 1967.

41. Mario Gutiérrez Ardaya (alias Julio) was born in Trinidad, Bolivia, on May 22, 1939. On March 10, 1967, he joined the guerrilla movement and was assigned to the vanguard section. He was killed in combat in the ambush by the Bolivian army at the pass in Batán on September 26, 1967.

42. see *The Bolivian Diary*.

43. Simón Cuba (alias Willy) was born in Cochabamba, Bolivia, in 1932. He joined the guerrilla movement in March 1967 and was assigned to the staff platoon. Together with Che, he took part in combat at the Quebrada del Yuro pass. On seeing Che wounded, he tried to get him out of the combat zone, but both were taken prisoner. He was assassinated in cold blood by the Bolivian army in the school at La Higuera on October 9, 1967.

44. Refers to the essay published by Che under this title in the *Tricontinental* magazine on April 16, 1967. It is considered by many as Che's political testament.

45. Ernesto Che Guevara, *Global Justice* (New York: Ocean Press, 2002), 62.

CHAPTER 13

1. *Última Hora*, September 8, 1967.
2. *La muchacha de la guerrilla del Che, Tania: Leyendas y realidades*, 80-81.
3. Ibid.
4. *Presencia*, September 11, 1967.
5. Ibid.
6. *La muchacha de la guerrilla del Che, Tania: Leyendas y realidades*, 80.
7. This version also appears in the libelous book by José Friedl Zapata, based on testimony by General Andrés Sélich's widow.
8. Refers to the events held on December 7, 1997, in every municipality of Cuba to render tribute and perpetuate the memory of the more than 200 Cuban internationalists who were killed in battles for the independence of Angola, Guinea Bissau, Namibia, and Zimbabwe, and in the struggle to overthrow the apartheid regime in South Africa.
9. Jaime Arana Campero (alias Chapaco) was born in Tarija, Bolivia, on October 31, 1938. He joined the guerrilla movement in March 1967 and remained in its ranks until October 8, 1967. Four days later, he died in combat when his unit was outnumbered in the Cajones region, where the Río Grande and Mizque River meet.
10. Dr. Octavio de la Concepción y de la Pedraja (alias Moro) was born in Havana, Cuba, on October 16, 1935. After accompanying Che in the Congo, he joined the internationalist guerrilla unit on December 11, 1966. He was killed in combat in the Cajones region of Bolivia on October 12, 1967, three days after Che was assassinated.
11. Francisco Huanca Flores (alias Pablito) was born in Oruro, Bolivia, on September 17, 1945. He joined the guerrilla movement in mid-1967. He formed part of the vanguard of the guerrilla column led by Che and was killed in combat in the Cajones region of Bolivia on October 12, 1967.
12. Aniceto Reinaga Gordillo was born in the Siglo XX mining district of Bolivia on June 26, 1940. In January 1967 he joined the international

guerrilla movement led by Che Guevara. He died in combat at the Quebrada del Yuro pass, Bolivia, on October 8, 1967.

13. Julio Luis Méndez Korne (alias Ñato) was born in Beni, Bolivia, on February 23, 1937. He was one of the first combatants of the guerrilla unit led by Che Guevara in March 1967 and was put in charge of supplies and armaments. He died in combat at Mataral, Bolivia, on October 15, 1967, seven days after the battle at the Quebrada del Yuro pass.

14. At this time, the group of survivors mentioned was composed of the Bolivians Inti and Dario, as well as the Cubans Pombo, Urbano, and Benigno. Around the date of the 30th anniversary of Che's ass-assination, the latter betrayed the Cuban Revolution by giving the CIA and some biographers of Che misinformation in an attempt to show that there were disagreements between Che and Fidel and Raúl Castro.

15. Walter Arencibia Ayala (alias Walter) was born in the village of Macha, Bolivia, on January 21, 1941, and arrived at the Ñacaguazu ranch on January 21, 1967. He died at Puerto Mauricio on August 31, 1967.

16. Apolinar Aquino Quispe (alias Apolo) was born in La Paz, Bolivia. He joined the guerrilla column in December, 1966. He died in combat in the ambush at Puerto Mauricio on August 31, 1967.

17. Eliseo Reyes Rodríguez (alias Rolando) was born in San Luis, Santiago de Cuba, on April 27, 1940. He joined the guerrilla column on December 20, 1966. He was appointed by Che as a captain in the staff platoon. He died in combat near the Iquira River on April 25, 1967.

18. Jesús Suárez Gayol (alias Rubio) was born in Havana, Cuba, on May 24, 1936. After working together with Che in the Ministry of Industry, he joined the guerrilla movement on December 19, 1966. He was killed in combat at Iripití on April 10, 1967. He was the first Cuban killed in combat in Bolivia.

19. Raúl Quispaya Choque was born in the city of Oruro, Bolivia, on December 31, 1939. He was one of the first Bolivians to join the

guerrilla movement. He belonged to the vanguard of the column under Che's leadership until his death on July 30, 1967, near the Rosita River.

20. Benjamín Coronado Córdova was born in Coro Coro, La Paz, Bolivia, on April 9, 1941. He arrived at the Ñacaguazu ranch on January 21, 1967, and some days later left as a member of the vanguard of the guerrilla column under Che's leadership to carry out his first reconnaissance of the operations zone. While undertaking this mission, Benjamín accidentally drowned on February 26, 1967, when attempting to cross the turbulent waters of the Río Grande. He was the first Bolivian to die during the conflict.

21. Lorgio Vaca Marchetti (alias Carlos) was born in Santa Cruz de la Sierra, Bolivia, in 1934. He joined the guerrilla column on December 11, 1966, and accompanied Che's column on its first reconnaissance of the operations zone. He drowned in the Río Grande when they were on their return journey to the Ñacaguazu ranch.

22. *La muchacha de la guerrilla del Che, Tania: Leyendas y realidades*, 114-115.

23. Refers to José Martí's quote, "Death is not final when one has accomplished one's life mission."

CHAPTER 14

1. Refers to the victorious march of the Rebel Army on January 2, 1959. Under the leadership of Che Guevara and Camilo Cienfuegos, it traveled to Havana to occupy the La Cabaña fortress and the Columbia garrison where, until the very last moment, the chief of staff of the Batista's armed forces had been installed.

2. Olaf is Tania's elder brother.

3. Refers to a speech made by Fidel Castro during the first days of November 1959 to inform the Cuban people of the death of Camilo Cienfuegos in an airplane crash. In the speech, Castro stated, "There are many Camilos among our people!"

APPENDIX **1**

1. The World Festivals of Youth and Students were held with the encouragement of the Soviet Union and other socialist countries in several European cities following the end of World War II. In 1959, this event was held in Vienna. Supported by the Cuban Revolution, these events continue to be held today.
2. In 1957, the World Festival of Youth and Students was held in Moscow. The World Federation of Democratic Youth was at that time composed mainly of organizations linked to communist parties.
3. There was a criminal repressive police force operating in Cuba during the dictatorship of General Fulgencio Batista from 1952 to 1958.
4. At that time, Antonio Núñez Jiménez, captain in the Rebel Army, was president of the recently founded National Institute for Agrarian Reform (INRA). A first lieutenant of the Rebel Army, Orlando Borrego, was second in command of the Department of Industrialization at INRA, which had been founded under the direction of Che Guevara.
5. The National Preparatory Commission of the Congress of the International Student Union was held in Havana, Cuba, in 1961.
6. The Sandinista National Liberation Front (FSLN) was founded by the guerrilla Carlos Fonseca, who later died in combat. The FSLN developed an armed revolutionary struggle against the ruthless Somoza family. With official US support, the Somozas had oppressed the Nicaraguan people from 1936 to 1979, the year in which the Sandinista revolution triumphed.

APPENDIX **2**

1. The times are left blank in the original document.
2. EICO refers to a brand name.

APPENDIX **3**

1. ASA is a unit of measurement used to identify the speed of a roll of film.
2. A *cristal* refers to a component for radio transmitters.
3. The letters refer to those in Morse code that are used in the reception and transmission of radiotelegraphy.
4. The Ch. Brigade refers to the countersurveillance team that Tania believed was observing her.

APPENDIX **5**

1. The way in which DD2 is pronounced in Spanish indicates that this was how Tania identified her *compañero* Diosdado in this message.
2. Refers to the anthem of the July 26 Movement, the first verse of which begins, "Onward Cubans, Cuba will reward your heroism, as we are the soldiers who will free our country…"
3. Tania mentions the titles of different songs by the Cuban bolero singer-songwriter César Portillo de la Luz, one of the promoters of the "feelings" genre that Tania liked so much.
4. A reference to *compañero* Papi, who Tania affectionately called Tarzan because of his strong physical build.
5. Tania is referring to her trip to West Berlin when she could look across the wall dividing the city and see the building where her parents lived.
6. When Tania mentions "the censor," she is referring to Diosdado, who, in accordance with the methods used in clandestine work, revised Tania's letters to avoid "a leak" of compromising information concerning her work in Prague.

APPENDIX **6**

1. These references to other people were used by Tania in the preparation of her cover. Certain personalities of individuals who formed part of Laura Gutiérrez Bauer's biography were based upon people that Tania knew.

APPENDIX **8**

1. The term public taxi refers to a collective taxi that follows fixed routes with a number of passengers on board.
2. Evidently there is a mistake in Mercy's report. According to the preceding paragraphs, he and Tania went to the beach at Itarare on March 1. After three weeks of training, Tania must have left for Montevideo, the capital of Uruguay, on March 24.

APPENDIX **9**

1. Blanca Chacón is a Peruvian woman who took part, together with Tania, in some events hosted by the Cuban Institute of Friendship with the Peoples (ICAP) at its office in Havana.
2. A reference to the triumph of the Cuban Revolution on January 1, 1959. Olive green was the color of the uniforms of Cuba's Rebel Army, led by Fidel Castro. Consequently, it became a symbol of identification with revolutionary Cuba.
3. The Peace Corps was founded by the John F. Kennedy administration in order to fulfill a variety of civil-military missions throughout the world and particularly in Latin American countries. In the period when Tania was giving her report it was presumed (not without reason) that US members of the Peace Corps had, in one way or another, links with the CIA and other US government espionage agencies.
4. General René Barrientos was the de facto president of Bolivia at that time.

5. *Carnaval* in Bolivia is a popular festival that precedes Lent. It is celebrated for the three days prior to Ash Wednesday.

6. The Nationalist Revolutionary Movement (MNR) was led from the time of its foundation in 1941 by Víctor Paz Estenssoro.

7. The Christian Popular Movement (MPC) was the name adopted by the reactionary political forces that supported the coup d'état led by General René Barrientos. This movement became an official political party after November 4, 1964.

8. The National Leftist Revolutionary Party (PRIN) was founded by the Trotskyist trade union leader Juan Lechín Oquendo. In the four-year period of 1960–64, Lechín was vice president of the Bolivian government, but due to disagreements with President Paz Estenssoro, he resigned from his post and joined the opposition.

9. The Bolivian Socialist Falange (FSB) was a right-wing political party that has since disappeared; it was inspired by the Spanish Falange and had fascist ideas. For a long period it was the main opposition party to the MNR government, established after the Bolivian Revolution in April 1952.

10. The government of General René Barrientos changed the value of the currency, and based on this reform, the new Bolivian peso was valued the same as 1,000 old pesos.

11. The Ministry of Education had registered the group of folklore researchers that Tania had made contact with a few days after her arrival in Bolivia.

12. Tania is referring to the immigration official at the El Alto international airport. As in other countries, immigration procedures in Bolivia were regulated by the Government Ministry.

13. The room where Tania was living at the end of February 1966 when she left Bolivia to undergo training in Brazil and subsequently to make the contact in Mexico was at 2521 Presbítero Medina Street, Sopocachi, La Paz.

14. The "Cárdenas era" refers to the six-year period of 1934–40, during which General Lázaro Cárdenas was the president of Mexico, noted

for his nationalist, anti-imperialist, and antifascist position. He was responsible for the nationalization of Mexican oil fields. In domestic politics, he initiated a wide-ranging agrarian reform that revitalized the principles put forward by the 1910–17 Mexican Revolution.

15. In May 1965, there were large-scale strikes and workers' protests in Bolivia against General René Barrientos's policies. In response, the dictatorship declared a state of emergency and troops occupied the famous tin mines of Catavi, Juanuni, and Siglo XX. During the occupations, hundreds of workers were massacred and the main leaders of the powerful Federation of Miners' Trade Unions were taken prisoner together with other leaders of the Bolivian left.

16. In April 1965, the United States intervened militarily in the Dominican Republic, aiming to overthrow the constitutional revolution led by Colonel Francisco Caamaño Deñó, who, with the support of the people and a range of left-wing organizations in the country, had defeated the reactionary sectors of the Dominican Republic armed forces led by General Elías Wessin Wessin.

17. At that time the US dollar was worth approximately 12.5 Bolivian pesos. Therefore, the pension paid to Sanjinés was equivalent to US$22.

18. This is the title of Fidel Castro's legal defense at his trial, following the failed attack on the Moncada garrison on July 26, 1953. This defense is considered to be the political manifesto of the July 26 Movement, of the Rebel Army and, later, of the first stage of the Cuban Revolution.

19. Conflicts in those years led the PCB to divide into two factions. Those who belonged to the Peking Line defended the policy of the Chinese Communist Party and the People's Republic of China. Those who belonged to the Moscow Line defended positions in support of what was called "peaceful coexistence" promoted by the Communist Party of the Soviet Union and approved by the majority in the Conference of Communist and Workers Parties, held in Moscow in 1960.

20. *Pisco* is a strong alcoholic beverage made by fermenting grapes. It originated in the region of the same name.
21. Large tin mines and other mines with associated minerals, such as bismuth, gold, silver, wolfram, and zinc, are in Huanuni, located in the region of Oruro, in the Bolivian eastern Andes.
22. Tania is referring to some documents that she had given Ariel during the meeting.
23. Tania's marriage to the Bolivian student Mario Antonio Martínez Álvarez took place at the end of February 1966, a few days prior to her departure for Brazil to undergo training with Mercy.
24. Tania is referring to the intensive plan of work that Mercy had given to her to carry out as soon as she returned to Bolivia.
25. The passport would cost 50,000 Argentine pesos, which is a more valuable currency than the Bolivian peso.
26. This is once again a reference to the instructions given to Tania by Mercy during their time together in Bolivia and Brazil.
27. Tania is referring to the practice of identifying, through different pieces of music, the person to whom the message is directed in clandestine radio communications. In order to achieve this, specialized departments of the VMT used legal frequencies of the international station Radio Havana.
28. At that time *Visión* was widely circulated throughout Latin America.
29. National Treasure Oil Reserves was at that time a state-owned organization responsible for locating and exploiting hydrocarbon (oil and gas) reserves.
30. The PCB was led by Mario Monje at that time.
31. The flag of Cuba's July 26 Movement is red and black; together with olive green, these colors are identified with the Rebel Army led by Fidel Castro.
32. A reference to Hernán Siles Zuazo (1914–96), a Bolivian politician who helped form the MNR and who supported the 1952 revolution. Immediately after this revolution took place, between 1952 and 1956,

he held the position of vice president of the republic. Subsequently, in 1956, he was elected president of the republic, a post he held until 1960. From his position in the government, he tried to maintain economic stability and reached agreements with the United States and the International Monetary Fund. At the end of his term, he was appointed Bolivian ambassador to Paraguay and to Spain. After the 1964 coup d'état, he went into exile. He did not return to Bolivia until the 1970s.

33. Ciro Humboldt was the last government minister of the overthrown president Víctor Paz Estenssoro.

34. November 4, 1964, was the date of the coup d'état that overthrew the second government of President Víctor Paz Estenssoro.

35. Juan Lechín Oquendo (1915–2001) was the vice president of the republic from 1960 to 1964 and the leader of PRIN. He was expelled from Bolivia following the widespread workers' strikes of May 1965, and he remained in exile in Argentina until 1980.

36. Tania is referring to one of the *compañeros* who accompanied Ariel to the meeting and who worked for the VMT branch of the MININT in the Cuban embassy.

37. Juan Manuel Ramírez worked in the Mexican embassy in La Paz.

38. This likely refers to *La Misa Criolla* (Creole Mass) performed by, among others, the well-known Peruvian singer-songwriter Chabuca Granda (1921–83). *La Misa Criolla* is a musical interpretation of a Catholic mass accompanied by typical Andean sounds and rhythms.

39. The calendar seemed at first to be a membership card of the Communist Youth Federation of Bolivia.

40. The Power is possibly a way of identifying one of the US monopolies specializing in electricity production.

41. The Four Point Program, an official US institution, was established to supposedly provide support for the development of Latin American countries. In fact, it acted as a front for infiltrating countries in the region. It was the fourth objective of a program from the Truman

administration (1945–53), made famous as one of the means of combating communism.

42. The term *góndola* is often used in Bolivia for buses and other means of public transportation.

43. Refers to the violent political conflicts that took place before, during, and immediately after the powerful miners' strikes of May 1965.

44. Tania made a trip to Cochabamba in February 1966 to try to find an apartment where she could have the operations training that was finally given to her in Brazil by Mercy.

45. Prensa Latina (Latin Press) is a Cuban press agency established a few months after the Cuban Revolution by the renowned Argentine journalist Jorge Ricardo Masetti. He was supported in this initiative by various Latin American journalists and intellectuals and by Che Guevara.

46. The first Tricontinental Conference was held in Havana in the beginning of January 1966. This conference approved the foundation of the Organization for Solidarity with the Peoples of Asia, Africa, and Latin America (OSPAAAL) and the journal *Tricontinental*, which is still published in Havana.

47. At that time, 900 Bolivian pesos were equivalent to US$72.

48. Montevideo is the capital of Uruguay, and Buenos Aires is the capital of Argentina. The cities are separated by the river named Río de la Plata, which facilitates communication between them. Uruguayan and Argentine citizens usually need only their identity cards, and not their passports, to enter either country.

49. *Coño* is an obscenity referring to female genitalia, loosely translated as "shit."

50. Oscar Zamora was the leader at that time of the group of dissidents from the PCB. This group announced its identification with the Peking Line. Tania and he were personally acquainted prior to her arrival in Bolivia because he, as a leader of the Communist Youth Federation of Bolivia, had taken part in events at the International Student Union, an international organization with headquarters in the Czech capital.

51. The article was published in *Información Periodística,* which was edited by Gonzalo López Muñoz before he joined the Information Services for the Bolivian presidency.
52. Mario Monje Molina was the general secretary of the PCB until December 1967. He was dismissed from his position because of his behavior toward the Bolivian ELN led by Che Guevara.
53. The PCB was founded in 1950.
54. Refers to the first months after the coup d'état against Víctor Paz Estenssoro.

APPENDIX **12**

1. PGU is the Central Intelligence Bureau of the KGB.

APPENDIX **17**

1. The Ciro Redondo invading column, under the leadership of Che Guevara, managed to move the guerrilla struggle forward in spite of enormous military and logistical difficulties. The column then united with the main detachments of the revolutionary forces to win the decisive battle of Santa Clara on December 31, 1958.
2. The Frank País Second Eastern Front, led by Raúl Castro Ruz, was the division of the Rebel Army that fought from the eastern-most region of the former Oriente Province.
3. Column 2, under the leadership of Camilo Cienfuegos, managed to take the guerrilla struggle north of the Las Villas Province to eventually help defeat Batista's forces at the battle of Santa Clara.
4. The sugar mill La Demajagua marks the start of the armed struggle by the Cuban people against Spanish colonialism on October 10, 1868, under the leadership of Carlos Manuel de Céspedes. On this date he proclaimed the independence of Cuba and gave freedom to his slaves.

LIST OF ACRONYMS

ASOFAMD: Bolivian Association of Disappeared Relatives and Martyrs
CDR: Committee for the Defense of the Revolution (Cuba)
CIA: Central Intelligence Agency
DIC: Criminal Investigations Headquarters (Bolivia)
ELN: National Liberation Army (Bolivia)
ELN: National Liberation Army (Peru)
FBI: Federal Bureau of Investigation
FGY: Free German Youth
FMC: Federation of Cuban Women
FSB: Bolivian Socialist Falange (Bolivia)
FSLN: Sandinista National Liberation Front (Nicaragua)
GDR: German Democratic Republic (East Germany)
GUWSP: German Unified Workers Socialist Party
ICAP: Cuban Institute of Friendship with the Peoples
INIT: National Institute of the Tourism Industry (Cuba)
IPE: Información Periodística (weekly Bolivian publication)
KGB: State Security Committee (Soviet Union)
MININT: Ministry of the Interior (Cuba)
MNR: Nationalist Revolutionary Movement (Bolivia)
MOE: Special Operations Division (Cuba)
MOEC: Peasant Student Worker Movement (Colombia)
MPC: Christian Popular Movement (Bolivia)
OAS: Organization of American States
PCC: Cuban Communist Party
PCB: Bolivian Communist Party
PRIN: National Leftist Revolutionary Party (Bolivia)
Stasi: State Secret Police (GDR)
UJC: Union of Young Communists (Cuba)
VMT: Technical Vice Ministry (Cuban MININT)

LIST OF ALIASES

- Abelardo Colomé (alias Fury)
- Alberto Fernández Montes de Oca (alias Pacho or Pachungo)
- Antonio Jiménez Tardío (alias Pan Divino)
- Antonio Sánchez Díaz (alias Marcos)
- Apolinar Aquino Quispe (alias Apolo)
- Carlos Alberto González Méndez (alias Pascual)
- Carlos Coello (alias Tuma or Tumaini)
- Carlos Conrado de Jesús Alvarado Marín (alias Mercy)
- Carlos Puig Espinosa (alias Manuel)
- Casildo Condori Vargas (alias Víctor)
- Ciro Roberto Bustos (alias Carlos or Pelao)
- Dariel Alarcón Ramírez (alias Benigno)
- David Adriazola Viezaga (alias Dario)
- Eliseo Reyes Rodríguez (alias Rolando)
- Francisco Huanca Flores (alias Pablito)
- Freddy Maymura Hurtado (alias Ernesto)
- Guido Peredo Liegue (Inti)
- Gustavo Machín Hoed de Beche (alias Alejandro)
- Harry Villegas Tamayo (alias Pombo)
- Haydée Tamara Bunke Bíder (alias Tania)
- Hugo Choque (alias Chingolo)
- Israel Reyes Zayas (alias Braulio)
- Iván Montero (alias Renán)
- Jaime Arana Campero (alias Chapaco)
- Jesús Suárez Gayol (alias Rubio)
- Jorge González Pérez (alias Popy)
- Jorge Vázquez Viaña (alias Loro or Bigotes)
- José Castillo Chávez (alias Paco)
- José Gómez Abad (alias Diosdado)
- José María Martínez Tamayo (alias Papi)
- José Ramón de Lázaro Bencomo (alias Delarra)
- Juan Carretero Ibáñez (alias Ariel)
- Juan Pablo Chang Navarro (alias Chino)

- Juan Vitalio "Vilo" Acuña Núñez (alias Joaquín)
- Julio Dagnino Pacheco (alias Sánchez)
- Julio Luis Méndez Korne (alias Ñato)
- Julio Velazco Montana (alias Pepe)
- Leonardo Tamayo Núñez (alias Urbano)
- Lorgio Vaca Marchetti (alias Carlos)
- Lucio Edilberto Galván Hidalgo (alias Eustaquio)
- Manuel Hernández Osorio (alias Miguel)
- Manuel Piñeiro (alias Barbarroja, XII, and Petronio)
- Mario Gutiérrez Ardaya (alias Julio)
- Neuris Trutié (alias Teobaldo)
- Octavio de la Concepción y de la Pedraja (alias Moro)
- Orlando Pantoja Tamayo (alias Olo)
- Ramón Oroza Naberán (alias Demetrio)
- René Martínez Tamayo (alias Arturo)
- Restituto José Cabrera Flores (alias Negro)
- Roberto Peredo Liegue (alias Coco)
- Roberto Rodríguez (alias Vaquerito)
- Salvador Prat (alias Juan Carlos)
- Serapio Aquino Tudela (alias Serafín)
- Simón Cuba Saravia (alias Willy)
- Walter Arencibia Ayala (alias Walter)

HAYDÉE SANTAMARÍA

Rebel Lives

Edited by Betsy Maclean

"Haydée Santamaría signifies a world, an attitude, a sensibility, as well as a revolution." —Mario Benedetti

Haydée first achieved notoriety by being one of two women who participated in the armed attack that sparked the Cuban Revolution. Later, as director of the world-renowned literary institution, Casa de las Américas, she embraced culture as a tool for social change and provided refuge for exiled Latin American artists and intellectuals.

Includes reflections by Ariel Dorfman, Eduardo Galeano, Alicia Alonso, Silvio Rodríguez, and Gabriel García Márquez.

ISBN 1-876175-59-1

LOUISE MICHEL

Rebel Lives

Edited by Nic Maclellan

"My only desire is to see Michel portrayed as she actually was: an extraordinary woman, a significant thinker, and a profound soul." —Emma Goldman

Louise Michel was the incendiary French leader of the 1871 Paris Commune. An anarchist and an irrepressible rebel, she spent much of her life on the run from police, in jail, or in danger of being locked away in mental asylums, as was the fate of so many feisty or defiant women. Here is Michel's own story, along with commentaries about her by Emma Goldman, Bertolt Brecht, Sheila Rowbotham, Howard Zinn, and her contemporaries Victor Hugo and Karl Marx.

ISBN 1-876175-76-1

HELEN KELLER

Rebel Lives

Edited by John Davis

"I have entered the fight against the economic system in which we live. It is to be a fight to the finish and I ask no quarter." —Helen Keller

Poor little blind girl or dangerous radical? This book challenges the sanitized image of Helen Keller, restoring her true history as a militant socialist. Here are her views on women's suffrage, her defense of the Industrial Workers of the World (IWW), her opposition to World War I, and her support for imprisoned socialist and anarchist leaders, as well as her analysis of disability and class.

ISBN 1-876175-60-5

ALBERT EINSTEIN

Rebel Lives

Edited by Jim Green

"What I like most about Albert Einstein is that he was a troublemaker."
—Fred Jerome, author of *The Einstein File*

You don't have to be Einstein... to know that he was a giant in the world of science and physics. Yet this book takes a new, subversive look at *Time* magazine's "Person of the Century," whose passionate opposition to war and racism, and advocacy of human rights, put him on the FBI's files as a socialist enemy of the state.

ISBN 1-876175-63-X

SACCO & VANZETTI

Rebel Lives

Edited by John Davis

"Sacco and Vanzetti died because they were anarchists... because they believed and preached human brotherhood and freedom. As such, they could expect neither justice nor humanity." —Emma Goldman

An illuminating example of how immigrants, anarchists, and communists were the "terrorists" of yesteryear, Nicola Sacco and Bartolomeo Vanzetti were convicted in a trial steeped in racial and ideological prejudice. Their case sparked an unprecedented defense campaign and became a symbol of the international struggle for justice, equality, and liberty.

ISBN 1-876175-85-0

Forthcoming REBEL LIVES titles include:

- Chris Hani
- Rosa Luxemburg
- Antonio Gramsci
- Camilo Torres
- Ho Chi Minh
- Toussaint L'Ouverture
- Nidia Diaz
- Amilcar Cabral

rebel lives

THE CUBA PROJECT

CIA Covert Operations 1959-62

Fabián Escalante

"Fabián Escalante is in a unique position to add significant insight and information about this crucial chapter of modern history. His review of CIA covert operations against Cuba is to be welcomed greatly, and should be widely read and pondered." —Noam Chomsky

ISBN 1-876175-99-0

CIA TARGETS FIDEL

The Secret Assassination Report

Introduction by Fabián Escalante

Only recently declassified and published for the first time, this secret report was prepared by the CIA in 1967 on its own plots to assassinate Cuba's President Fidel Castro. Introduction by General Fabián Escalante, former head of Cuban counterintelligence.

ISBN 1-875284-90-7

COLD WAR

Warnings for a Unipolar World

Fidel Castro

Who won the Cold War? In this astonishingly frank interview with CNN, Cuba's Fidel Castro makes some extraordinary revelations about the conflict that took the world to the brink of annihilation.

ISBN 1-876175-77-X *(Also available in Spanish 1-876175-91-5)*

LETTERS OF LOVE AND HOPE

The Story of the Cuban Five

Alice Walker with the Families of the Cuban Five

The diaries and letters of the five Cubans imprisoned in the United States for the "crime" of trying to prevent terrorism against Cuba. This book provides a glimpse of how ordinary families strive to maintain connections in extraordinary circumstances. Includes a succinct legal analysis of the case by attorney Leonard Weinglass, outlining how US courts have significantly violated both international law and the US constitution.

ISBN 1-920888-23-3

TRICONTINENTAL REBELLION
Voices of the Wretched of the Earth
Edited by Ulises Estrada and Luis Suárez
An inspiring anthology of the revolt of Third World peoples in Africa, Asia, and Latin America. Contains a selection of the best of *Tricontinental* magazine, as well as full color reproductions of some of the classic political posters *Tricontinental* was known for. Contributors to this anthology read like a "Who's Who" of world revolutionaries.
ISBN 1-876175-78-8

CENTURY OF TERROR IN LATIN AMERICA
A Chronicle of US Crimes Against Humanity
Luis Suárez
This is a comprehensive history of US intervention in Latin America, from the Monroe Doctrine through the "dirty wars" in Cuba and Central America, to the neoliberal agenda being imposed with such explosive consequences today.
ISBN 1-920888-37-3

LATIN AMERICA
From Colonization to Globalization
Noam Chomsky in conversation with Heinz Dietrich
An indispensable book for those interested in Latin America and the politics and history of the region. As Latin America hovers on the brink of a major social and economic crisis, Noam Chomsky discusses some of the principal political events in recent years.
ISBN 1-876175-13-3

CHÁVEZ
Venezuela and the New Latin America
Hugo Chávez, interviewed by Aleida Guevara
Is Venezuela the new Cuba? Elected by overwhelming popular mandate in 1998, Hugo Chávez is now one of Latin America's most outspoken political figures.

In this extraordinary interview with Aleida Guevara, Chávez expresses a fiercely nationalist vision for Venezuela and a commitment to a united Latin America.
ISBN 1-920888-00-4 *(Also available in Spanish 1-920888-22-5)*

GLOBAL JUSTICE
Liberation and Socialism
Ernesto Che Guevara

Is there an alternative to the neoliberal globalization ravaging our planet? Collected here are three of Guevara's classic works, presenting his revolutionary view of a different world in which human solidarity and understanding replace imperialist aggression and exploitation.
ISBN 1-876175-45-1 *(Also available in Spanish 1-876175-46-X)*

MANIFESTO
Three Classic Essays on How to Change the World
Ernesto Che Guevara, Rosa Luxemburg, Karl Marx and Friedrich Engels

"If you are curious and open to the life around you, if you are troubled as to why, how, and by whom political power is held and used... if your curiosity and openness drive you toward wishing to 'do something,' you already have much in common with the writers of the essays in this book."
—Adrienne Rich, from her preface to *Manifesto*
ISBN 1-876175-98-2 *(Also available in Spanish 1-920888-13-6)*

OUR AMERICA AND THEIRS
Kennedy, the Alliance for Progress, and the Debate on Free Trade
Ernesto Che Guevara

To check the growing rebellion in Latin America after the Cuban Revolution, Kennedy initiated the Alliance for Progress—a program for free trade and development in the Americas. Che Guevara, representing the Cuban revolutionary government, condemned the plan as a new strategy to subjugate the continent to US interests.
ISBN 1-876175-91-8 *(Also available in Spanish 1-876175-65-6)*

CUBAN REVOLUTION READER
A Documentary History of 45 Key Moments in the Cuban Revolution
Edited by Julio García Luis

From the euphoria of the early years of the revolution to its near collapse in the 1990s, the editor selects a broad range of material, providing a sweeping vision of revolutionary Cuba—its challenges, its defeats, its impact on the world.
ISBN 1-920888-05-5 *(Also available in Spanish 1-920888-08-X)*

CHE GUEVARA READER

Writings on Politics and Revolution

Edited by David Deutschmann

A new, updated edition of this extraordinary and comprehensive selection of Guevara's writings, letters, and speeches. Not a biography, or a book of reminiscences by others—this book offers Che Guevara in his own words.

ISBN 1-876175-69-9 *(Also available in Spanish 1-876175-93-1)*

SELF-PORTRAIT

Ernesto Che Guevara

An intimate look at the man behind the icon. This remarkable photographic and literary memoir draws on the rich seam of diaries, letters, poems, journalism, and short stories Che Guevara left behind him in Cuba. The photographs, some never before published and chosen from the Guevara family albums, bring to light a surprisingly sensitive and artistic edge of the legendary revolutionary.

ISBN 1-876175-82-6 *(Also available in Spanish 1-876175-89-3)*

THE MOTORCYCLE DIARIES

Notes on Latin American Journey

Ernesto Che Guevara

This bestselling classic features a moving preface by Che Guevara's eldest daughter, Aleida Guevara, and exclusive, unpublished photos taken by Che and his traveling companion, Alberto Granado, throughout their 1952 adventure around Latin America.

ISBN 1-876175-70-2 *(Also available in Spanish 1-920888-11-X)*

REMINISCENCES OF THE CUBAN REVOLUTIONARY WAR

The authorized edition with corrections made by Che Guevara

Ernesto Che Guevara

Preface by Aleida Guevara

The dramatic art and acute perception evident in Che Guevara's early diaries fully blossom in this highly readable and often entertaining account of the guerrilla war that led to the 1959 Cuban Revolution. Steven Soderbergh's forthcoming film on Che Guevara is based on this book, along with *The Bolivian Diary.*

ISBN 1-920888-33-0 *(Also available in Spanish 1-920888-36-5)*

ALSO FROM OCEAN PRESS

THE BOLIVIAN DIARY

The Authorized Edition

Ernesto Che Guevara

Preface by Camilo Guevara

This is Che's last diary, compiled from the notebooks found in his knapsack when he was captured and executed by the Bolivian army in October 1967. Revised by Che's widow (who originally transcribed the diary), this is the definitive account of the attempt to spark a continent-wide revolution in Latin America. One of the two books used as a basis for Steven Soderbergh's forthcoming movie on Che Guevara.

ISBN 1-920888-24-1 (Also available in Spanish 1-920888-30-6)

LATIN AMERICA

Awakening of a Continent

Ernesto Che Guevara

Here, for the first time in one volume, is a comprehensive overview of Che Guevara's unique perspective on the continent of Latin America, showing his cultural depth and rigorous intellect.

ISBN 1-920888-38-1 *(Also available in Spanish 1-876175-71-0)*

CHE: A MEMOIR

Fidel Castro

For the first time Fidel Castro writes with candor and affection of his relationship with Ernesto Che Guevara, documenting Che's extraordinary bond with Cuba from the revolution's early days to the final guerrilla expeditions to Africa and Bolivia.

ISBN 1-920888-25-X *(Also available in Spanish 1-875284-83-4)*

oceanpress

e-mail info@oceanbooks.com.au

www.oceanbooks.com.au